Reich, Jung, Regardie And Me:

The Unhealed Healer

Reich, Jung, Regardie And Me:

The Unhealed Healer

BY

J. MARVIN SPIEGELMAN, PH.D.

1992
NEW FALCON PUBLICATIONS
SCOTTSDALE, ARIZONA, USA

International Standard Book Number: 1-56184-032-7

Library of Congress Catalog Card Number: 91-67382

First Edition 1992

NEW FALCON PUBLICATIONS
7025 East 1st Avenue, Suite 5
Scottsdale, Arizona 85251 U.S.A.
(602) 246-3546

TABLE OF CONTENTS

The Unhealed Healer is primarily a record of my experiences while undergoing the first four years of an eight year Reichian therapy with the famed chiropractor, occultist and Reichian therapist Dr. Francis Israel Regardie.

It details the "nuts and bolts" of procedure and content of very many of the sessions, along with reflections and fantasy work which I did on my own during those painful years of my mid-forties, almost twenty years ago.

Secondarily to this, and as means of an introduction, I have included a brief essay which I have entitled *BODY AND SOUL: REICH AND JUNG*. This paper is an inquiry into the body-soul problem by means of an examination of the work of Wilhelm Reich from the point of view of a Jungian analyst who has also had extensive Reichian work.

I explore Reich's personal and intellectual development, similarities and differences in the views of Reich and Jung, and their implications for the body-soul problem, with special reference to my own experience.

My credentials as a Jungian are as follows: eight years of Jungian analysis (upwards of seven hundred hours), training and graduation at the C.G. Jung Institute in Zurich (1959), and twenty-plus years of experience in private practice. My Reichian work consisted of eight years of personal therapy (about three hundred fifty hours), six years of practice, some seminars, but by no means as full a training as would be expected of an orgonomist.

The Unhealed Healer is aimed at psychotherapists, my fellow Jungians, Neo-Reichians, and to the patients of all of us, who might derive some solace, insight, fellow-feeling, and wonder, respectively. I do this with trepidation, of course, but my publisher and others think that this would be a extraordinarily useful thing to do.

Why, in heaven's name, am I foolhardy enough to do this? What dark motive of exhibitionism, masochism, or other ism lurks there to risk the judgment, opprobrium, scorn and contempt of my fellow healers or, just as bad, their pity? I must be out of my mind! Precisely. I undertook Reichian therapy to get "out of my mind" and into my body. I did not originally plan this. Rather, I had visited my future therapist, Francis Israel Regardie, along with my friend and colleague, L, to learn more about the general occult field, in which he was internationally known. When we spoke to him about our desire to learn more about that field, ("magic," sometimes spelled as "magick" to distinguish this spiritual path from entertainment), he responded that such powerful energies are released in magical work that it would be wise to undergo Reichian therapy first or along with our study, since "body-armor" causes great trouble when not released or resolved. We both found his views convincing and undertook the work.

But why write about it, my fantasized interlocutor questions? I wrote for my own edification and because, for many years, before and since, I did so as part of my own developmental process. I even fancied myself as a potentially publishable writer of fiction, an "illusion" also documented in a companion volume of this series of "Failures," namely, *The Unpublished Writer*.

And why publish? Because I am in a unique position to withstand the anticipated scorn of colleagues and others. This is because I have "earned my dues" as a recognized clinical psychologist (Ph.D., University of California, Los Angeles, 1952, Diplomate, American Board, 1959), Jungian Analyst (Diplomate, C.G. Jung Institute Zurich, 1959), teacher (UCLA seven years plus seven at USC; lecturing in England, Japan, Israel, and the U.S.), consultant at hospitals, and successful private practitioner. I have also had published some sixty journal articles, and eleven books. So I seemed to have "arrived" and been successful, including areas of my personal family life. And this "success" was true! Also true was the fact of grief in my life, as everyone has, including the loss of my connection with professional colleagues at the time I undertook the Reichian therapy (repaired some years later). So I was unsuccessful as well.

A lot of the misery and pain shown in the record of this work, I think, was a result of the therapy itself. I am saddened as I look at the suffering chap I was, those years ago, but I am gladdened to be able to have compassion for him/me and to point out that the link-up with the body, as Jung taught us, and resides in the alchemical metaphor of our work, comes not so easily. My own pains with "body" and "world" were a paradigm for this psychological fact.

Secondly, I publish because most other patients can not or do not —and I was one in those years. Sure enough, I had had extensive personal and training analysis in Los Angeles and Zürich, to the tune of eight years, so I, like all analysts, knew what it meant to be a patient, but here I was, in an alien field, one I had previously held in contempt myself! My therapist was also trained as a chiropractor; another blow to my vaunted superiority! All of this was very useful to my re-definition and "embodying." My extensive previous Jungian analyses and practice had enabled me to embrace my soul and discover my Self, and there was no question of my deep and abiding commitment to what I had experienced in that work. Yet I clearly had troubles in connection with body and world, which Reichian therapy helped significantly, particularly the former; the latter is still in process, part of it is in the risky appearance of this very book!

Thirdly, I publish because I am very skeptical of all accounts of what happens in therapy as reported by therapists. We all make use of events and conditions in our articles—I have done so myself—as if these were true or authoritative. Maybe so. But what does the patient think of all of this? How often (ever?) is there an article in which both patient and healer write about how and what they experienced in the work? Freud reported certain things about the Wolf Man which subsequently turned out to be utterly wrong and not nearly as favorable as he thought. Nor is he alone in this! I cringe when I think of those favorable incidents I have reported in articles, indicating significant change or cure which, subsequently, turned out not to be as I had imagined. I am sure that others have experienced something similar. Therefore, I write about my own experience, from the vantage point of one who is patient and therapist simultaneously. Surely there is value in this for some researcher, not so embedded in it all as I am, to advance our knowledge in this damnably complex and inter-subjective field where it is so difficult to arrive at mutually agreed-upon verities.

So, I have convinced myself of the value of letting this book be published. It remains for the reader to make his own judgment. I can only add that the *Unhealed Healer* of this book wrote (and continues to write) a book about "Successes" and other developments in our healing profession and that these books will also ultimately appear. Finally I conclude this apologia with the heartfelt sharing of the pain and joy of this psychotherapeutic process, whether of body or of soul, whether one is patient or healer for, in truth, we are always both.

I want to salute my analysts and teachers, living and dead, healers all, and thank them. First and foremost is C.G. Jung, followed by Max Zeller, Bruno Klopfer, Margaret McClean, C.A. Meier, Marie-Louise Von Franz, Liliane Frey, Rivkah Kluger, Hilde Kirsch, all Jungians. And latterly, come Wilhelm Reich and Francis Israel Regardie.

Finally, it is patients I thank. You have taught me everything!

J. Marvin Spiegelman
Fall 1991

INTRODUCTION

BODY AND SOUL: REICH AND JUNG

[The following paper was written in 1980, some time after my Reichian therapy was completed, and has not been published heretofore. It was an attempt to reconcile the views of the two researchers, aimed primarily at an audience knowledgeable about analytical psychology, to both inform them about Reich and compare him with Jung. It has been re-edited, in the spring of 1991, largely removing the quotations and diagrams drawn from Reich's original work. The reason for this is that those who are the inheritors of the copyrights of Reich's books and papers, I am informed, are extremely sensitive as to how this work is presented and who does so. They, I am told, are friendly neither to non-medically trained orgonomists, nor to those "spiritually" inclined. I belong to both categories. I can understand their sensitivity, since Reich was so maligned and misrepresented in life and after death, but I do regret not being able to present his own words. In the course of the presentation, I refer the reader to the relevant quotations.]

This paper is an inquiry into the body-soul problem by means of an examination of the work of Wilhelm Reich from the point of view of a Jungian analyst who has also had extensive Reichian work. My credentials as a Jungian are eight years of Jungian analysis (upwards of seven hundred hours), training and graduation at the C.G. Jung Institute in Zurich (1959), and twenty-plus years of experience in private practice. My Reichian work consisted of eight years of personal therapy (about three hundred fifty hours), six years of practice, some seminars, but not the training undergone by orgonomists.

I will explore Reich's personal and intellectual development, similarities and differences in the views of Reich and Jung, and their implications for the body-soul problem, with special reference to my own experience.

REICH'S PERSONAL DEVELOPMENT

Wilhelm Reich was born on a farm in the German-Ukrainian part of Austria on March 24, 1897 to non-practicing Jewish parents. His childhood was atypical, for Jews of his time and place, in a number of ways; he rode horses, hunted, kept animals, had a private teacher who also helped him tend a laboratory for insects and plants. Even more atypical--and tragically so--was his experience of his mother's suicide when he was only fourteen. This self-destructive act happened after Reich told his father about his mother's affair with the boy's tutor. Three years later, Reich's father died of tuberculosis and the seventeen year-old was left alone to run the family farm. The enterprising and gifted young man managed this while also continuing his studies. World War I interfered with this work and he spent three years in the army where he rose to lieutenant and was decorated in Italy.

After the war, Reich attended medical school in Vienna, earning his living by tutoring fellow students. He also studied with Freud. Reich not only graduated with honors (1922), in four years instead of the usual six, he also was admitted to the Vienna Psychoanalytic Society in October 1920 while still a student!

Reich began a private practice in psychoanalysis and psychiatry in 1922, continuing his postgraduate education in neuropsychiatry for two years, under Professors Wagner-Jauregg and Paul Schilder. He was the first Clinical Assistant at Freud's Psychoanalytic Polyclinic in Vienna from its foundation in 1922, rising to its director in 1930. During this period, Reich became attracted to the social and sexual causation of neurosis and founded mental hygiene centers both in Vienna and Berlin, where he worked from 1930 to 1933.

It was during these years that he formulated his views on character analysis. He threw himself with vigor and energy into his work and into fighting political and social conditions he felt caused emotional crippling. He lectured on sexual hygiene and was outspoken on issues which are still hot and controversial today, such as abolition of laws against abortion, homosexuality and birth control. Seeing the misery, poverty and political inequities that he had not perceived previously, he became an advocate of social and sexual reform, even affiliating himself with Marxists and teaching at Workers' Colleges. He wanted to provide sex education, nurseries, and sex counselling facilities in factories and business, and advocated home leave for prisoners.

The reward for Reich's passionate work on these social and psychological issues in the nineteen twenties and early thirties was expulsion from both the International Psychoanalytic Association (1934) and the Communist Party. To what extent his own personality played a role in this rejection and to what extent his views caused it is not clear. But Reich himself noted that from early on among the psychoanalysts he thought himself as a sharp, killer fish among placid, less combative ones (10, p.40). He was clever, opinionated, judgmental and arrogant, but Freud liked his vitality and intelligence. It seems that power-struggles as well as differences in viewpoint were the chief feature in his separation from these movements which had given him sustenance and a home.

In 1933, Reich left Germany to find a temporary haven in Oslo, Norway, where he continued his researches full time (giving up the private practice of therapy) until he was invited to the United States in 1939.

By 1942, Reich had acquired a two-hundred acre estate in Maine for his laboratory and research. He gave it the name "Organon," after the energy he believed he had discovered. Students came and some success, as well, but he was prosecuted by the Federal Food and Drug Administration for his claims regarding his orgone energy accumulator. His defense that he was pursuing natural science and not conventional law was utterly unacceptable to the agency and his home was invaded, his books burned, his lab locked, and he was finally imprisoned, only to die there in 1957, a broken man. (The details of Reich's trial and jailing can be found in Jerome Greenfield's book, *Wilhelm Reich vs. the U.S.A.*, [1]. There is also a very beautiful personal book by Reich's son who lived through this period with him, called, *A Book of Dreams* [6].)

To read Reich's responses to the charges of the F.D.A. (9, Appendix), is to see a man fruitlessly engaged in a defense against the very forces he tried to combat throughout his life via education and reform. The gradual increase in suspicion, sense of persecution, feelings of extraordinary specialness and grandeur finally became quite pathological. Reich made extravagant statements about his powers, felt that UFO's were interested in his work, that President Eisenhower was secretly supporting him, and that he could significantly modify the weather. The extent to which his personality brought on his persecution, or that the real persecution that he received finally caused his deterioration, is hard to assess. I share the impression of Kovalenko and Brown (4) that no one was really willing or able to confront Reich at the "deep level of challenge and outspoken emotional exchange which was apparently natural and comfortable for him." This is particularly apparent in his interview about Freud (10), which we will discuss later on. Here, however, we must note that Reich's isolation and broken love bonds, experienced from early life onwards, and the tragic effects of moralistic judgment, haunted him throughout his life. He was attacked unmercifully and unfairly by individuals and groups who often twisted the spirit of his work. He was to comment on this activity in the concept of "emotional plague," which we will describe later.

REICH'S INTELLECTUAL DEVELOPMENT

Early in his career, Reich found that patients would talk endlessly about their symptoms and problems, but that when the possibility arose of changing the way they lived or the structure of their personality, there was enormous resistance. He then shifted his attention to the analysis of the patient's character traits, much as symptoms had been worked with. By "character," Reich understood a stereotyped or characteristic way a person had of approaching life. This rigid responsiveness was seen as defensive in function and in the service of controlling and blocking off unacceptable feelings from within and, simultaneously, to defend against threats from outside. He called such modes of being "character armor" and found that these began early in life, later to become the foundation for neurosis and the blockage of any spontaneous response to life. The book, *Character Analysis* (7), appeared in 1929 and was both attacked and hailed, but was ultimately incorporated into the body of psychoanalysis. It was during this period (1923-1934) that he also developed his orgasm theory (see below), the idea of "stasis neurosis," sex-economic self-regulation of primary natural drives as distinguished from secondary perverted drives, and explored the role of irrationalism and human sex-economy in the origin of political and personal dictatorship.

Most importantly, however, Reich extended his concept of psychic or character armor into that of muscular armor. By this idea, he meant that muscular tension and rigidities not only served the same purpose as did neurotic character structure, but that indeed they were functionally identical. A retracted pelvis is inhibitory of sexual drives as much as is a strait-laced attitude. The same holds true for a perennially sweet smile, or an elevated stiff chest: all serve to inhibit feelings and drives which training had labeled bad, e.g., rage, anxiety, resentments, sexual desire and, on the other hand, grief, love, pleasure, sympathy. Rigidity of musculature, in short, represents frozen emotion (5). This frozen emotion finds its expression in neuromuscular tension, postural defects and visceral disfunction.

Reich's therapy was devised gradually as he began to touch patients where he saw tension and rigidity. He gradually invented non-verbal techniques that penetrated bodily/armored resistance and had a reorganizing effect. The therapy is based on methods of breathing, movement, and relaxation which have the aim of dissolving the horizontal bands of tension which cross the body. He discovered these bands of tension which can be seen as segments: ocular, oral, neck, chest, diaphragm, abdomen, pelvis. Later researchers, such as Alexander Lowen, have added the knees and the feet ("grounding"). In the respiratory block, for example, the person may have a chronic condition of holding the breath, or shallow breathing, originating in childhood fears and aimed at keeping control. Through the breathing methods in Reichian therapy, there is a gradual relaxing of this "holding," and the underlying feelings of anxiety, etc., can be released.

As the bands of tension dissolve, the autonomic nervous system becomes able to react strongly and powerful sensations, "streamings" (see below) and feelings emerge. Many people find such active sensations frightening and uncomfortable. If the therapy continues, however, the patient will ultimately find total release of tension, and experience what Reich referred to as the "orgasm reflex," a relaxation of the organism accompanied by a shivering, much as a cat does when it relaxes. This full release, occurring on the couch as the patient lets go of control, brings an enormous sense of well-being, re-organizes the character structure, and enables the individual to enjoy deep, open tenderness with others. Vulnerability is accepted, as well as the capacity to experience exchanges in which the core of their being is in connection with others. A natural sexuality is central in this exchange, as well as a natural morality.

A person's armor is what either precludes sensations which should be erotic or pleasurable, or prevents build-up and discharge alike, leaving people in a chronic condition of unreleasable tension. Aggression and hate are among the few emotions that heavily armored people express. Their eroticism is converted into hate, just as does the surrounding armored culture. One of the most characteristic changes in Reichian therapy is that people begin to refuse to continue relationships which were exploitative, battering, or injurious. Yet the culture is full of such negative relationships, and Reich called the collective condition of armor the "emotional plague." He felt that such a label was accurate because of its chain-like reaction, when people are involved with flurries of truth-twisting, rumors, gossip, persecution and automatic rejection of the new, as well as a fear of freedom.

The very vivid tingling sensations which people experience in therapy, called "streamings," along with clonisms and other somatic phenomena, occurring in various regions of the body, become expressions of the bio-electric energy which Reich felt he had discovered. This quite concrete development of the libido idea, Reich called "orgone." At first, Reich recognized that these tinglings and prickling sensations were caused by the free-flowing orgone which had been kept latent because of the chronic muscular tensions.

Gradually, by experimentation, Reich concluded that these energies also existed external to people. He believed that he had discovered an energy which is part of the living, pulsating world, a basis and source of life. This bio-electric energy streams among persons, earth's environment and the stars. There is, therefore, a cosmic stream of orgone energy which can be experienced in the organism, demonstrated in the laboratory, visible as "bions" and also seen in the atmosphere.

From 1940 onwards, Reich's work shifted from a clinical and therapeutic interest to what he felt was an increasingly biological and natural science endeavor. This resulted in increasing ostracism and antagonism toward him. Notable here was his work in cancer (*The Cancer Biopathy*, excerpted in the Writings, 9). He felt that cancer was a matter of biological frustration, an organismic shrinking and withdrawal, which occurred, as did other somatic diseases, in just those areas where armoring was most severe. This view of cancer, along with his use and advocacy of an "orgone energy accumulator"—a box-like device he believed could increase the orgone energy surrounding a person and help to relieve illness--brought on the wrath of the medical establishment.

As if these threats to current biological and medical thought were not enough, he also researched an area which he called "cosmic orgone engineering" (C.O.R.E.), which led him to speculations about smog, storm-control, weather in general, drought and desert conditions. He even produced a tentative technique for the production of rain in arid areas.

I am in no position to evaluate his biological and engineering research, but it is relevant to note that the attack which he received for his views was formidable--even though he described in detail how his experiments were conducted and asserted a natural science basis. None of his critics sought to replicate his work. This attack finally led to his imprisonment and death: a concrete and tragic example of emotional plague.

It is important to ask how isolated was Reich in what he discovered? His energy concept is remarkably similar to that described in East Indian, Asian, and western occult literature, even to the parallel of his armor segments with the chakra centers. Reich's vegetative streamings are not unlike the vertical meridians of acupuncture or the energy experienced in Kundalini Yoga. Reich seemed not to know of these parallels. Indeed, he showed no interest in comparing his findings and views with other material in contemporary or ancient physiology or psychology. His biological conception of core and periphery seems overly simple to biologically trained people, and his language often seemed too authoritarian and alienating.

Yet his work was vast and profound. All the body therapies of today owe much of their origin to his thinking and discoveries. Reich's personal and social isolation was tragic and one still does not know when his theories and discoveries can be put to an adequate outside test.

REICH AND JUNG: SIMILARITIES AND DIFFERENCES

I begin this discussion of Reich and Jung, regretfully, with Reich's feeling about Jung, to whom he, like many others, erroneously attributed both a naive, unscientific mysticism and anti-semitism. In the interview with him by Kurt Eissler (10, pp. 88-89), Reich said that Jung was correct in discovering a universal libido or energy, but Freud was right in saying that it was unscientific. Reich believed that he, himself, had proved it scientifically, being able to measure it with a Geiger counter, thus taking away its "mystical" connotation. Reich also merely accepted that Jung was labelled anti-semitic, without further inquiry.

Reich continues the misconception in *The Function of the Orgasm* (8, p. 127), in which he criticizes Jung for taking all the sexual aspect out of the concept of the libido and ending up with the concept of the collective unconscious, which Reich saw as merely mystical or in line with Nazi ideology.

Great men do not always read each other and, alas, may not understand their rivals any better than the rest of us do. But, in fairness, Reich did not have access to such works as that of Jaffe (3), who corrects in depth that mistaken impression of anti-semitism or national socialist predilections. He could have seen an earlier corrective effort by Ernest Harms, however, in 1946 (2).

Despite this negative judgment, there are a number of ideas or areas in which Reich comes close to formulating his conclusions quite parallel with those of Jung. The first of these is to be found in the basic formulation of opposites (see 9, p. 102). He observed that neurotic patients develop stiff body peripheries, while maintaining an inner core of aliveness. Such patients feel uncomfortable within themselves, inhibited, unable to be themselves, feel cut off. Sometimes they are so tense with this unexpressed energy that they feel like bursting; they long to move toward the world, but can not do so. These efforts toward contact with life are frequently so painful that disappointments are unbearable and the person prefers to crawl into himself. Reich concludes from this that the basic biological function of moving outward toward the world and life is counteracted by a moving away from it, or a withdrawal into self.

A moment later, Reich notes that these opposites are to be particularly noted in a functional antithesis between sexuality and anxiety. He observes that the very experience of pleasure, of expansion, can not be disconnected from healthy living functioning (9, p.105). Still later, he says that psychological attitudes are themselves derived from the amount of energy arising from such excitation. And most succinctly, he concludes that sexuality itself is equivalent of the biological function of expansion, while anxiety is the opposite of this, involving a return from the periphery toward the center, the antithesis of this process of excitation (p. 107).

Finally, he reduces the opposition "toward the world" vs. "toward the self" and sexuality vs. anxiety to the simplest terms: the fundamental pair of opposites are the sympathetic and parasympathetic nervous system.

Reich continues the discussion of polarities in his *Function of the Orgasm* with the chapter heading, "Pleasure (expansion) and anxiety (contraction):

Primary antithesis of Vegetative Life." In this chapter, he reports that by 1933 he recognized a unity between psychic and somatic functioning. He makes it a cardinal point that the primary biological opposites of contraction and expansion are identical in both the somatic and psychic realms. He goes on to present tables of comparisons, such as the antithesis between potassium (parasympathetic) and calcium (sympathetic) in the autonomic nervous system as variants of expansion and contraction. He notes that parasympathetic innervations are accompanied by dilatation, turgor, pleasure, etc. whereas sympathetic nerves come into play whenever there is contraction, blood is withdrawn from the periphery, pallor and pain appear. He concludes from this that life itself is a continuous process of expansion and contraction, pleasure and joy in moving out of self toward the world, and sadness and contraction in moving away from it, into the self (9, p. 125-6).

In later books, *Ether, God and Devil* and *Cosmic Superimposition* (in 9, p. 299 for quote), Reich subsumes these oppositions in a basic principle, pulsation. Pulsation, he says, is the fundamental characteristic of orgone energy, itself, which can be then be subdivided into two opposite and antagonistic part-functions--expansion and contraction. One can also synthesize orgone energy from them, he says, most interestingly.

We can readily see that Reich, like Jung, was very much impressed by the polarities in nature and the psyche, but, with his biological bent (even bias?), he saw these as expressions of the autonomic nervous system and the pulsation of life itself. I think this is a useful extension of Jung's polarities and may suggest some research of a physiological nature into Jung's introversion-extraversion typology. Reich's partial bias, I think, can be seen in his equation of displeasure with the introverting aspect of the polarity, although I do not think that he was an extravert. If so, how did he manage to get himself into such terrible difficulty with the world around him? His biological reductionism, however, also shows itself in his rejection of meaning, purpose or goal. In several places (e.g. 9, p. 104) he says, that life merely functions; it has no goal or meaning. And again (p. 106), he says that biology knows only functioning and development, follows a natural course without any other significance. Such a view fits better with traditional biology than with psychology, where the archetype of meaning is already supplied with the archetype of the spirit. It seems to me that, later in life, Reich came closer to the meaningful perspective with his conception of bio-psychological unity, as we shall see.

We may now look at Reich's extension of his bio-psychological polarities into what one might call his "basic symbol." This symbol crops up in several different books and with different pairs of opposites. In it, he formulates a process of initial unity, followed by differentiation and opposition, followed by a tendency toward another, higher level of unity. This Hegelian variation of thesis-antithesis-synthesis was also a basis of Jung's thought, as we know. The diagram that Reich used for depicting psychosomatic identity and antithesis can be visualized as a basic dot, considered the source of biological energy, out of which rises an arrow, representing this same identity, which then separates into a pair of opposites, psyche and soma, carrying the opposition (e.g. 9, p.106). Later on, he uses a similar diagram in connection with the autonomic nervous system (9, p. 132). The lower arrow is now vegetative life itself and the opposites are the sympathetic and parasympathetic systems.

In a later book, *The Cancer Biopathy* (9, p. 260), Reich again uses his schema to describe his orgone therapy as neither a psychological nor a physiological-chemical therapy. Instead he sees it as a strictly biological therapy having to do with disturbances of pulsation in the autonomic system. In this diagram, the opposites are mechanical lesion and chemical-physical therapy on the somatic side, with psychotherapy and neurosis on the side of the psyche.

Reich uses this diagram not only in the opposition psyche-soma, the nervous system and in healing, he continues to employ it in a distinction between "good" and "evil"—in the sense of good and bad energy (9, p. 456). "Dor" is the evil energy. Reich is here referring to the antagonism inherent in life energy functions themselves. Evil, he feels arises out of stalemated or immobilized life energy.

Reich's trinitarian symbol--if one can use such a term for his intensely biological imagery--leads over into a four-fold formulation as he discusses the phases of his "orgasm formula": mechanical tension--electrical charge--electrical discharge--mechanical relaxation (p. 114). It is this four-fold system that leads him into using images of union, of circles and spheres.

There are remarkable statements, even in his early and classic *Character Analysis* (9, pp. 148-150) which only too clearly present a representation of the image of the uroborous, of the organism as snake biting its own tail!He describes the organism, particularly in the experience of the orgasm, as striving to unite together head and tail, the embryologically important mouth and anus. This is so fundamental as to be basis of the orgasm reflex. He presents a drawing which resembles a worm with head and tail trying to come close together and calls this the emotional expression of the orgasm reflex. When the organism surrenders itself to its sensations of flowing, it can also surrender itself completely to the partner in the sexual embrace.

Reich then asks what function is served by this moving together of the two ends of the trunk, making for this orgasmic pulsation? He then asserts that the answer goes deeper than the individual biological organism. He sees this as suprapersonal, but not metaphysical nor spiritual. All the same, Reich's denial does not stop him from calling that yearning for surrender and union, "cosmic." He goes on to say that if these two ends of the trunk bend backward, away from each other, instead forward and toward one another, the organism will not be capable of surrendering itself to any experience, whether love or work. Muscular armor, the result of this lack of surrender, essentially prevents this orgasm reflex.

That the symbol of the snake biting its own tail, the uroborous, so dear to alchemy and to Jung, should also be at the base of Reich's work, is remarkable. But since he, too, is struggling to get a grasp of the psyche in matter and its biology, it may not be so surprising after all.

It may also not be surprising when we find that the circle becomes a central image for Reich, both in his depiction of the egg-shape of the "orgonome," the basic form of living matter, and in his portrayal of pathology. For example, he describes (9, p. 337) the most conspicuous aspect of the orgasm reflex—the coming together of mouth and genitals—as having led him to the origin of the orgonome form, which is a circle.He had noted the orgasmic convulsions of animals or the swimming of jellyfish in such a way that the body tends to sag in the center, facilitating this union.

Reich frequently uses the circle symbol, from center to periphery, with the impulse coming from the center, to be deflected by a circle of armor into deviations (e.g. 9, p. 132). When Reich describes his idea of "superimposition" in the genital embrace, one clearly apprehends a biological level of the *coniunctio* archetype (9, pp. 354-355). He describes the preorgasmic body movements, particularly the orgasmic convulsions, as extreme attempts of the organisms and their energy to fuse with each other. He even avers that the orgone energy, in such cases, actually succeeds in transcending the limits of material orgonome. This reaches, I think, a clear perception of the desire of the ego to transcend itself in what Reich previously rejected as mystical experiences. He finally can speak of orgasmic longing as a yearning to strive beyond one's self, and even becomes the answer to riddle of why dying is often represented in the orgasm (9, p. 355). In increasingly poetic language, Reich brings forward the mystical ideas of "salvation in the hereafter," "liberating death" and even nirvana, as ways of expressing that the naturally functioning organism is fulfilled in the orgasm reflex and in the sexual superimposition that accompanies it.

Reich's disclaimer not to the contrary, the *coniunctio* image is deeply imbedded in this concept. This will be even more clearly seen below as I discuss his later understanding of Christ. At this point, it may suffice to indicate that there are several crucial images which Jung has written about extensively and which form the core to Reich's attempt at making psychology biological.

I turn now, to other views of Reich which are of interest to a Jungian. His view of fantasy, for example, which he earlier decried in the sexual act (9, p. 210), is contained in the statement that a person can not imagine anything that does not have a real or objective existence in one form or another, since sense perception is a part of the natural functionings of organisms and follows natural laws, hence "real."

And how is fantasy real? Self perception is an essential part of the life process, says Reich. Very much along the lines of Jung, one might say, and yet a very far cry, indeed, from the elaborate and differentiated way that Jung worked with image and fantasy and their archetypal roots. Could one not venture the guess that what Jung had worked out on the psychological (soul) level, Reich was working on at the biological (body) level? I shall examine this question later on.

There are very real differences between the two thinkers, however, which can be seen, for example, in Reich's view that the function of sensation is everything. Jung said that there are at least three other ways of apprehending existence: feeling, thinking, and intuition. Reich's idea of functionalism transcended both mechanistic thinking and mysticism, however. He noted that science came to the realization that sensation was the key to understanding nature, that that function is the bridge between the ego and the outer world (9, p. 281). The unity of psyche and soma, he referred to as the principle of orgonomic functionalism and this unity, of emotion and excitation, of sensation and stimulus, was its basis. He rejected any form of transcendentalism, he said (9, p. 291), although we have seen where his language goes beyond this.

Reich had no use for a mechanistic attitude toward the body-psyche, which for him was an indication of an armored condition, nor for mysticism, which he saw as merely a consequence of the blocking of direct organ sensations and the subsequent manifestation of these sensations as pathological perception of supernatural powers (9, p. 293).

This leads us into other examples of Reich's view of religion. He believed that, since enduring suffering is the result of the organic incapacity for pleasure, religious ecstasy was essentially masochistic—that is to say, release from sin was the same as release from inner sexual tension. Since the armored person can not do this himself, release is desired or expected from an all-powerful authority, namely God (9, pp. 97-8). Reich, no doubt correct about some suffering, stated that his formulation applied to all religions and suffering, therefore performing the kind of reductionism he learned from Freud.

A fuller statement of his views about religion and sexuality is to be found in his work on orgonomic functionalism (9, p. 305). There, he says that the sharp distinction between sexuality and religion leads to their irreconcilability, and is to be found in both mechanistic and mystical thinking. This is carried to such extremes that the Catholic Church, for example, sees sexual pleasure as a sin, even when sanctified by marriage. The functionalist resolves this contradiction by realizing that the principle common to sexuality and religion is the sensation of nature in one's own organism. When natural sexual expressions were repressed in the human animal during the development of the patriarchy, this produced a severe, unbridgeable contradiction between sexuality as sin and religion as liberation from sin. In primitive religions, says Reich, religion and sexuality were not separated, were one. With the patriarchy, this was split into sin and God. The functionalist understands the identity of emotions in sexuality and religion, the origin of the estrangement and the dichotomy it created, as well as the fear of sexuality among religious people. He also understands the degeneration of sexuality in pornography. The mechanist and the mystic are a product of this contradiction, remain trapped in it, and perpetuate it. The functionalist breaks through the barriers of this rigid contradiction by finding the common features in emotion, origin, and nature.

This is a clear statement by Reich which, like the previous reduction, leaves us seeing its limitations. His understanding of religious experience is small and he projects wholeness onto primitives. But Reich is clear in taking his stand on the image of a "natural" religion based on a "natural" biology. We shall see later on how well this vision was to sustain him. But now we can follow how his intended biological and functional thinking begins to take on other imagery. For example, in that same book, (9, p. 317), he believed that he had found the answer to the hatred and destructive thinking of both mechanistic and mystical thinking: this was the realm of the devil.

This equation of the sadism and destruction, attendant upon armoring, with the Devil, finds its counterpart when Reich, in his later book on the Emotional Plague (9, p. 473), equates "life" with Christ. There, he wishes to subsume, under the heading "murder of Christ," the hatred of all that is alive. For Reich, Christ becomes the principle of life itself, free of armor and, therefore, like a red flag for a bull. A far leap for the functionalist, one thinks. And was it not also Reich's fate to be "crucified," because in his own way he tried to support and identify with this "principle of life" against those who he claimed supported armor and the emotional plague, the "devil?"

I want to turn now to some other areas which show a similarity between Reich's conclusions and Jung's. Here, first, are Reich's views on energy knowing itself (9, p. 517). He not only thinks that the very quest for knowledge is the attempt of orgone energy in the living organism to know itself, to become conscious, but it, in itself, is a piece of that large cosmic orgone energy in action. Becoming almost rhapsodic, once more, Reich feels that he has touched upon the greatest riddle of life, namely that of self-perception and awareness. All striving for perfection appears as a striving for integration of emotion and intellect, for the greatest freedom and flow of bio-energy without blockage. In this quest, one becomes aware that the self is only a bit of organized cosmic orgone energy and, from a more profound perspective, is a step in the functional development of the cosmic orgone itself.

This statement of cosmic orgone energy becoming aware of itself is very much like that of Jung's, is it not, of the Self knowing itself through the encounter with the human ego? Reich even goes so far as to recognize this process as a religious one (p. 518): He even says that the human animal will slowly get used to the fact that *he has discovered his God* and can now begin to learn the ways of God in a very practical manner. Still later, in describing his own developing experiences, but in an impersonal way, Reich says that the image of God, at one point, appeared to be the perfectly logical result of man's awareness of the existence of an objective functional logic in the universe (p. 521). Reich's discovery of this "functional logic" then approaches Jung's formulation of synchronicity (pp. 522-23), when he states that there is a functional identity of objective and subjective natural logic, which is active and of which the investigator felt himself to be a faithful tool. Reich even admits that he followed this path wherever it led him, with awe, as well as a deep sense of responsibility and humility. He uses the image of a "symphony" to express this identity of biological and cosmic superimposition. If these thoughts do not constitute a religious connection with the soma-psyche and universe, then there is none!

I would like to close this section, describing Reich's views as they become similar to some of Jung's, with a paraphrase of a statement which is an eloquent support of what Jung would call individuation (9, pp. 504 ff). There he advises us to follow our own truth, as if it were our brain or liver and in no way try to live a truth which is not fully our own. He also advises us not to preach, but to live our truth and, thereby, by example, show people how to find their own way to truthful living. No two truths are alike, there are no absolutes, but there are some which are common to all. All trees have roots in the soil, for example, but no tree can draw on the roots of another for nourishment. Therefore, we have to find our own. The way to do this is by listening patiently to ourselves. This does not lead to chaos, but to the place where all common truth is found, the sap common to all livings things, beyond animal and man. In a final poetic burst which, for the present reviewer, constitutes evidence that Reich did, indeed, find his truth, he enjoins us to forego other prophets and attend to how we feel when we love dearly, when we are creative or build our home, give birth to our children or look at the the stars at night.

DISCUSSION

As we watch the change in Reich's views over time, we see an anti-religious, anti-mystical viewpoint change to expressions which are almost ecstatic in style, if not in content. Yet this ecstatic and hortatory style does not escape a deep pessimism about the possibility of therapy, including his own, to change anything, really, in the human condition. When interviewed by Eisler in 1952, Reich went so far as to say that there was no use in individual therapy at all, except to help a little bit here and there or for therapists to make money. But for the larger, social situation, it was hopeless. That was why he gave it up. Only in infants was there any hope, in unspoiled protoplasm (10, pps. 46-47).

One sees Reich's despair at the impossibility of changing the social conditions that make for armor and neurosis. We can hardly blame him when we consider that all the insights of depth psychology over the last century have had hardly any impact on the world's social condition at all! Yet is such hopelessness totally warranted? Jung did not seem to think so, which I will discuss in a moment. Let us first continue with these observations from Reich, but now bringing his experiences in connection with Freud, who also was rather despairing about the ultimate capacity of analysis to modify people fundamentally.

Reich tells Eisler that when he first heard Freud say that it was not the purpose of the therapist or anyone else to save the world, Reich disagreed. But, after many years of agony and suffering emotional plague from people's armor, Reich agreed. He came to this agreement only after attempting the changes; Freud gave up without trying.

In this book, Reich makes a considerable point of Freud's pessimism, based on his failure to resolve the character armor resident in his structure, but this did not prevent Reich from arriving at the same conclusion. He continues (10, pp. 69-70) on the topic of therapy, telling how treatment at the beginning of his career was three months, on the average, becoming longer and longer, until Freud left therapy altogether. Freud was clearly disappointed. Reich came to the same conclusion, he tells us, but only after much experience. In his view, adults are hopeless. He uses the analogy, once more, of a tree. Once it has grown crooked, you can't straighten it out. Then Reich startlingly concludes that the biological plasma of the human race has been spoiled for millennia!

Why then, do we pay any attention to the views of Freud and Reich if they, at the end, became so pessimistic about the possible benefits of therapy? Because, I think, they discovered partial truths, if not whole truths. They have advanced psychological understanding and thinking in depth, an innovation which has had considerable reverberation far beyond the impact they experienced during the course of their lives. If they have not deeply effected the political world, they have at least effected the growing corps of therapists and their patients.

For those of us to whom the Jungian viewpoint—with its lack of scientific materialism and its freedom from dogmatism—is more congenial, we can appreciate what these thinkers have to offer. In the present context, I am particularly impressed with Reich's penetration into the body and its tensions, rigidities, and energies. For me, Jung expanded in the depths of the soul the initial discovery of Freud of the unconscious, and Reich has deepened that discovery into the body.

My own experiences of Reichian therapy leads me both to appreciate and agree with what Reich found. It was very clear to me, from the outset, that the breathing and movement techniques of Reichian therapy brought me into contact with my own body rigidities and the possibility of their relief. The resultant deep affects and experiences were not different in kind from those I experienced in Jungian analysis, but they were certainly dissimilar in the quality of connecting these affects most intimately with body sensations. One might say that, for me, as an introverted intuitive type, the Reichian method helped me to get even more in touch with my fourth function of sensation than did the usual Jungian methods of reflection, dream interpretation and active imagination. This procedure of working from the body directly, from sensation and movement to image, rather than the reverse, as usually happens in active imagination, was valuable for me.

Yet I am also in agreement about the limits of Reichian therapy. I did not experience, for example, a final orgasmic reflex about which Reich speaks, although this did occur periodically. After every session there was considerable relaxation, relief and deepening of connection with a psycho-biological core of being. Yet these periods of wholeness were relatively brief, and soon there was a return to some experience of tension, armor, rigidity in some region of my body. Was this because of my own nature, perhaps? Did the astrological condition in my horoscope (Grand Square of Fixed signs) contribute to this situation in a particular way? Or was it a measure of physiological inheritance? A physiatrist (an orthopedic specialist) was of the opinion that people of eastern European origin had more muscular rigidity and stiffness than other groups. Or was it some other aspect of my individual psychology? I think that all of this is true, in large measure. Yet my observation of other patients who have undergone Reichian therapy and even those who may be said to have achieved permanent orgasmic reflex leads me to believe that they are no more free and unarmored than are the bulk of Jungians individuated!

I have written elsewhere (11, p. 101-116) that each therapeutic modality seems to have something specific to offer, yet each system's result seems to entail its opposite, failure! So that, for example, Freudians do not seem to be sexually freer or more genitally mature than others, nor are Adlerians less free of the power drive, nor Reichians less rigid, nor are Jungians more individual. Yet those of us who adhere to a viewpoint or a system have obviously gained considerably from our work therewith.

My conclusion is that each of us, and each view, have some piece of a larger totality of the human experience, just as the various religions seem to apprehend the divine in a particular way. Insofar as we can experience these various therapeutic approaches and findings in ourselves, we transcend provincialism. There are probably as few of us who can do this as there are people who can appreciate the divine experience in the variety of religions! Still, some of us need to try and, for the sake of the evolution of human consciousness, there may be some merit in explicating some of the overlap. It is in this connection that I see Reich and Jung.

Reich, from my standpoint, presents the possibility of expanding Jung's idea of psychic energy, libido, into the biological and body domain directly. It is not by chance, in my opinion, that so much of Reich's conceptions as to the polarities of psychobiology, of synchronicity, of the value of the individual, of freedom and the need to experiment with one's nature, are congenial with Jung's view. I suspect that both men experienced a certain depth of the soul by going deeply into themselves, and both suffered difficulty in communicating their findings and gaining recognition in their lifetimes. Yet we who follow need not be stuck in parochialisms.

I can aver, for example, that it was very clear to me, lying on that Reichian couch for many years, that the "streamings" and flow of energy that I experienced thereon was a most concrete and viable example of the psychic energy that I had for years encountered in terms of images in dreams, fantasies and affects. "Fourth function" or no, this coming to grips with the direct experience of body-energy in the form that Reich describes is most convincing, just as the direct impact of the archetypes can be experienced if one seriously commits himself or herself to the process of active imagination. How these two quite empirical approaches of the soul can then be linked up with the traditional experiences in kundalini yoga, kabbalistic meditation techniques, occult practices and the like remains to be accomplished. I can only say that it is to be regretted that Reich seemed not to know that the energy he described had also been experienced by others in many traditions. He, however, was unique in showing a technique whereby this can readily be produced, and he was also a pioneer in linking such energy and its blocking to the segments and their armoring.

I would like to see further research done in the area of the energies. For example, the linking of typology with autonomic nervous system dominance would be helpful. Yet the basic research for therapists, of course, is with ourselves and with our patients. It is in the spirit of sharing these findings with other therapists that I present this paper.

For me, there is no doubt that the Jungian perspective and findings are the most congenial to my own psychology and experience. Yet it was particularly in the area of my own fourth function, sensation, that the Jungian perspective seemed (and still does seem) insufficient. I was personally helped by Reichian therapy to improve my awareness of sensation, both introverted and extraverted, but I still see little impact from any of the depth psychologies on the facts of the world (extraverted sensation function), the environment, or the societies in which they live. This is not the fault of these psychologies, but it is incumbent upon us to recognize, as do Brown and Kovalenko (4, pp. 10-11) that:

> There is growing existential despair, disillusion with authorities, continued arms build up, inflation, ecological and environmental disaster, terrorism, inability to solve starvation and world health problems or apply the wonders our technology has produced to practical world conditions. It should not be surprising that people are filled with anxiety, depression and stress.

Given such a condition of existence, both Freud and Reich grew pessimistic, even bitter. Jung, on the other hand, seems to have had a sufficiently large world-view to take in the obvious negativities and transcend them. He did this by linking up his own experiences historically and cross-culturally, so that he felt less isolated and alone. He also did so, I believe, by grappling with the problem of evil in a psychological and historical manner which helped him see our condition as an evolutionary one. His magnificent book, *Answer to Job*, is one that has revolutionized our understanding of the problem of evil and made it available to us as a psychological problem with which an individual can grapple. With Jung, therefore, one can struggle with these issues in the depths of one's own soul. It is from our own work with evil that an enhanced consciousness can result in some change in the collective, inner or outer.

At the day to day level of therapeutic work, I can report that I have used Reichian methods, either alone or in conjunction with Jungian work, with perhaps one-quarter of my patients over a period of six years. More recently, I have generally given up Reichian methods and look to find other ways and views whereby sensation, body and world can impact my analysands and myself within the traditional analytical work. I do this partly from the realization that I am not as skilled or as "natural" a Reichian as I would like, and partly because the asymmetrical stance of the therapy (doctor "treating" or "working on" the patient) is less congenial to me at this time than the work in symmetry (mutual process). This in no way leads me to value the Reichian work less, any more than I denigrate the traditional asymmetric stance of Freudian and Jungian colleagues. Rather, I do this from a sense of individual talent and temperament. I am strongly of the opinion that a knowledge and experience of Reich's work would be of great value to many Jungians—as great, perhaps, at the physical level, as the knowledge of alchemy has been at an intellectual level.

REFERENCES

1. Greenfield, Jerome. *Wilhelm Reich vs. The U.S.A.* W.W Norton & Co., New York, 1974
2. Harms, Ernest. "C.G. Jung—Defender of Freud and the Jews." *Psychiatric Quarterly*, April 1946.
3. Jaffe, A. "C.G. Jung and National Socialism" in *From the Life and Work of C.G. Jung.* Harper and Row, New York, 1971.
4. Kovalenko, Lawrene and Brown, D. "A Talk about Reich, Jung, and Contemporary Times" for Saddleback Community College, May 1979.
5. Regardie, Francis. *A Chiropractic Therapy for the Emotional Disorders.* (privately printed, no date)
6. Reich, Peter. *A Book of Dreams.* Harper and Row, New York, 1973.
7. Reich, Wilhelm. *Character Analysis.* Orgone Institute Press. New York, 1949. (Original in 1933 and 1929)
8. Reich, Wilhelm. *The Function of the Orgasm.* Noonday Press, New York, 1971. (Original in 1927 and 1942)
9. Reich, Wilhelm. *Selected Writings.* Farrar, Strauss and Giroux, New York, 1973.
10. Reich, Wilhelm. *Reich Speaks of Freud.* Farrar, Strauss and Giroux, New York, 1967.
11. Spiegelman, J. Marvin. "The Image of the Jungian Analyst and the Problem of Authority." *Spring*, 1980, pp. 101-116.

CHAPTER ONE

SESSIONS 1 AND 2: SEPTEMBER 16, 1971

Well, I have had my first official "treatment." I had had an introductory session with Regardie earlier, in which we chatted and he took my history. It was strange indeed to "tell my story" and later, to write a more extensive history for him, after having taken so many myself, during the earlier years of my own training as both therapist and analyst... More recently—knowing that histories are as much fantasy as fact, and that the history changes as attitudes change—I do not take such formal surveys with patients anymore, but let the memories, experiences, and facts emerge as we work with dreams, feelings, and so on. So now, to give my own history and to write it also is peculiar.

Also peculiar have been my own feelings before this first "official" session. As I had acknowledged to Regardie, I was quite ambivalent about undertaking this work again. I was reluctant to pay for help, though knowing full well that the healer (like myself) was entitled to his fee. I was also reluctant to put myself under the jurisdiction of someone else again, after having had very bad experiences with colleagues who thought they were in a position to judge me. This was somewhat aggravated by Regardie addressing me by my first name and asking that I call him by his last name. Again, a power or status struggle. He is older it is true...but no, I shall ask him to call me also by my last name. There, I shall compel a kind of equality!

But I do find the man warm and interested. He pokes, manipulates, stretches. He asks me to breathe continually and deeply, including a hyperventilation which makes me dizzy. Yes, I know that this is a kind of breathing to induce more emotionality, less defensiveness. I accept it. All that poking, and his request that I respond to pain by screaming out and by pounding his table...this is strange. But it had a good effect. Strange reactions: tingling of hands, limbs, and, at one point, feeling my mouth congeal into a condition which felt like "I will not cry!" There was no affect with it, but a muscular tension of my mouth, along with a memory from childhood wherein I said this to myself. When my mother would—in my feeling—excessively enquire of me as in an inquisition, or berate me, I would stand firm and silent, neither answering nor crying. It was my dignity and courage. And now this thought: I will not cry. But, in response to my healer's question, no, I have not held back the tears in my life. I have cried. Indeed, as my mother has said about my childhood, and my wife and other people have also known, I have been a man of emotion and express feelings readily. If anything, I cry to excess. I cry at performances, I cry at the pain of patients. I cry with joy. I cry when I see my children in their beautifully open and spontaneous ways. So, then, the statement, "I will not cry" is a residue, a piece of the "flesh" speaking from an ancient time, when I was not so emotional.

26

After the session, I feel strangely happy. I feel less tense than before, less rigid. And I am gayer. It is soon, though, for any true effect. I smile. I notice that I am already in a kind of projecting transference with my healer, just as I was many, many years ago when I first underwent analysis myself, and just as I have seen many patients undergo it. I tell him things about a book of his I have read, complimenting it. He mentions an author, and I resolve to read this book, just to learn more about him. There is a going forward of my psyche as a kind of cloud or smoke to envelop him, know him, like him, and to be known, pleased and liked in return. Yes, indeed, this is the beginning of the famous embroilment of healer and patient, which I now experience again, after many years, from the side of patient. I do not mind. We shall see.

POST SESSION : REFLECTIONS: SEPTEMBER 22, 1971

But also there is sadness. There is a feeling of no longer being able to be a healer myself, no longer believing that my way of working is right and efficacious. A new patient enquires, a parent wonders if I can help his adolescent son, one who is compelled to wash and clean himself, has to stay away from youngsters his own age. He has been to other healers without help, can I help? I speak to the father, am touched by the plight of the son who, strangely, bears the same first name as my own son, but can I help? I do not know. I even think of sending this man to my own healer, rather than myself. But then a priest comes to see me, a man of God. Him, I can help, having heard his dreams. Yes, there I can help: God people, religious people, soul people. I can help by understanding, by empathy, by the widening of consciousness. But, can I help pain, when my own is so great? I do not know. I have helped and I have not. I have been helped and I have not. So it is; let be what is.

SESSION 3: SEPTEMBER 22, 1971

Today I experienced a clonism. This is a spontaneous shaking and moving of a part of the body, a muscle or other area. After working on couch and table, breathing and crying out, being gouged and pushed in belly and legs, I suddenly dropped my legs in a relaxation as natural and unanticipated as my previous tensing of the leg was automatic. At that point, there began a heaving at the diaphragm, a wave-like motion of the stomach, an experience which can be best described as a weeping of the belly without tears. The emotional content that accompanied this experience was one in which my being was saying, "There has been tension, tension, all my life; conflict, conflict, all my life. Let me relax, let me rest!" And, for a moment, there was rest. But the rest was brief, tension returned, and longing resumed. But it happened. I had always been able to weep freely from the eyes and from the chest (sobs), but not from my belly. Now my belly was weeping on its own, was freeing itself from being tense, so tight.

Earlier on, we discussed my horoscope. The doctor said, as have astrologers before him, that the several squares of opposition, the four squares which coalesce at the center of my chart, make my psyche and my life quite difficult. This continuity of conflict might kill another man, he said, but my own inheritance of physical and spiritual vitality enables me to survive and turn it into a creative expression. But, all the same, a life of continual conflict... This I knew in my own soul, and with this I am reconciled. For I have, indeed, embraced this battle of the soul. It is in the flesh that this conflict now pains me so, in the struggle of the muscles to be tense and relax, to ward off and to fight, to want to rest and submit. But, continued the healer, the horoscope is one of a very big personality. The chart shows the possibility of a disturbed mother— Neptune in the fourth house, which can produce madness, addiction, or genius. With me, perhaps it has produced something of all three. I know that in my moral-instinctual conflicts, there has indeed been a kind of madness of pain. I know, too, that I have been suspicious and attacking at times, which is mad since it is sometimes not in accord with reality. Struggle with excessive eating and drinking is in my background. As to genius? Well, who can say of himself that he is, or also, is not? It is better, I think, to speak of one's own genius, in the sense of the spirit, or, in the stories of the genie in the bottle, the mercurial demon-spirit who lives in us. That, of course, is the genius of the soul, the particularity and strangeness which is our individuality and specialness. But, I do not want to dwell on my struggles with the abandonment of ego to Self, nor the realization of Self in ego—not because these are not true and valuable, but because I wish to stay away from ideas and images, fantasy and reflection, and dwell in the physical reality of muscle, pain and clonisms, the weeping of belly, the frozenness of mouth which is a dark apprehension of the sorrow of the universe, the pain of depression, the knowing in my depths that there has been no rest, no release, no feeling of "there, there, it is all right."

But still, there are ideas and patterns and forces. And there is the horoscope, too. It is not, perhaps, that I am too much in the world of ideas, for the horoscope shows much fire and water as well as air signs, but very little earth. Mercury, only, dwells in Taurus, in the earth, so I am like the Hanged Man in the Tarot, whose head is in the earth. That means much to me, for have I not always dwelt upon the problems of "earth," of instinct and desire, passion and realization? And yet, as Regardie says, I am bound to be impractical and not effective with things. Despite these struggles and lacks, Jupiter rules benevolently for me, just as my father was benevolent, and there is much help from outside, from women, and from spontaneous creative events. I must, by nature, work hard, but the redemption comes not from my own work! A friend tells me that the "Hanged Man," in Tarot, is a symbol of non-vicarious salvation, as opposed to the Christian symbol.

So be it, if true. Most emotional am I, says the doctor, from the horoscope. I knew that. But, I ask, can this tension and conflict be reduced in the flesh? Yes, says he; anyway a great deal of it. My psyche has adjusted to conflict creatively, can the body be healed of it? There is hope.

POST SESSION : REFLECTIONS: OCTOBER 6, 1971

It is in between sessions. But I wish to speak a little about what I have often experienced—a strange depression. Sometimes, when I read the work of other healers, the views and theories of some of them, I grow a little agitated and then depressed. As if I am wrong and they are right, and I am in error or illusion. Yet

I also think it is they who do not see what I have seen, know what I have known. My own way seems unique—it is not for most people. And then I dream: I dream that I walk into a clinic, a hospital where I both studied and taught, and where my father both studied and taught. Another healer is there and does not know me. He asks what I do and I tell him. He replies, coolly, that my way of work is doomed, old-fashioned. His method, leaving the soul altogether behind, is the new wave. There is no soul at all, of course, says he, the very definition is unscientific and useless. I feel strangely destroyed, wiped out. Like a very old worker whose hand is replaced by machines. I awaken sad, and sad am I now. Shall I engage this sadness, as I did of old? Shall I, rather, enquire of the Gods of Healing, as has been my plan? Or is it, as a loving colleague has said to me, that it is like an animal in his territory? He is in his space and if another animal appears, there is threat and battle. At that level of the soul, at the level of the animal and dark struggle, there is only either/or. It is only when I am in my high spiritual life that I can espouse the value: "Let many flowers bloom; let many theories and beliefs and experiences fill the scene and help us to come to that manifold truth where individuality and complexity can live with the singleness of the one truth, the community of all." There, on high, is tolerance, bigness. Down low, in the belly, perhaps, there is fear and mistrust, holding one's territory. So says the colleague. This seems true. But what of the sadness? I shall let it speak, let it tell me itself of its condition. In this, I shall be true to my original great master, Jung, whose spirit I have followed and revered since a youth.

I am in the fantasy. It is the end of the dream, in which I leave the University and Clinic and walk alone. I walk to the sea and gaze out at it. I puzzle; why do I feel so broken and defeated by these differences of view, even though it is understandable that each "sect" believes, as in religion, that it is the true one? My sadness is like a dark cloud which covers the sun. And, at that moment, even outside, the sun is indeed covered by a single dark cloud, which makes the world dark and dreary for a moment and goes by. It is light again. I must go into that cloud, I think. I can travel astrally in my dreams, why not in this fantasy, which is a reality of the soul? This I do. I go up, up, and find myself in this dark cloud. I rest in it, and find it soft, like a bed. An old idea, of course and, to those ancients who knew nothing of direct experiences with clouds, a reasonable idea. This cloud is like a bed. I rest in it. What does it mean, that I rest in it? That I am merely passive in my depressions and do nothing? Yes. That I am spoiled in them? Perhaps. But perhaps I can make something of them. I take some cloud and mold it into a little man, a sculpture of a depressed little man. That is it! I shall be like the Greek artist Pygmalion and create for myself a new life! I shall be like God Himself and create a partner for a dialogue with me. He, this creature born out of my depression, will speak with me, accompany me, be my friend and brother. Or will he be a child? Will he be my own hurt child, my own wounds and madness? But why leap ahead? Let me make this creature and see what emerges.

I mold and mold. An animal emerges. It is an ox, or a bull. He is not fierce, but looks at me as if he were a cow or steer. The eyes are sad. It is a castrated bull. I can see that this is a bull whose powers are destroyed, his fierce capacity for battle has been taken away. Is that the sadness? Is this the passionate fighter I once was? Merely defeated by all these other animals, or, better, by little men who had the power, had the scythe or weapon, to take away my power in the world?

The steer nods. Yes, I must admit defeat. Others were stronger than I. The battle is lost. But not the war, perhaps. Better yet, why fight at all? Is it victory that I seek? Vengeance? Perhaps, but that is a lesser need than the desire to know more deeply. So, then, I must take in this bull, assimilate this steer, realize that I was defeated. I embrace the steer, look deeply into his eyes and say:

"I know old battler, old friend. We are defeated, you and I, we have lost. But it does not matter any more. We shall sit peacefully and reflect. We shall approach the Gods. You, great defeated bull, are not to be blamed because goaded and harmed by those who like to play that game. I shall sit upon your back like a Zen monk, and I shall play my flute for you."

I do this and the steer brightens, his eyes take on pleasure and joy. He looks up with happiness and I sit upon his back in comfort. He is a strong ox, after all, with a capacity for pulling loads. He has endurance. He will outlast those who go from fad to fad, idea to idea. He, indeed, can pull the cart, the chariot of my warrior spirit, in a tamed way... No, he looks sad again at being "tamed." Rather, he responds to warmth, to love, to my care. The defeated bull of my soul is to be embraced by me. Defeated in battle, he will pull my chariot with his vitality and endurance, carry this bruised body with dignity and care. And the warrior in me will no longer be a bull, but a man! Very good, the bull and I are happy.

So, this is the first creature which emerges out of the cloud of my depression, the despair of my being a defeated healer. The battle is no longer at the bull, or territorial level, but at a more human one, perhaps. But we both acknowledge defeat. Others have the victory in the world. We can go on with dignity, not victory. Still, the spectacle of no testicles on my bull is too sad. The bull smiles; yes he smiles. For it is the man who has testicles not the bull! Yes... And, as they say, "the bull has gone out of sight." He has become the energy carrier of this body-chariot of mine. And we shall see what other creature comes from the dark cloud. But not today, not today.

SESSION 4: OCTOBER 6, 1971

Today, I felt a need to breathe from the belly, deeply. I longed for a deep breath. How aware I was that I normally breathe from mouth and chest, from lungs. I knew, of course, the value of belly-breathing and was well able to do it, but only by force, by conscious attention to it. Now I felt a longing to let it breathe of itself, let the relaxation take into itself the great *prana* of the world without having to control or force.

But I could not. Regardie's pressure on my stomach elicited tension in my back, control and protection in the same belly-center, Svaddhisthana chakra, the same back-belly place where my pain, hunger, longing, and struggle is. Oh Leviathan, Oh Makara, oh fish of desire and ravenous moon-glow in the depths of the ocean of unconsciousness, you dwell in me so deeply and darkly! Despite all my efforts, you leave me in pain, in ceaseless struggle between devouring and fasting, between control and a surrender which will not happen—or happens only as surrender to self-destructive devouring forces!

And my screaming does not come in rage and pain. Rather, as he works, I find myself trying to fight back with my breath, countering the pressure of his hands, his thumbs, his fists. But the fighting, the counter-pressure, did not lead me to relax. I saw that my way was counter-productive, not helpful. Help for me, it seems, is active, devoted, working, never relaxed, never surrendering. How sad for me!

My chest? Stiff. As if from fear, the healer said. Was I frightened very much as a child from my mother's words? No, I was not. I remember her saying that she was afraid she would kill me, and her saying that she asked her own mother to take a knife from her hands, but I do not recall being afraid of her actually doing so. How much was fantasy? How much was the true word of her mouth? Rather, I was afraid of her temper, her words and anger, not her physical strength. But, yes, a memory comes: of humiliation, of my soiled undergarments thrust in my face. Poor woman, distraught over this "passive-aggressive" child who resumed soiling his pants as the only way, perhaps, to show aggression and anger, keeping it stilled in his chest. Poor woman, sensing the rage and battle, counter defeats, counter humiliates. I recall that feeling, the pain. Now it comes as an inner battle: control versus letting go, keeping tight versus surrender. Now too, there comes a need to break wind in the session, to let go, relax sphincters, but afraid. I do so and the healer, of course, says it is only natural, no problem. Yet that is no release, no surrender, really. Come now, wounded healer, I say to myself, this is not "child's play." You longed for relaxation, your sought-for surrender, your belly-breath and child-healing will not come so easily!

Further enquiries from the healer: no chest illnesses? Yes, in a way. Hay fever, of course, serious. And cured many times: by me alone when I left home in my youth; and two other times when I began deep work on my own soul with healers. Cured, but, of course, a tendency there. What was the word? Predisposition? I recall that hay fever, like asthma, is interpreted as a cry of the soul, an anger of the child, a rage at the mothering. I recalled too, the attempt at control of my sneezing. Mother, once again, not understanding, tried to "help" by getting me to stop sneezing. Again control, control: "Control your sphincters, control your sneezing, control, indeed, your breathing!" Yes, the message came through clearly. And a message to myself, control your anger, control your temper! But with analysis, I gave up such control and raged freely. But other controls, other messages, are still there: Control breathing and sphincters.

I think that my breaking wind, like the temper outbursts, is a freeing. Perhaps it has the same contempt and explosive character that it had in childhood. But the breath held is the heart constricted, the chest raised high. To control, to maintain pride. I was helping my mother and myself, fine compromise! Too much control in my child-life: sphincters, breathing, temper...Now I can breathe more fully, and the soft loving flows. Is this "soft flowing" a breath, feces, or feeling? No matter. It flows and even though the constriction returns, there is expectation, says the healer, that at some point the body will cooperate in the healing and not fight. I can cooperate by...I do not know how.

But we spoke too, about another healer of the body, a woman who needs only ten double-hours to accomplish all that Reichians would desire. I knew her, says Regardie. I saw her years ago. Yes, her method helps some people, is based, indeed, upon a similar viewpoint and attitude, but the cure is limited. There is only a superficial releasing of the muscles, the deep emotional freeing does not take place. For some, of course, this is enough, but not enough for most people. He, himself, would abandon his own method and embrace hers if it were truly sufficient. Of course, so would I. But would I?

Which brings me to the wonderings, again, about my own talking, dreaming, fantasy method. Should I, would I, abandon it? Not likely, even if the results are marvellous. Too much at stake. And so it would be for most practitioners. We are a conservative and fearful lot. Too much status to lose, too much livelihood and, of course, like the old apes, too rigid in our ways. But I will adapt, change, move. First, I say to myself, first "heal thyself."

I conclude from this 4th session, a need for deep breath and soft flow. And I taste sweet spit, but also a taste of medicine, or smelling something. Does he use something, like rubbing oil, or is it only in my fantasy?

SESSION 5: OCTOBER 13, 1971

During this past week, I suddenly grew ill. Rarely one to suffer physical illness, one evening I felt stomach cramps, nausea, which increased in the morning and, by the end of the day, I was a little dizzy, weak. When I came home, I had several degrees of fever. Strange to say, my wife suffered from a similar ailment. At first I attributed this to excessive eating the night before when, to make my sister-in-law feel good, I ate too much of her good dinner, more than I wished. Oh, how many times I had done this (still do this), in relation to my mother's cooking! I eat the good food and, knowing that this is the way they show love and care, knowing that my eating a lot and enjoying it is a care-showing back, I overdo it and later regret it!

But this time it was not the case, since my wife did not overeat. In truth, I suppose, the psychological fact of my eating on the basis of distorted love needs was correct, but not the physical input. In a day or two it passed, but I felt strongly that this disease of the belly, rare as it is with me, although surely an intestinal flu, was also a meaningful coincidence with the struggles with the belly center that I had been undergoing. Hunger, food, love, eating, cramps, nausea—all together. To say nothing of the diarrhea! And, withal, my lower back ailment suddenly recurred after many months of relative surcease! So, Svadhisthana was surely disturbed, and I felt it deeply in the flesh.

So then, upon beginning the fifth session with the healer, I was feeling better from my illness, but prepared for further work on it. Sure enough, the healer found my whole side out of line, and it required deeper adjustments to get it back. He agreed as to the meaningful coincidence of illness and belly-center. And so, once aligned, we began the "work," with which I was now becoming slowly familiar. But first, he had me jumping in place, breathing deeply, and bending, in front of the mirror; how ungainly I looked! How ungraceful, and how stiff I was also. Once on the table, the breathing, the calling out. The pain...of neck...of chest...of legs, as he systematically and slowly pressed them down with each breath. And then the familiar tingling in arms and legs, and the smells and tastes of uncertain memory. I asked, later, whether he had something on his hands that gave this somewhat pungent, medicinal smell. He said no. Some unknown memory, perhaps.

So we worked, until...At one moment, the healer struck me a blow on the stomach, a punch, I felt, which—he later assured me—was only an unexpected tap which facilitated the response. And what a response! Spasms of belly and chest, sobs from heart and throat! And, unlike the previous time, tears. Tears and sobs, racking and heaving sobs and weeping, while my belly spasmically heaved and my legs fell, relaxed. Most striking of all—memory. With the blow, with the spasm, with the tears, as if stored up in a brain belonging to that same belly, there appeared a memory of a time long ago...

I was not much more than eleven years old, newly arrived in a different junior high school, the result of my family's move from a working class neighborhood to a middle class one. This school was so much better. No rough and brutal children, no daily fear of fights, no latent or overt antisemitism. Or, so I thought. But I was wrong. Soon after my entrance into this new school, there seemed to be a necessity that I establish myself, be initiated or something. Whatever it was, there was another boy, nasty and tough—I thought at first— but really as frightened and pathetic and needy as I, whom I had to fight. I really did not know why. It just was so. In the non-rational world of initiation among boys, even among the enlightened, the middle-class, there needed to be initiation, struggle, combat. And so I fought. Now my memory showed a scene on the grass outside the school after classes. Several boys gathered around the other lad and myself as we fought: he hitting me, I hitting him; he knocking me down, me knocking him down. Finally he struck a hard blow to my stomach, which drove the air out of me. I was unable to breathe for a moment, nor cry, nor speak. But then the fight was over and we embraced. The need for battle and initiation was accomplished and I was alright. But here in the healer's room, there now flowed the tears for that poor lad that was I. Now what I felt was the futility of that battle, the sorrow, the loss of air, the needing to cry. And the disappointment that I had to fight, the feeling that I was not a good fighter. The memory of that poor lad that was I, so one-sidedly developed, having skipped two whole years of school and advanced intellectually but not emotionally and socially. I was also large for my age, but not so strong. I wept for the futility and the pain of that boy. I wept the held-in tears of frustration that this lad could not show. This poor lad, living in my belly, cramped up.

I wept for a time and then stopped, quiet. But only for a bit. Once again the sobs began, with more belly spasms, and another memory presented itself of an earlier time. Now I recalled an earlier fight, when I was just nine years old. My parents had sent me to a summer camp, "for my own good." I was sent away for a whole month—for the first time—and this was all right, but they had no idea of what they were sending me to. It was the camp of a military school! Of all things for a nice Jewish boy, intelligent and shy! The school was for rough children of broken homes, mainly, with not one Jew. I suppose my parents were attracted by the idea that there was time spent in the mountains and time spent at the seashore—ideal, no doubt, in their minds, but utterly unconnected, as usual, with both my inner reality, and the reality of what a boy's life was in America.

The memory: Being assigned work, which was alright, for all had some "chores." But mine? To feed the pigs, of course. What other job would the thoughtful and considerate French director of this camp select? Naturally! He must have had his initial intellectual training in the same French school which produced the Dreifuss trial and Devil's Island! So, I objected, weakly. From this weak objection, it emerged that I must fight. I do not know, even now, how this was so. Perhaps I was allowed another job, but only if I win the fight. In any case, I found myself in a boxing ring, this time with a boy who was both larger than myself and, certainly, more physically differentiated, strong.

I remembered it now on the healer's couch. We are in the ring. I swing at the boy and try to hit him, without success, for he manages to keep his head close to his chest. Meanwhile, he hits me, and I am both hurt by his blows and frustrated at my own impotence. Finally, again, a blow in the stomach, and I can hardly breathe. I am defeated, ignominiously. But it is all right. Again, the defeat brings me a certain acceptance. But still, no change: the Jew must feed the pigs! no justice, but less harassment. And now I shut up. But, on the table, I recall: the futility of battle, the impotence, the humiliation, all of these together. And I weep and weep, no words. Silence.

With silence, comes…what? Understanding? No, not entirely. I understand the need for initiation, for battle, for boys to be tough. I understand, even, the anti-semitism, without rancor now. Now, very physical myself and well able to defeat any such boy or man my own size—certainly that brutal Frenchman—no longer humiliated physically, or as a male person, I am silent because I understand the primitive necessity of the boys, of men, and I can weep for that poor lad that I was: needing real help in developing in the male world of battle and force, and not having it. I understand and feel. Now my tears are for the futility of it all. Even my understanding does not heal the feeling of futility. I respect the physical and emotional need of the natural man and weep at the futility of how it is fulfilled. So, no rituals; no initiations for that primitive world. I had to do it myself, later on, with my own discipline and fighting. Not so much physical fights, but battles to become more physical, strong, and less fearful. But something in me knows that the weeping and heaving, the remembering and understanding, are not enough. Something in me knows that this voyage into the past, the memory of the muscles, the belly brain, are still at work. There are things which are even more painful, known but not known. I had, after all, been over much of my childhood and youth with previous analysis, had I not? But these muscle memories? These belly affects? No, not weeping like that, not heaving like that. And there is surely more.

Then a dream comes to verify my suspicion about myself. A dream comes, as if to say, "Look, you are still deceiving yourself, deluding yourself in some way: there is still more of the problem of Father and Son, of Maleness, to be found in this muscle-memory, brain belly."

The dream: I am in the healer's office with my father. There is something that I am not telling the healer; that I am also going to another healer with my father, and that I make daily notes, where I sign my signature. Interpretation? Easy. For I do, in fact, write these notes and reflections apart from the healer, as if there is, indeed, a "second healer" to which I go. And, I am sure the outer healer would not mind this. Indeed, I mentioned this to him casually once. Also, I am, indeed, with "my father" in the healing, in both places, working on the problem of male identification, failure, need. I do, indeed, pay the "healer" outside and inside each time, and "sign my name." So it is. My psyche announces the fact, but also announces that there is a deception, there is a discrepancy between the two, just as I intuited. I accept this discrepancy, but need to learn more about it.

SESSION 6: OCTOBER 20, 1971

During this past week, I felt all right. The day before this sixth treatment, however, after working well and hard with my own patients, I felt detached, a little weird—cut-off, dissociated, non-connected. Then today, after my usual running, there was a pain in my chest, as if asthma, a wheezing. I had bronchitis as a child, is this a recurrence?

In the session, I begin as usual: straightening of spine, jumping. Then the couch: gouging, pushing, pressing. Legs spread and the breathing. Then came a trembling of the legs. I felt it, after the healer called attention to it, and also a tightening of the upper leg muscles as if to restrain and control this trembling. The affects: hopelessness (from childhood, said the healer), longing for the father (recall the dream of last week), and memories, but without affect. "Memory without affect is without effect" says Freud, as so says Regardie, too. True. Feeling of resistance.

With the end of the session comes a sense of disappointment, wanting more. More drama, perhaps, or more of father. It all has a cumulative effect, says the healer, "insidious."

Now, as I write, outside the healer's place, as I am accustomed to doing, there is quiet, but an unknown, sad feeling. I suddenly feel that I haven't paid for the session, but I have.

Away I go, for the week-end enjoyment; good with friends, good with my wife, but unhappy when alone. Unusual. More need for alone time—for active imagination, perhaps.

A dream comes, in which a woman is subject to a man who does not care about other people. I am afraid that she will support him, be exploited, too. I awaken angry, angry at patients who have exploited me, not paid me. Angry and impotent.

Now, daytime and daylight. I want to go into that rage and sadness, for the sadness is there also. The sadness comes at not being connected with, not having my own needs met. The anger is that others present their needs, and I must "understand!" Rage and sadness.

Now, back to that cloud, that dark cloud which I visited before, where I encountered that poor ox, that sad-eyed, castrated, impotent ox of my potent soul who had been brow-beaten and defeated, retaining only his endurance and his strength, but who could no longer snort and roar. Poor, good, tamed, knowing ox. But now there is a rage in me, in this cloud, this "cloud of unknowing." There is a rage and a pain at the endless taking care of others, having to put aside my own needs, endless having to "understand!"

So, cloud, show me what the rage looks like! Show me the form of this rage and what it protects, what it wants, what I must attend to! I call upon thee! I summon and request, pray and demand!

I see the sad-eyed ox once again, but these sad eyes now belong to a child, a little lad. This dark, curly-haired boy, between five and eight, looks sadly at me. He has no words. He looks only sad. And I feel sad. But where is the rage, where is that wild affect? All gone—at the moment. Only the sad boy is here. Sad and hopeless. Were these the affects of last week? The boy is sad and hopeless. He will never be free, never be understood, never be really happy. Is that how I felt between five and eight? Those sad days when we moved to the empty fields on Jefferson. Those lonely, friendless days of a year or so, before we moved back to Potomac Street. Yes, I recall seeing those weed-filled lots, those lonely hills, later to be painted by my friend, Martin, and the painting given me by him. But that boy, that sad, friendless boy: let me speak with him.

"Oh, lad, tell me why you are sad. Tell me of your sorrow." He only weeps, as I hold him in my arms.

Later on, I am back in the cloud, with the sad-eyed ox and the sad-eyed boy, but free from the rage. I see, rising, an angry spirit, a wisp, as if a genie in a bottle. Is it the spirit Mercurius, Himself? Is he a Genie, with wishes? No, he is a smoke-made creature, with eyes as dark as the ox and the boy, but fierce. He arises from the bottle as if he is the cloud himself, not so solid as the ox or boy.

"Speak to me Spirit, speak to me Rage-King, and tell me who you are, what you want!"

"I shall speak to you knave, jack of trumps," he says, "I shall speak. Jack of trumps is charioteer, so mount! Mount, chariot-man and take a journey with me. Take your ox and your silent boy, and journey with me."

"Gladly, Spirit, gladly, for I feel, already, a certain relief in the chest, as if the spirit of oppression lifts itself in me. But tell me, first, about yourself. How can I try you, to 'scry you,' as they say, to see if you are real, favorable, or what?"

"Ask away, Jack, ask away."

"Jack is not my name, nor am I a Tarot card. I can take the trip, but first, why the rage, and who are you?"

"I am the voice of evil, it is said. I am the voice of rage. I am the voice that justice demands, I am the voice so sad. Changeable am I and vitriol. Steadfast am I and sturdy. Ask what you will of me, but more confused will you be. I can be known through vision and scene, through taste and smell, through senses all. Knights knew me, and so can you."

"But why rage, why evil?"

"Evil is rage, they say, and rage evil."

"Who says?"

"You say!"

"I do?"

"You do. And yet I protect you, note the deviltry in others. I can see. If you would but listen, listen and protect..."

"But you rage out in me, call out and demand, proclaim, judge and shriek so that all run from me when you are in me."

" 'Tis true, I suppose, 'tis true. Enough talk. Come with me and see. All questions will be answered. Trust me now and see what change will be."

"I will trust, then, for I strangely do. What else can I trust? Besides, I am alone, alone with ox and child. So we will come with you."

I walk along a sky-path with the child on the ox's back. He and the ox are both less sad now, just quiet, rather expectant. I walk along, holding a string attached to the ox's nose, loosely. The spirit goes on ahead of us. I ask that he lead us, though now I want to run away! What perversity, what two-sidedness!

"Just like me!" says the spirit, and laughs. Less fierce. "Two-sided."

But now we walk where the spirit leads. We walk in the air. We are in the astral region, where one can walk in air. It is the walkable air, as contrasted with the outer air itself. We walk high up, led by the spirit. Round we walk, round and round...distractions come in. Other thoughts, places...conflict...As I experience this, I fall to earth, the ox and boy also fall also. The spirit vanishes in a wisp, and I clutch the ground. Ox and boy are tiny, but the earth is warm and we weep into it. I need to be held by it. The spirit laughs at me, laughs at the need. Soar with me, he seems to say, fly with me into heights and beyond, follow me, have no regard for those petty, vulnerable, childhood, earthy needs. The spirit cares nought for those things, it seems. But I have to. Someone has to. Else rage. But I thought that the rage came from the spirit.

"It does. When the earthy part is not cared for."

"Puzzling, puzzling. I am confused."

CHAPTER TWO

SESSION 7: OCTOBER 27, 1971

Today, the healer began as usual: straightening my back, but he noticed that the adjustment was far faster today than, say, one month ago. It was encouraging. Then, jumping, breathing, calling out, screaming. As he works hard upon my painful neck and upper shoulders, I feel great pain and I call out, "Please, please, I want to get away from the pain." Then I have a need to bite, to bite hard. The healer gives me a towel upon which to bite, and I do so, but then the feeling again of "it is useless to fight, to bite, aggression is futile," and then tears and sobs. A sense of deep aloneness.

Regardie remarks that in childhood I probably heard, "Big boys don't cry." No, not that. That is not the place of this pain that I feel; not the stupid statement about masculinity, nor even the place that I was with my mother, when I said to myself at five and six and seven and ten: "Don't cry and be humiliated." Or again, "Don't cry and give her the satisfaction." Yes, I remember those feelings, those experiences and attitudes, but this silent place is not any of those. It is a deep, non-verbal place. It is not a place of infancy, but of an *aloneness with God*! I tell the healer this. I know this place and yet do not know it, why the sadness of it, the sense of futility. For it is not the futility of God, but the futility of fighting. But I do not know why or what...Then, the healer notes that my back is truly touching the table, that there is a deeper relaxation and a softness in the tears and affect. I sense this, but very soon I feel the arch again, the raising of this same back at the belly center, at the Svaddhisthana region. At the same moment, I am aware of feeling for the healer, not wanting him to feel bad that he was mistaken, that he not feel that he has failed, or that what I am saying is a complaint. As I move out toward him in my feeling and concern, I sense that my now flattened back has arched again. This is my split, I tell him. I cannot relax, attend to myself and go out toward him at the same time! It is a split between belly and heart, between caring for oneself and for another. I can not do both at the same time! How often this is so with my patients! How often I go out toward them even when needy or bloody myself!

I try to convey this to Regardie. Does he understand? Can he really see the energy centers? Can he notice the flow of the forces? For this is the magic I wish to learn from him. I also want to give him some things, to teach him about methods of active imagination. Does he really understand?

Yes, says the healer, he understands. He can, in truth, see the flow of the energies, he can teach it, but in time. He can even see the block between the two centers, he says. "It has a frown in it."

Now I sense the importance of it, and why the wordless depth. I hope that I am on my way to healing this split, which goes deep into me, reaches, even, into the deepest place of all: not mother, not father, but into my relationship with God.

At the end of the session, I note that I have forgotten to pay again. But now I leave the check in his mailbox and am happy.

But it is not so easy to reconnect, nor to be healed. For that same evening, my back is out again, and the next day I am swept of rage.

The only peace is to turn inward with rage. This rage is Mercurius Himself, is it not? Is this not the duplex, inside-outside figure who leads me to go out, to relate, to project, to leave myself? I turn to him, ask him, in the rage, to protect me, as he hinted. So, I turn again to the cloud. I turn once more to that creative cloud of smoke-water which has produced ox and child, and the Duplex himself. I look and see a bottle containing smoke. There is no cloud now, but an ancient green bottle which contains the smoke of Mercurius, the cloud-water of his being which can be summoned by me, as I rub this bottle, cold and crisp and hard. It sticks to the touch, as if it has been long in a frozen place, an ice-cavern under the earth or a cold cloud, high in the sky. I hold this bottle and warm it with my hands, which then stick to it like glue. Slowly the bottle warms, slowly it gains heat from my hands, my own energy, my own rage, maybe. Perhaps this bottle needed to be frozen, just as my rage did. Perhaps the bottle, too, is a vessel for this writing, which I use to contain the wild and fiery spirit of Mercurius which I know as rage at the outside and despair within. I rub, and the spirit appears. He flies out in his smoky being and laughs.

"Well done! You have already learned a lot in a short time, have you not? You have learned of the split, and learned that rage is to take you away from the pain outside and to turn you toward a place within which will help you."

"Yes, I have learnt that. But are you, really, a helper or a devil? Are you not he who leads me outside as well as within? He who brings rage and despair?"

"Yes, I am he. It is true. Because I lead to heights and depths, to the maximum, the maximum." Here he sounds the word, maximum, with a long U, reminding me of the Hassidic singer I once heard who called for the "maximoom" in human living, in the fullness of life. I can agree.

"Oh Spirit Mercurius, I know you. For you stretch me high and low, in and out. I know you are a kind of Gemini which makes for my multiplicity and stretching. And yet, I lose my earth, I lose my reality, I lose my ox and my child, my energy and my smallness, when I follow you alone in your wanderings. Please help protect me, great spirit, and not only stretch me!"

"I will, oh man, I will, wrestler with the Angel of God."

"I see, spirit. I see that you are that self-same Angel with whom I have always wrestled, emissary of the divine, stretcher and pusher who comes from God. I see it."

"Yes."

"But where were you when I was on the healer's table? When I was sensing that deep, non-verbal aloneness, that hopeless place of being with God? Were you there?"

"I was there." Mercurius' face now looks more serious and grave, and shows pain itself, as if he is aware of my suffering and pain, and is sorry for it.

"I was there," he continues, "but it is too soon to speak of those things. Too soon. For I, even I, know that to speak of these when you are not in the place of pain and flesh, is to lose the very earth that you fell to, the very reality where ox and child are more at home! I do care for you, in truth, even though you do not seem to know it! Angels care, after all, for we come from the Most High, do we not? We do, please be assured."

"I am assured. And I trust. Just as I trust the healer. I trust you, too, Angel, even though, like the healer, you hurt me and lead me into greater pain. You, I am sure, are in the service of God, just as the healer is in the service of his God and my healing. So, lead on."

"No trip today. It is taken. We are friends. No trip today. The trip is friendship. Rest."

SESSION 8: NOVEMBER 3, 1971

Spinal adjustment was easy this time. It seems as if my back may be ready to cooperate a little at last. All the same, I had suffered back pain this week, but it had seemed more like a pain between back and belly, a kind of burning sensation which could have been, as another healer once called it, a pancreas inflammation.

The healer said that I, as a "compulsive" type (whose character, adds Reich, is over-orderly and prone to both excessive guilt and sympathy), experiences certain symptoms in the early part of therapy including insomnia, indigestion, and impotence. Last night I was, as is most unusual for me, insomniac, my present pains may be "indigestion" and, in fact, although not impotent, I have had less intercourse recently than in the past.

The session was more quiet this time. I yawned a number of times, which event was greeted by Regardie as a good sign of increasing relaxation. He did the usual pummeling, gouging, while I breathed and shouted. At the end, I felt more relaxed. This time, when he stroked my feet, this felt pleasurable, rather than the previous unpleasant tickling sensation. He suggested that such pleasure would increase and that "other things would happen," as well.

Meanwhile, my life continues. I try to stay in touch with the "boy," who still remains mostly inarticulate, speaking only in my sensations and body reactions, and the poor castrated ox, who still looks mostly mournful in his eyes. As to the great and changeable Angel Mercurius, he is there and gone. Having resolved to make this record of my healing one of a careful reportage of my treatment on the one hand, attending to the body, I also agreed to carefully report and continue with the attention to the soul, an account of my voyage with child and ox or, at least, what would emerge from the initial cloud.

So then, I return to the cloud. Long ago, a Knight always returned to a forest when he began a new adventure. I, it seems, return to the cloud. My "forest" or nature, I think, belongs in the work with the body, and is to be found in the boy, the ox, and my own flesh.

I am in the Cloud. It seems to have a firm floor, made of wood. All around me are soft cloud-pillows; that is to say, these are forms made from the cloud itself, like cotton. I lean against these cloud-pillows and sit on the hard floor in a circular space high above the earth. The boy is there, large-eyed, thoughtful. The ox is small now. I contemplate these seemingly weak beings and think about the days when I experienced myself as a most potent man, in spirit and flesh. I look at them and see my own smallness therein. Now I hear a laugh. It is the Angel Mercurius. He rises and unfolds, just as he did from the bottle, and I remember that it was he who was both the origin of the cloud and he who rose out of it, a paradox that I did not feel inclined to deal with at the moment. Now, however, the room or floating platform of the cloud seems to be independent of the Angel Mercurius. He rises up anyway, and laughs.

"Now, sweet Prince, you experience your impotence, your smallness. A far cry from that lad who thought he was chosen, what?"

"Yes, Angel Mercurius, it is true," I said, remembering that 'chosen' feeling.

As I spoke, a telephone call came from a patient, resistant about the fee. He had expected the same fee as several years ago. His need-demand, my need-demand, stubbornness. He said that he could not afford it, but I wonder. He is single and alone. Others who work with me pay the same fee even when they have children to support. So then, the battle of "need." He would like me to "give in" and be a good daddy-mommy, but I will not. And yet, my practice is down, I need the money.

"So then, Mercurius, Angel of mine, you no doubt saw all that. You see my struggle with money, with matter, with all that level of 'flesh,' not of the body, but of security, of rightful return for work, of giving and receiving, of recognition, of all those problems which have been wounds for the lad, for the ox, and for me."

"Yes, Prince of Paupers. I see."

"You smile. You seem to both sneer at me, but also to smile, as if you are sorry for me."

"I am indeed. How can I convey it to you? It is as if three dimensional reality has to be contained within the two, of this page, this fantasy, this time. As if the four dimensional reality I come from has the same difficulty expressing itself in the three. But I will not dwell on that. Look now to your own belly, your own hurt."

"Yes, I do. I feel it. I feel the pain of my belly, tears in my eyes. If I affirm my need and my worth, then I may lose all. If I charge less, then I surrender my true need and worth. True need and worth in recognition versus reduction in both and only a little help in security, then resentment besides. I could not work well, resentful. Better nothing at all than that I should reduce my fee and 'be nice'."

"Can you stand for that?"

"Can I stand for that? I don't know. If my practice went down a lot, I suppose I would have to eat crow. But, must I eat crow before…hurt intrudes. Bleeding… I look at the boy. He is sorrowful. I look at the ox. He, too. They are sorrowful for me! It is I who needs to be pitied; I, the ego, not the boy of need, not the ox of vital self, but I. Can I pity myself, poor ego? Can I, myself, an ego, embrace and love that ego? Not the child in me, not the wounded ox-energy, but I, myself? Can I stand for my own ego need? Yes, I can, but at the price perhaps, of not having enough money for my family? No, not that. But it hasn't come that far yet, has it? For once, I can say, 'Yes, I embrace my ego.' Not God, nor the Sun, as when I was 'chosen.' I can say 'I am entitled to that fee,' I earned it and I deserve it. If he cannot pay, or does not want to, all right. I am sorry. But I need it for my ego and myself. Period!"

"Bravo, Prince, bravo! You have embraced yourself. You have become a bit like me, taking on a bit of the devil, n'est ce pas?"

"Yes, Mercurius, I suppose I have. But, because the Devil is egotistical, does it mean that I am a devil? I do not think so."

"I hope that is true, Prince… But, what is that sad feeling lingering in your belly and eyes? What is that sorrow of heart that remains?"

"Non-recognition, Angel. I, it is true, can embrace myself, but it remains that the world does not. The fact of unfilled therapy hours remains. It is not enough that I embrace myself. Now an anger comes. Why, indeed, should I have to defend myself? I think of that physician who urged his/my patient to sell everything for treatment, and himself charges high fees as well. Why defend at all? If I know that it is worth it, then so be it.

"But perhaps it is not worth it. Am I not going to another healer now? (And I wrote that "I" with a small "i," as well!) Is that not a confession that I am not healer enough to heal myself? If I am not healed, why such an embrace of self as healer? Not worth it. A confession… But my lack of healing is in the body, not the spirit…! Oh, Mercurius, help me in this! I was once chosen by the God from whom you come. I was once a true Prince, an heir to the kingdom. Help me! Please!"

"Just as you offered to help your patient? What about my fee?"

"Are you the devil after all? You want my soul? What is your fee for help?"

"My fee? You want to pay it?"

"No, never mind. I need to be independent, even of you. I need to embrace myself. And I do so!"

Then, as I sank to the floor of this circular cloud-room, the dark-eyed boy and ox both came and warmed me. The boy stroked me and embraced me, the ox licked me, as if he were a dog. As they warmed me and loved me wordlessly, I felt them grow smaller and smaller, until they were mere specks. They then entered my body through my navel and were inside me, the boy at the belly center, the ox at the solar plexus, where indeed, they both belonged. They now could become a living part of me, not external.

What could that mean? My silent child-side could now also love and warm me; my energy self, raging, could also warm and love me; they could now become true functions and not be split-off, autonomous parts. I could listen to them. God had once chosen me, no more. Now I could choose myself.

"Why?" came the insinuating voice of Mercurius. "Why?"

"For God," came my answer unbidden. "For God."

Another telephone call comes. This time from a friend who cares for me, one who has never felt 'chosen.' But she, in truth, has chosen herself. I, apparently, have not. What does it mean, to chose myself "for God?"

God chose me, no longer does. Evidence? No recognition, not being chosen by others as He has. Also, betrayal from those who I thought 'recognized' me. I must choose myself, then...but, for the sake of God? What does that mean? Maybe it means that if God can no longer 'choose me,' I must carry that function myself. All right. But how does that help God? By making His task lighter? Perhaps. Or that I must be more active in asserting my value, because I acknowledge, to myself, that God chose me? Yes...I can see it. As if a young man would proclaim through the streets with great joy, "she loves me, she loves me." Or would I proclaim through the streets, "God chose me, God chose me!" But no longer, no longer.

Tears, confusion. More tears, more confusion. Ego, choose ego, to help God. Somebody help me! God help me!

What appears are cries from the belly and the solar plexus. I hear cries. I call for God, and I hear the cries of the boy and of the ox. Now they have voices! I call for God and they answer! Are they God? Maybe. The ox, of course, is an aleph, the ox of the Zen Ox-Herding Pictures, is the vital energy of the self, anyway. What if they are God? And what if they help only when I embrace my ego, as it was shown? When I call out to God, they call out, too. Do they call out in me, or are they the answering call of God? I ruminate, I am like the ox, or like an obsessive compulsive. I am in pain.

A long silence ensues. The answer does not readily appear. I hear the cries of the boy in me and of the ox. They chant. It is a ringing chant, calling out to God. Need and passion, creatureliness and emotion, cry out to the Lord. Lower centers cry out to higher...but, no answer. Left with pain, I call out. I mumble, concretely. I raise my voice. In a three-fold manner, I call, Hm-Hm-Hm... But that too fails, for it becomes a humming of Three Blind Mice. Three blind mice, indeed: the boy, the ox, myself. All blind. All feeble. All broken.

All right, Mercurius. We are crushed. What do you say...? Only a smile, rueful, not so sneering, but not kind either. And he goes back into battle, by Himself. No answer.

I am left, sitting on the platform. No Mercurius now, no ox and no child: alone. No, not quite right. The child and the ox are within me, in belly and solar plexus. But alone all the same, it seems. Alone... So, I embrace myself. I hug myself, and rock, singing a lullaby of love.

I do not know the answer. I do not call out to God, nor do this for Him. I do it because I need to embrace myself, my ego, and my need. And I do. I do, great Lord, I do.

"And, in so doing," comes an answer, "you do it for Me."

SESSION 9: NOVEMBER 10, 1971

Today I screamed and screamed. This was no ordinary scream. No forced attempt as in the past, to shout while deep breathing, responding to his relatively mild pushing and pummeling. I needed no encouragement at all, today, since the healer squeezed and gouged and picked at some very tender and tight muscles, my "wing" muscles. You know, the place in the back where man's wings were once attached, and where they leave only a painful, sore, and tender memory of our "fall" and their detachment. Well, the healer worked on those, and I screamed and called out to Jesus, to God, and finally had to sit up and scream some more, in order to get him to stop that torture. And he did stop for a moment, but began again. And again. Finally, I was on my haunches, pounding the cot, pounding and screaming, and he stopped. He, thankfully, stopped. And then, for a minute perhaps, I felt a blessed peace, and noticed that I had perfectly normal posture. My chest had fallen from its normal military position, but my shoulders had not thrust forward, nor had my head flopped forward either. I was, in short, after the pounding of the wings and neck muscles, relaxed and "natural." It was amazing.

The healer said, "One day you will have that all the time." He suggested that I read the essay by Groddeck, who preceded Freud and Reich, called "Exploration of the Unconscious," which speaks about these same wing muscles and how they hurt. Huge energy is expended by most people to keep the pain unconscious, so that one will not feel the agony of the armoring. And what does it armor, I inquired of the healer?

"Well, pride," he said. And pride, no doubt, it is. Pride to keep that chest up, to know that one is still a person, a being, and not a nothing, an indescribable, non-entity, speck of nothing.

Are we not "fallen angels," beings whose wings have been taken away, whose spirit and closeness to God has been removed, doomed to live here on earth, close to the dust, made of dust, and suffering the agony of the "fallen ones?" It is probably true, and that is why we are in such pain. Reich, I suppose, does not say it that way, nor, I imagine would Groddeck, but so it seems to me...

But such pain. How will I feel when I am in the pain in full earnest? Could I bear it? Today, he gave me more pain than I had had altogether until now. If he had done these things in the first session, I said, I doubt whether I would have returned. He laughed and said, "Of course." But many people are so armored, keep their pain repressed so much that they do not even cry out at this! Imagine, keeping the affect back so deeply! Imagine, allowing oneself to be so self-torturing! But, what can I say...I, who am just as self-torturing as anyone I know.

This too, came out in the session. Earlier on in the session, as we talked about the paper on fantasy by Jung which I gave to him, earlier as I jumped and tried to get limber, he spoke to me of Reich on this matter, and the view of magic. He said that Jung suggested active fantasy when people had no dreams. A way that he used was merely to have patients look in the mirror. Look in the mirror, suggested Regardie, and tell what you see.

I looked. I saw a middle-aged man, tense, rigid, puffy around the jaws, with rigid shoulders, rigid chest, tight muscles, and flabby about the middle. I saw a thin-lipped, scornful mouth, angry, and then pained eyes. Suffering, tight, rigid. I saw this creature and scorned him myself. I felt only scorn for him, no compassion. Thus did I seem to myself. And I remembered filling out a questionnaire on the "self-concept." In that questionnaire, I no doubt emerged as self-accepting and very healthy. And here I was, at this moment, in the healer's room, full of the lowest self-concept imaginable. There it was, true. But so was the other truth, I said. One is interior and the other exterior, I said to the healer. Not true, he replied, Kether is in Malkuth, Nirvana is in Samsara, Inside and Outside are one, for that is Zen, too, isn't it? Yes, and a Tree is a Tree at the end, I replied. But I knew that this is so only at those moments where the split is overcome. At this moment, alas, the split exists for me. I sat there, wounded and miserable, in this healer's office. And I knew him as a son-of-a-bitch also, just like me, for this is what I called him when he was hurting me; he laughed and said, "You know my name!"

Sons of bitches are we, it is true. But my face was not only scornful and angry, rigid and wretched, it was also sad. Sad it was, and weakened. For I am a fallen angel, a sore-winged creature who cries out to God, "why hast thou abandoned me who was chosen?" I remembered my fantasy of the days before.

Now, as I record my experiences, continue this never-to-be-seen chronicle of the healing of a healer, I think of my fantasy. But no, I harbor a secret hope that one day my chronicle will be known. You who read this will know that I hoped that you would know.

I return to the "look in the mirror," pain and sharing of my self-revulsion with another. Then a memory from adolescence arises, when I looked into such a mirror alone. I remember a time when the Rosicrucians taught a 14 year-old boy to look into the mirror with candles at both sides, so that one could see one's previous incarnations. I saw first a poet, with flaming tie. I saw a handsome youth, like Byron, perhaps. And then I saw an older man, a sad and bitter philosopher, a Kierkegaard. Not so modest was I? Not so modest at all, to see great writers and philosophers, at 14? And now, at 45, perhaps I was not so wrong. There was the writer in me then, who seeks and emotes and reflects, but above all, feels. And there is the old philosopher who knows, who sees, who is bitter and full of anxiety, the "sickness unto death," who compulsively ruminates. Both are there. No Byron am I, nor Kierkegaard, but a young poet and old philosopher all the same. The face that I saw in the mirror was of the bitter philosopher, the poet grown old. That indeed was what I saw.

"Mercurius, now that I sit here alone, what did happen with my self-embrace when God did not? What happened to the introjecting and realizing of the boy and ox in belly and solar plexus? What happened to the self-embrace, so easily lost? Speak Mercurius, Angel of God who falls not! Speak, Devil of the Lord who laughs at man and goads him!"

"You would have me speak, would you? Command me, would you? How long, and what does it take for you to submit? What? Pain, a look at the foolish face? The realization of fallen angel? What?"

"Just what it took you, fallen angel! You, devil, who fell and somehow achieved wings once again, probably because you could goad and punish us poor mortals. What, indeed, does it take? I cry out and demand. And you, like people, take my imperious cries and demands and reject them. I cry out and demand of God, as if entitled, and so do I demand of men, too. They reject, naturally, and my boy and ox are pained. Well, that is how it is, I suppose. I do feel "entitled," I suppose, and as "he-who-has-given-so-much." But there is such self-reproach, such self-rejection in me, along with the pride and "entitledness." It is a mystery and a pain, a paradox which I can not solve for myself. Both are true, just as the two self-concepts were true. Just as you, Mercurius, are double-edged, doubled sided.

"Yes, Prince, yes. For you are my shepherd."

"I am your shepherd? The Lord is my Shepherd, they say. But Mercurius says that I am his shepherd, I am his Lord. But you, too are mine, oh Angel. Shepherd me, for I do, indeed, shepherd you by mimicking you, being you, being so two-sided and angelically fallen. I am you and you are me."

"True."

"Then what?"

"We're the same?"

"We're the same."

"The same. In pain."

"A man am I, in pain."

"A devil am I, in pain."

Mercurius, God-forsaken.

Mercurius, God-chosen.

No wonder we break our backs.

No wonder we suffer our wings.

No wonder.

No more wonder, Lord. No more wonder.

Peace.

Man is a frail creature. Devil created, devil shaped.

God's fool and God's creation. His eldest son and shepherd.

Wings break, hearts cry and heads roll.

No wonder.

And when the world ends, when sleep brings surcease to suffering, Dukha dulls and no wonder.

Sleep.

SESSION 10: NOVEMBER 17, 1971

We got to work with "flat-foot Charlie" and I finally understood the flat-footed, heels-on-floor, flexible knees, jumping exercise. I managed to do it with more freedom and grace than in previous weeks, particularly last week with my acrimony, bitterness, and criticism of my rigid and flaccid body!

Nor did Regardie let up here. He bent my back, which made for sweet pain as the muscles relaxed, as my pelvis was stretched, my legs held down as I arched and bent back. And then I dropped my arms the reverse way, touching the floor with my hands, gradually, letting the rigid mid-section taste the flavor of stretching. It was good.

He did not forget the poking, the pummeling, the touching, the kneading. Once again, I screamed in earnest, called out and raged. This time, miraculously, I did not have to hold my breath all the time, in defensive posture against anticipated pain. Pain was there, but now I could breathe during the pummeling, I could gasp for air and cry out in between the horrid shrieks. Best of all, when there was a moment of rest in between, I found myself laughing, laughing and giggling. I laughed with relief, with pleasure that there was a momentary surcease from pain. I laughed because I was intoxicated from the hyperventilation. Most of all, I laughed at the marvelously crazy fantasy that I was having.

I was imagining that Regardie was tuned in to the Masters of the psychic realm, the astral regions, and that they were now helping both my suffering spirit and my suffering flesh. I laughed at the absurdity of the projection, yet had pleasure and hope as well. Relief and hopes of continuing on the path of uniting body and soul, spirit with flesh. It was this that I told Regardie during the last period, the time when he usually ceased his activity and had me report what was happening to me, what the sensations were. The laughter and the fantasy were more real, more cogent, than the little tremblings of flesh, the already-known numbness of fingers, tingling.

Before this, I had also imagined that Regardie was looking at the circulation of the light, the flow of the energies of the centers. So I asked him. "No," he said, not that. Nothing so deep as that at this point. He was merely looking at the muscles, at how the belly muscles were bringing down that prideful chest, that chest which was already, he said with satisfaction, returning to quite a normal place. Yes, he seemed pleased with the work.

I was pleased too. Because things were moving. I felt a change in my chest and pride, too. My psyche was also moving. How? Well, I had arranged for a series of sessions for me with the Rabbi of the temple where my son was going to be Bar-Mitzvah. I had done this in order to get closer to the ritual for my son, to extend my knowledge and appreciation of traditional Judaism, and to play a deeper part in my son's forthcoming initiation. The Rabbi assented, and meetings were now beginning.

The Rabbi and I met alone, while people, children, came in and out at will. We spoke of the basis of Judaism being ritual and action: behavior and observance were the foundation of life and law, rather than belief and image. We talked and shared, agreed and disagreed, and he gave me a book which spoke against evolution. He sounded like a conservative Roman Catholic, and I said so, knowing that Orthodoxy was orthodoxy. But our conversation was in good spirit. I felt a strain in both relating to this good Rabbi, while not selling out my own views, nor engaging in battle.

That night I dreamed that I was in a room with many men, including the Rabbi. A young woman was speaking her own views quietly and with conviction. I went over to her and put my arms around her lovingly, and felt very good about it. I was happy when I awakened, because my feeling for her was not paternal, nor heroic, nor defensive, but of an equal, brotherly quality. I was connected with my own feminine nature in the midst of all the patriarchal masculinity. That was what I wished to do, in my relations with men. Whether I talked of Adam and Eve and the Fall of Man with an orthodox Rabbi, or of Buddhism with my Buddhist-priest friend. One-on-one I could do this, but in a group?

But what had this to do with the work with my healer? My chest had fallen anyway, and a quiet assurance of the soul was taking place.

SESSION 11: NOVEMBER 24, 1971

Before the eleventh session, I had a battle with a patient and came to the session in pieces and in pain.

I did the usual: breathing, jumping, getting a better hang of it. But this time, during the last period, the time when one merely attends to what is going on in the sensations of the body, I found many more sensations, tremblings and coursings than before—in my feet, legs, sides. Suddenly I felt a great weight upon my chest, as if it supported a huge stone. Then a vise about my neck. Now I knew what the armoring was like: heavy, heavy paralysis. I began to feel this paralysis throughout my body, now on one side, now on the other. The paralysis seemed to cover everything except my genitals, at one time or another (to which the healer said, "Thank God"). The paralysis shifted, and I felt myself in a deep, deep place. Only my mouth could move, and I whispered: "I cannot speak, I cannot move. I must not speak, I must not move." This came as a ritual, repeating itself again and again. A touch of the healer, on my belly perhaps, would free the paralysis there, or a laugh would do so, only to come back. I thought of death, of being paralyzed. I remembered the fear of a patient that I once had, a nun. This excellent Sister had a great fear of being buried before she was truly dead. She was not afraid of death itself: she had too much faith and did much valuable religious activity in the world. Rather, she was afraid that she would awaken in the tomb and, for an instant or longer, realize that she was trapped and would then despair. It was the despair that she feared, for such despondency would lead to lack of perfect trust in God at the moment of death which, in turn, would rob her of heaven. Poor thing, I thought. Poor thing; having been regaled in childhood by her mother of tales of people being buried alive. This had stayed with her, combining with religious belief.

Now I understood her. My muscles and bones understood her. For I, too, could not move, was suffering a living death. I remembered, at that moment, a time during World War II, when I was at sea. I half-awakened from a dream and found myself in my bunk with no light on, no windows, and unable to find them. I was panicked, for I felt trapped, about to die from lack of air. I was mortally afraid. Here again, I was unable to move. I could breathe only from my throat, in little, non-noticeable breaths. All else was still. "I must not breathe. I must not speak. I must not move." Mortal stillness.

"A great early trauma," said the healer, "or several of them." That was why the chest was so high and in a constant state of defense against something, he said. An early mortal fear. "I must not move or speak." The memory did not come. But it will come, he said, do not fret.

But fret I did. I was in great fear that I would forget what just had happened. I was aware of a kind of censor, a brush that tended to wipe out memories and painful events. Freud was right. No matter. The memory would come one day, when I was ready for it. Yes, now I sensed the censor. It was not like the war-time figure, expunging facts and places. It was more like a broom of forgetfulness, sweeping away whole memories. That was repression, of course, the broom of mind-cleaning! But, the body would return the memory one day. The body would restore the psyche. What a thought! I who had valued the psyche above all, would soon know and appreciate the body's mind!

I was drunk with the air, I was intoxicated with the hyperventilation, but I was even more profoundly drunk with the realization that there were memories and thoughts, behaviors and compulsions, obsessions and feelings, stored in these poor muscles, tired with strain, taut with tension. Little by little, though, I would be free! I would be free!

POST SESSION: NOVEMBER 27, 1971

But what of the cloud? What of the boy and the ox?

"Oh cloud! Form yourself and speak to me. Form and show me the way in my path of hazy vision, desire and failure. Show me, I beg you."

There comes a vision of Mercurius as sorcerer. He is astrologer, magician, and laughing punster. He wraps his star-silk robe about himself, just as would any archetypal rumination, and he laughs.

"Ho! Marvin! Here I am, as summoned. You summon easily and I answer readily. Just like any ghost. Just like any fool who is called by his master. But you forget. It is I who am master, and not your silly little ego. Still worrying about fame and fortune, my man? You already have it! More than most. More, even, than you deserve. You miserable cur!"

"Miserable am I? Do you start that abuse? Is it not enough that the rejection and abuse come from outside and from other insiders who are even more judgmental and diabolical than you? Must you join in the abuse?"

"No, I need not. But I thought I might as well abuse you, since others do and you seem to thrive on it. Either you are the chosen one himself, or you are the chosen bad one, himself. Either one, my man. Either one. The reality is that you are both. You are miserable, are you not? (he laughs) You are miserable indeed! So, come now out of your miseries and play. Play the game of joy in life. Play. The cloud is not only a dark gloomy one, but light and fluffy, soft and gay."

So, I go with him and play. Now I see the boy, playing a flute and walking along happily. The ox, still like a large dog, also goes along with a smile upon his face. Mercurius is in the lead, walking and flying, with winged feet. And I, in back, scamper about, looking and jumping. There is pleasure.

SESSION 12: DECEMBER 1, 1971

During the next session, after experiencing excruciating pain where my neck and the muscles adjacent are being deeply worked on, I shout and complain, but again I break the hold. During the period of observation of my sensations, I once again experience the paralysis on the left side, one eye open. I am told that both hands have been rigid, in tetany. I felt paralysis, but more: I felt continued pressure of fingers on my neck and neck muscles, long after they were removed. I feel it and remember wanting to choke someone who had piled labels and interpretations upon me, unjustly. The healer asks, "Suppose you had not pushed my hands away, what would happen?"

"I could not go on bearing the pain," said I. "I suppose that I would have fainted."

"No," he responded. "Finally, you would weep, you would cry."

I thought about this and wondered. Perhaps so. I would cry and just give in with pain and hurt and despair and bitterness. My rage, surely, has not been a good defense. Regardie went on to say that if I did that then people who unconsciously hurt me would be astonished. Anger only brings on anger, rage and battle the same. But tears would astonish them and they would desist. Would they? I do not know. But then there would be humiliation, defeat, rather than the battle and confrontation...Well, we agreed, the healer and I, that in time the boy would tell. I have been of the opinion that it is my anxiety that does not get expressed, that he stops too soon in pushing down my thighs, for example, in fear that my anxiety would be too much. He says that there are tears behind the rage. The angry feelings must get out and then the tears. He knows that I can cry, but still he waits for...Well, we shall see.

Now I sit with rage and pain, the suspicion and the poor defense, the horror at being projected upon and deviled. What can I do for myself? What can I do with endlessly disturbing relationships? I can sink into the pain of the muscles, perhaps. Or ascend to the cloud once again. What shall it be? To ascend or descend, are they the same in the end? Let us see.

First down. Down into the pain of the body. Memory of the muscle ache in neck and upper shoulders. I feel the fingers once again, the paralysis. I am in the grip of a person with huge hands who is squeezing me. Not choking really, but squeezing, squeezing. It is the healer, yet is not. I do not cry out anymore. I just cry. "Kill me if you must," say I, and the columns fall in.

"No use, no use," come the words from the Cloud. And I feel pain in my neck near my ear. "No use," says Mercurius. All is doomed, I suppose. Whether I struggle or not, surrender or not, all is doomed. No use. I will suffer the endless frustration of never being healed. Hell it is; shit heaped upon me. The shit is compounded of names and descriptions of me: paranoid, kike, aggressive, bright, genius, all names and interpretations, too many. I sit and take this abuse and pain. Then I holler back. What pours out of me is more throw-up, vomit. Now the pain is in my shoulder. A real, physical pain has descended to right shoulder. I will be still.

Quiet, do not speak. Nospeak. The new language of pain: nospeak. It is the language of bearing up under abuse and not answering back, not crying out in anger, not even leaving. Nospeak is the language of 1984, of Communist States and Fascists. Nospeak, the language reserved for the tyrant. For the tyrant Devil, or the tyrant God. Nospeak. Still.

POST SESSION: DECEMBER 8, 1971

Last night I had a dream. I had read, beforehand, in Dion Fortune's book on Psychic Attack, about Vampirism, about the materialization of elementals and such. My dream was simple. I dreamt that I saw a nice man, with glasses and curly hair, gentle, who had somehow materialized another man who was a copy of himself. He had not meant to do this, but did so anyway. The Copy-Man was a nuisance to the first man and I seemed to know something about such things. I offered to help, and suggested that the first man simply re-absorb the Copy-Man. But he did not want to do so and just ran off. I, therefore, was left with this Copy-Man, who was neither man nor spirit, but a sort of elemental ectoplasm. I thought I might be able to absorb him into myself (just as I had read the previous night as was done by Dion Fortune's adept friend.) As I set about doing so, the character of this elemental changed: his face grew hairy and devilish, his teeth became fangs, and I was confronted with a demonic creature who frightened me very much. I did not think that I could truly absorb him and thought that I must send him off, dissolve him. This I tried to do, in my fear, and I awakened as this was happening. Now, fully awake, I still saw this figure as an apparition. I tried, indeed, to dissolve him and I was not sure if I did. All evening there had been a fierce wind and the house had creaked, so the atmosphere was right for ghosts and such.

And now, the dilemma between magic and psyche. If I try to speak to this Copy-Man-Demon, will he be a figure from the astral level, the purgatorial zone which manifests? Well, I shall deal now with the psychic level, for that I know, and the dream is surely one that I must work with, belongs in the context of my struggles of the past days.

So, then, Copy-Man-Demon, I summon you. But I summon you in my full waking consciousness! I summon you to stand here beside me and before me in the charmed circle of my psychological work. Come and speak! There you are now. I see you. Rather man-animal-like, stupid-looking, head hung low, as if something is wrong with your neck, can't hold your head up. I think of the arguments of the Orthodox Rabbi against evolution: there are no such creatures of half-man, half-animal, says he. Well, here you are. Not living on the earth, it is true, but in the mind of man and perhaps, in an astral place.

"We live, it is true, and are not so stupid as you think. Do I not change from man to monster? Do not I change from fierce to weak? Do I not appear both in a ghostly reality and a psychic one? Not so stupid. Nor are we what your Rabbi thinks, though he is partly right. We exist, it is true, and in the evolution of the soul, not on the level of the concrete earth, though we can effect things there. There is no conflict between your psychology and magic. It is all merely created."

"All merely created, you say. Yes, indeed, all the hand of creation, God's or man's. Have I created you, I wonder, or did you exist already?"

"I, of course, exist already. You have invited me into your soul by your interest in my realm."

"Yes, and now what to do with you."

"What indeed."

"You are like an Englishman in speech, gentle. And like a monster in appearance, fierce. You are glass-wearing and curly, Jewish. And you are sharp-fanged and gross, animal!"

"I am, of course, you, am I not? Are you not Jewish, gentle, and eye-troubled? Are you not animal, fierce and ravenous? Are you not, really me?"

"Is it so? Has the gentle Jew created his own image which, in turn, brings forth a fierce Fagin? Is it so? And, if so, what does it mean? With whom can I speak? For I do not trust this creature, this figment and reality."

"Hah. You create me, I am you, and you do not trust me! Well, then, absorb me, adsorb me, take me in and I will dissolve and be no more!"

"Yes, I will. Whatever the truths of being or non-being, you surely came out of my dream, and you surely do have similarities with me, so I feel confident that I can absorb you, in the light of day! Come in...! I feel you come in and there is a shiver in my back. There is a coldness, a wetness. I breathe deeply. I breathe and relax. The monster has come back in, gentle and fierce, man and animal, cultivated Jew and missing-link monster. I am calm. Enough. He dissolves and the parts go throughout my system, in cells, in bones, in muscles and madness. Let it be."

SESSION 13: DECEMBER 8, 1971

The session began as the others, rather, but soon changed into a dialogue. The healer noticed that my chest was back up high. Anyway, he remarked that my chest dropped after our conversation; affect had come out a little. I understood. Some relief from expression, from not having to "hold in" so much.

Now, a day later, I am back in a muddle with the dream and experience of the day before, the magical-creation dream of the gentle Jew and Monster. I mentioned this dream to Regardie at the end of the session, in speaking of how my image of God had changed. Anyway, there is a need to confront this dream and these figures once again.

The other day, I had absorbed the gentle-Jew-monster. It had come into cells and bones and muscles. But I have no sign of its true change, inner or outer. Was it a "mere fantasy," or was there a true change in reality, psychic reality or outer reality?

My insight in between is that the gentle-Jew-cum-monster who made a being just like himself, was rather like the Jehovah of the Bible, who "made man in his own image!" And, as a friend remarked, he is like the Atlanteans of old who made such creations and were washed away in the flood after misusing their powers. Was this what Adam did? No, that is different.

...Straying thoughts, loss of concentration. I come back to the figure in my dream.

"Oh, figure, whatever your name is, I absorbed you into my system, but I have need to...to...change you...me. Please present yourself as you are at this time."

What appears is flowing blood, a river of blood. In it are little red balls, like enlarged corpuscles. Each ball contains something of the figure. "But I was always there, in every cell," I hear him whisper. "I was always there! God the father, negative-judge and devil has always been in every blood cell of your being. And blood cell it is, for it is the emotional, dark, passionate, patriarchal, Saturn that you have always known. With sharp Eye-in-Triangle and sharp judging tongue in his mouth. In every cell, in every cell."

This voice spoke both as if he/it were God, and also about God. A veritable Hierophant of two-sidedness, personal and objective. All right then, I shall engage this voice of blood.

"Speak, blood-judge, speak and be a whole voice, a voice of love and prophecy, instead of dismal darkness."

"What a fool you are to expect it! Did you not see my monstrousness? Did you not see? Does not my voice come gently, intelligently, cultivatedly, as a gentle Jew? And does it not also come as a wild and ravenous, monstrously judging and devilling creature?"

"But, God-figure, if you did, indeed, make man in your own image, just as the dream hints, did you not make man and then run off? Not take responsibility for your monstrous side?"

"Just as you do, my friend, just as you do. Were you not told how you are like your old teacher, 'taking care,' being 'nice,' and then slipping out these opinions and feelings about people?"

"Yes, but it is in response to...no...that is not the answer. I guess I do not become aware enough of how I do this, how I gossip and slander as well...pain in belly."

The old morality is gone, that of the "Law," both Jewish and Christian. The Impersonal law is dead. But not quite. There remains the death throes of agony, of re-absorption of a figure which is not God, but the Jewish man of the dream. But was he not a magician? Was he not a strange magician who inadvertently made man in his own image by mistake? And here he is, a gentle, cultivated Jew who flees from his monstrous side. As do I. But I, in the dream, am not that. I offer to help, to absorb. I am a veritable Jesus Christ! Taking on other's shadows, or...the shadow of my shadow! Flat on my face, down... All right. Rest.

CHAPTER THREE

SESSION 14: DECEMBER 15, 1971

Little talk today, back to body work. My back was improved, more flexible, had not gone out. But Regardie reported that the recent period of six weeks was a difficult and dangerous one for me. Uranus and Mars squaring, and thus danger of accidents. That I could corroborate, for last Sunday, in driving the boys to synagogue, I went through a red light—most unusual for me—and I was spared an accident by other drivers.

Regardie remarked that I was more relaxed now. My back had the bend of the reader-scholar and the doctor, he said. Jewish hump, I asked? No, that is higher up, he replied. Also, compensated by my high chest arrogance, I said. He agreed. We did not talk more because it is foolish to do so while the chest is still up. Resistance, I supposed; we left it at that. After the work, there was much more relaxation, and I was reluctant to speak. Exactly, said the healer. The more relaxed one becomes, the more one does not wish to speak. I could even touch my head to the couch when sitting up, showing much improvement in the back. Flexibility is much greater, a quiet, working session. Well, most work is slow, step by step; miracles or dramas are rather like the torches of the devil, I suppose: much fire and smoke, not much transformation!

SESSION 15: DECEMBER 22, 1971

Today's session was rather routine. Jumping Charlie, or whatever it is called, was looser to the healer's satisfaction. My back was out again, combination of poor posture at work and all that excessive eating which fouls up the belly, I thought, and he agreed. Take vitamins and minerals, he opinioned. Work on back and chest and belly, with breathing and shouting. It does help each time, now. There is pain and pleasure in his work on those muscles, especially in the back: first the rubbing and soothing, a bit like massage; then the molding and kneading of those same muscles which make me scream in pain and bang on the couch or squeeze hard. Then rest and greater relaxation. Today he even went for the muscles on the inner thigh. Well, I jumped at that! Not yet ready to deal with castration anxiety, I suppose. But all the same, it must have been an advance, just as Orson Bean felt, that he even worked at that level. So, some relaxation, long reportage of sensations—and I could tell that he was not interested when I started to get into fantasy—and ending. Two weeks of holiday coming up and I think I will miss the sessions. Well, I can jump myself after all! And drop, and moan and breathe. Maybe get a friend to knead my back. At the end, I asked, "Are you a little depressed? You seem quieter today." He laughed and merely said no. So, am I projecting, am I into the transference of several weeks ago? He does not bite, so I'll gratefully wait, and let my concern for him just rest.

More important, I think, than the session itself, are the dreams I have been having. I dreamt that I was on a trip with my wife. We come to a transitional place, a border region through which we must pass. This region is both a park and a factory, and has various buildings. We must pass by a man who is the inspector. I think that we are either in a car or on horseback. The man is not pleasant to us and sends us off to various buildings where we see brutal things: horses killed, poles with nail after nail stuck in them, senselessly; in general, an atmosphere of violence. I get the feeling that these are somehow meant to instruct us or show us something. I ask the man about why is he doing this, and he suddenly changes his attitude. He says he thought that I belonged to one of those "Semites" (he pronounced it to sound like "some meat" with the accent on the meat) with my Frank Buck hat, my short pants. He now realizes otherwise, I supposed. Anyway, he had a raft of assumptions about groups, races, nationalities, and religions, and brutally treated those who fell into certain groups. Having recognized the error of his judgment, he was apologetic. End of dream.

Well, now, my unconscious reacts, apparently, to the work I have done. The judge of an earlier dream is now manifest as an inspector, a kind of border guard one meets as one goes into the new world. Now I come, not with an alter ego, but with my wife. It is true that I have experienced the judge strongly in relation to my wife. Not that I am judgmental of her or she of me—it is the reverse, I think. She and I are enormously tender of each other and want so much not to hurt. Yet it is true that the brutal judge has arisen in connection with her. I have judged myself harshly for transgressions, for any hurt I have caused her.

Curious how he labels me "Semite," as if he were some "honkie anti-semite," all right. Those people I knew who hated Jews were against Jewish mind and heart, Jewish religion, but also usually insensitive to women, etc. So, there he is, a border guard. He is one who kills horses, damages a man's connection with his animal nature; one who drives nails into posts just for fun, one of those like the Roman soldiers who enjoyed crucifixions, perhaps. A sadist and narrow-minded bigot, anti-semitic. Yet, my guilt has been for not fully following Jewish Law, the Ten Commandments, for being "anti-semitic," in a way. He acknowledges that he misjudges me. What do I need to make this crossing? To confront my wife with my nature? I have already done so in the past. No, it is to protect or do something with the inner wife, the loyal and true and devoted feminine in myself, as well. To go with her, together, into the new world. So now, I have to try and speak with this border guard.

"Border guard! You have called me 'Semite' unjustly. I am a Semite, it is true, but not contained in any system that way, and you have been brutal to me, and to others too, with your narrow-minded outlook. You are powerful, you guard the gate to the new world, the place of new experience. Yet you beat me up, and my horses. You see, now, that you have misjudged me. I implore you to stop being so brutal, to give up these archaic beliefs and prejudices. I implore you to examine each newcomer to the new land, the new place, inner and outer, with more care and less quick judgment. Can you do that?"

"I can do that, of course. For I am trained to look at people, passports, and make quick judgments. I am usually accurate. It is only you that I have misjudged so badly—and perhaps, some others."

"But if you have misjudged me, you could do the same to others. Look at how brutal you have been to the animals!"

"Wait, I did not kill the horses. They died by themselves, having little nerve for the crossing. Think now, of how cautious you and your wife have been with horses."

"True enough. But as a child I was fearless with them. I would regain that feeling!"

"You will, I suppose. For few can pass by me, survive to go to the other side, and not feel free!"

"But what of your judgments? Can you agree to simply look more carefully and slowly at newcomers to the other land? Examine without such quick judgment? Look at the person and his passport in such a way as not to fall into the trap of hating the strange and different?

…An outer situation presented itself, which showed very clearly that my judgment is vulnerable and, when shaken, I become somewhat irresponsible. I now must also pause with this effort, either to return, or to anticipate another dream experience which will aid me on the road to dealing with the judge, who is now border guard. Would it not be strange and appropriate that he who has endangered me and hurt me in relation to others, and myself, could become the positive keeper of the border, the protector, rather than the destroyer? How great this would be! I pray that this may be so! Oh, Lord of All, beyond all ken, let your judging part be a protector and helper, a positive keeper of the veil between regions! Let your wisdom prevail and protect, not destroy! Let it be so I pray. I can not improve the judge, only You great God, Lord of All, can do so. Let the Self, and God, be the leader in giving His wisdom to the Keeper of the Gate, and let this Keeper be fair and just, protect the within and the without, not wantonly and foolishly judge and destroy! Oh, Lord, I pray!

LATER

"You, Border Guard, I see your violent streak, your teeth clenched, your quick judgmental violence to what exists, your lashing out! Too quick is your judgment! Too quick is your reaction, your harsh hand. No one gets in, say you, no one passes the region of your protection, but they do! They get in and hurt me, and you hurt me too, with your quick violent reactions. These others get in because I mistrust your judgment and because many sneak by you, did you know that?"

"I know. My strong right arm, my beady eye, my guards, even, are not enough. Dead horses, too, I know, are too much. But look at me, this strong hairy arm. Look at me, this strong heavy body, look at me!"

"I look."

"You have striven manfully to realize me, my strength."

"I have?"

"Yes, you have. For you have let me have the final say. You do not discuss with me, you did not examine and criticize. You just react!"

"But that is what you do, I thought. Again, you put on me what I find in you! You are quick to judge, and then call me judgmental, you just react, and accuse me!"

"Exactly!"

"Exactly. I see. It is as if I do that to myself, through you. I am quick to judge myself as well."

"And you do not pay attention... Listen, wait...and my eyes shall grow less beady. Listen, wait, and judgment shall grow deeper."

I feel a shallowness of my reaction here. So, I resolve not to be 'too quick' right now. I must do this more deeply, less halfheartedly.

JANUARY 12, 1972

It is several weeks since I have written in these pages or seen Regardie, but life goes on, dreams go on, as do pain and conflict. What to put down here? That which cries out for freedom in me, that's what.

I dreamt once more that my own judgment was questioned by others. My wife questioned it, and many young people, "hippies," said that I was wrong. I said that a person needs to be responsible for himself, to do what he wishes, and be self-supporting, but also responsible. They denied this, and I was forced to consider if I was wrong. Then again, I dreamed that I was with a woman, trying to find a place to be with her. She was blond and Teutonic and arrogant, but her skin was very special, like the marble of statues, but fleshly, semi-human. Her flesh was like a Michelangelo statue come to life, as if Dawn were now in my hands! The woman was only half-human, semi-divine. A friend suggested to me that she was Saturn in the form of a woman, that same judging, demonic, sexualized old man in the form of a woman, and The World. Is she not so in the Tarot Cards? Maybe one day I should confront her in that form, or in the form of the Emperor in those same cards. Better now, to continue with this figure, this judge and keeper of the gate who resists change.

"Go back," I hear. "Go back," says what seems like my Guardian Angel. "Go back to the Cloud." I return to the Cloud, the place of beginning. I sit and contemplate. Before me are a series of seats, upon which are several people. One is the Keeper of the Gate, and next is a little man with the little man's psychology—power hungry and pompous. Finally, there is the woman, Saturn, as marble-flesh. They all sit in big chairs, Judges. There they are, Bigot, Keeper of the Gate, Little Man, and Marble Flesh. Now Hermes-Mercurius comes and walks through them, around them, as they sit heavily in their Judge chairs. As he moves about them, I think of how I often go around and through such people, they are so heavy and dense and slow. So am I, so slow in overcoming or transforming the Judge. I look at them, as Mercurius laughs at me. I look at the heaviness of the Bigot, with his bald head and thick neck. I look at the roughness and beady eyes of the Keeper of the Gate, see his brutality. I look at the silliness of the Little-Man, with his power-hunger and stupid pomposity. I look at Miss Marble-Flesh, with her cupidity and arrogance. I see them all and get sick to my stomach, want to throw up.

"Wretch," says Mercurius. "Wretch! That will help you throw up and off all the garbage and folderol that these types have dumped upon you. Wretch! For that, too, is a tool of the Magic Man, the Magician-Healer with whom you work!"

I do so, concretely, until there is a reflex in my belly, and I wonder if that will help me.

"But what, oh Mercurius, great Magician of them all, can I do about these slow ones, these representatives of Saturn the Body, Saturn the Slow, the Narrow, the Arrogant and Pompous? How can I cope with them, 'handle them' as they say, though the very word offends me."

"Do as I do. Go in and out of them, around them, through them, above and below and everywhere. For they stand still and move slowly. They remain in the concreteness of flesh and being, they hold firm in the past and the present. They stay with the sensations. You and I can fly through space and time, to future and past, go everywhere."

"I have done so, but the world has resisted me. Flesh has, reality has, sensation has. I need to be a new kind of Magician, one who not only flows through and around and quickly, but one who can change and mold and effect these creatures. I must be an Abraxas of change, a maker of effect or, at least, to be in touch with such a one. Mercurius, can you do such things?"

"I can. Watch!" He knocks down the chairs, but the people do not move. "You see?"

"Yes, you can knock them down, I have seen that. I have seen that in myself also, but they do not change. Distraction. Things break in…telephone calls too. A woman who almost devoured me, from my youth, whom I helped and then had to protect myself from, called to say that she loved the boy in her, redeemed. And, indeed, she sounded less resentful, demanding, hostile. She also had her face peeled, she said; a new year, like a snake. Change, again. I come back to the living reality of these inner figures. Mercurius, help me. These figures do not change for me. They may talk with me, apparently change, but not really. Don't you see?"

"I see. Have it out with them, as your old master said."

"But I tried that too, but there is no change!"

"I know…Not real enough. Not concrete enough."

SESSION 16: JANUARY 12, 1972

After a two week lay-off, it showed. We started off with small talk about my skiing, his holiday which didn't get going, London fog, my mild regression, but then we got into it.

Work on forehead, usual belly and chest—a long time, it seemed. At the end, during the observation period, I felt my back to be perfectly flat. No pain. For two minutes, perhaps, there was the first absence of the perpetual dull ache which had been going on for more than five years. I mentioned it, and he said, yes, it was the relaxation that came from the work with the inner thighs. Yet there had been fear and pain there, even though he had worked on my thighs for only a moment or two.

"Castration anxiety," I said. As soon as I spoke, my back was slightly arched again. Oh, that Judge, that labeller! That narrow-minded bigot; as soon as I said the boxing-in words, he was there in my back again! The healer nodded. That, he said, came from way, way back, from before the word "time." I thought of my circumcision time, and that the doctor who had delivered me had been a drunk, and probably a bigot as well. Had he performed the circumcision? Or was it a *mohel*? No matter, the judge was there of course.

The healer put a mirror before my face, after all the work he had done on my forehead and eyes. Enormous relaxation was shown. "Ten years younger," he said. Fewer lines were on my forehead, and softer, and in the face, too. But my eyes looked a bit afraid. "Yes," he thought so too, but much life in them. I remembered when we had looked at the mirror together before: there was the Judge, indeed! I was so critical of how I looked, and I saw the critic there, brutal, and hard. He had softened in my face now. But only briefly, because the tension came back.

Now, I felt tenderness and warmth for the doctor, of which I spoke. He acknowledged it and returned it. As if the freeing from the rigidity of the Judge brought forth more loving.

I spoke too, about my struggle with the Judge, thinking to go back and confront those places where it had been heavily constellated, with men who had cared for me and betrayed me, were indifferent, or stupidly judgmental, or whom I had betrayed. But Regardie said the horoscope was bad for that just now. During this first month I was back in a negative Saturn condition (the Judge), with Saturn in Scorpio (just as in my chart), and that I really ought not to do so. I assented.

I still thought, "Well, some headway, that I can even conceive of going back and trying to work out this archetypal complex with one of these men. Foolhardy, perhaps, but I knew that fantasy would not be enough: there needed to be the concrete working on the body or in relationship. The limits of fantasy work lay just here. Those deepest wounds, sub-verbal and sub-imaginal conflicts, could not be solved at the "upper centers" alone: lower centers were necessary, concrete, belly, back, and chest.

We spoke, too, about magic, about his teaching me. He thought we could do that also. Start with the pentagram of banishing ritual, or simplified horoscope that he uses. But go slow. Better to solve the body tensions the Reichian way first.

JANUARY 17, 1972

Feeling better since last session, but still, uncertainty and slowness in dealing with the Judge. Two instances, in my practice, show how men can constellate that with me, and fail to work it out. The first case, a "Little Man," just wanted to get things and then leave. The second case, still working with me, had a dream in which I was scoffing at him; we got into a fight and struggle. I was glad about this dream, talked of working through the judge in him and me, but the upshot was, that he wasn't getting enough out of the therapy; he could have discussions with male friends and judging-work was available with colleagues. So, it shows that some men come for support, for help with their lady problems, but do not care much about relationship, working through the negative transference, or "mutual process." In a way, I can not blame them: why pay money for this, when they can get it free with friends? But can they? I wonder. The second of the two, professional in psychology, possibly can, but perhaps not as skilled as I in working on relationship. He, in turn, had fantasies of this being an ego matter for me, where I shine and sparkle as a star. Funny, for that is just where my wound is; but in "mutual process," I may be a star, and could help others, but they apparently do not wish to. Then, a friend-colleague called and said he would like to work on judge problems with me!

Another dream came in which the Bigot appeared. This time, I am at a party, and the Bigot is there with his wife. He is formally dressed, in tuxedo. His bald head and wide face, his hating eyes, his self-satisfied look, suggest a reactionary political stance. In my dream, he offers me a cigarette. I say, "No thank you." But he says, "But I offered you one," as if to imply that if he offers, then one must accept. I do not try to argue with him, sensing it is hopeless, and take the cigarette. In fact, two come out of the pack, and I put them in my shirt. I do not plan to smoke them. I accept his forcing his "gift" upon me, but I will not smoke it, self-destructively. End of dream. Let me continue the dream in fantasy.

"Mr. Bigot, you appear repeatedly in my dreams and in my psyche, now as Judge, now as Bigot, as Keeper of the Gate, or formal and reactionary, as you did in this last dream. You have even been an Eye of God. What is it you wish from me, why do you stay to haunt me?"

"I wish only to give you something."

"And what, pray tell, might that be?"

"I wish to give you a sense of history, of the past, of the hard-earned values of tradition, of conservatism, really."

"I thought I had those things. I went through such a period in both my analyses. Remember (or were you there?) when I took up Eisenhower and all that. And I have, indeed, continued loyally with both the Jewish and American traditions. Nor have I been a bigot in return to reactionaries in my work."

"That is true, and I know it. But there is another sense in which you have not been true to tradition."

"And what is that?"

"To the conservation of the soul."

"What is that? I have also done my utmost in that area."

"You have not."

"What do you mean?"

"You could sacrifice your life for the true values. You could give up all joy, all pleasure, all pursuit of self."

"I could, but I think that is senseless. Do you do that? With your tuxedo and grand self-indulgence, you do not look like it."

"I do not self-indulge. I am tough. As you can guess."

"Then I do not understand you. I am lost again. You ask me something, espouse a view, and then change it. You act like Mercurius Himself! Please be straight with me. What do you want of me?"

"I want nothing. Only to give."

"What do you wish to give? Cigarettes? Self-destruction?"

"I want to give..."

And he is gone, nothing remains. Only frustration. I can not speak with him. I can not move him or have a rational dialogue with him. We do not understand each other...That, at least, is "mutual." Neither of us understands the other, though each of us thinks that he does.

Now my thoughts move to my own nourishment, move away from the frustration experience with the Judge. I yawn, I think of reading something, of being passive. Just, perhaps, like those two men: wanting something, not relationship. All right then. Read a little.

JANUARY 19, 1972

In the interim, I have had both good and bad times. Had the sense of having drunk too much when a former maid came back to visit with her two-year old. The child, continually demanding, the woman in a terrible state of need herself, and I, trying to care for both, missing my dinner, drinking and finally going to bed. Afterwards, a hangover, unpleasantness,—bad for the system, loss of sensitivity of the centers, the various energies in each of the plexi. Good, in that I recovered from that, had a very good talk and evening with my wife, feeling our re-connection and own "mutual process," and back on track of the proper functioning of the system. What emerged was the possibility of using that Judge, that conservative fellow, as a Regulator of the system, as one who could let me know limits. What joy it would be to have that Judge evaluate what is bad for the system, when it is overloaded, when there is too much food, drink, sex, talk...or whatever. That sounded exciting indeed.

As I reflected about the prospect of Saturn as regulator rather than destroyer, I felt that would be very fine, but would he do so? I read back over what I had written a couple of days earlier. This time, the reaction of the Conservative seemed less maddening, he wanted to conserve the soul, after all. That matter about not being for self-indulgence but for sacrifice, seen in the light of regulation of the system, seemed not so bad. So then, let me reach back into the Cloud of the Soul and see the face of Saturn, if he will work as a Regulator, in a positive way. Yes, I can see it, Saturn limiting Gemini, so that Scorpio can go deep. Let me see if he will.

"Mr. Conservative, formal man, are you aware of my lucubrations? You nod, you are. Do you think that you could serve as this regulator, this Saturnine limit-maker who could protect the system from breaking down? Do you think your judgment or 'conservatism' could truly conserve against breakdown?"

"I do."

"And do you, Judge, Keeper of the Gate"...I had begun to say 'take this person as your bride' or some such thing, but my intuition already leaped ahead. I already saw Saturn behind all of these and I had a vision of Saturn and

Mercurius, the rulers of Limitation and Expanse, of lowest center versus highest, and in relation to each other. But before I leap ahead to such a union, I must ask these figures if, indeed, they are ready to perform such a regulatory function.

The Formal man nods, the Bigot looks out of small eyes, suspiciously, but nods a little. The Keeper of the Gate says yes, and they all tend to meld into one figure—a King, an old King. He is hard, wears his crown, has a beard, sits like my grandfather or my Swiss analyst. He sits, crowned, and nods his agreement to serve as regulator, silently. Should I but listen, he will give a clue, a sense that there is danger of excess. Alongside is the youthful, laughing spirit of Mercurius, the Fool. The young king and the old, the ruler of Gemini and the ruler of the Nether world. Paradise is where Zeus and Kronos, Jupiter and Saturn, intuition and possibility, sensation and limitation, are together. The myth says that but now to live it, to find it in my own life, my own human functioning! Surely it is possible, but the images are not quite real. What are the real ones, effective ones?

...Time passes. I read. I read of Primal Therapy, of screams and arrogance. So many "truths." All have a piece of it, of course, since the claims are metaphysical rather than scientific, largely, and monodogmatic rather than plural. And every man's psychology may speak to a common condition. Better, it seems to me, to find a quiet truth, one that enhances understanding, or one that is good for oneself, without thinking that it is the Only One. So many think so. But, Only is so Jewish, isn't it? Just like the Orthodox Temple of my son. Better, though, to be an orthodox Jew than an orthodox psychologist! The Authority of the Self is central for oneself, of course. Janov is rich and famous after all, and I am probably just envious, remembering our time in high school together.

But I am back with limitation. What image suffices? Stick with the last: the formal, tuxedoed man, a cowboy in modern dress. Will you serve?

"I do serve. The trouble is that you do not listen. As in your fantasy, you chose to hear what I had to say as crazy-making or reactionary. The only thing I said was that I was for the conservation of the soul and against self-indulgence. Now you are for those two aims. Being against self-indulgence does not mean anti-Dionysian at all. It is merely being for limitation and order. Is Apollo so far off from where I am? I am merely a mortal version of such Gods."

"But if you are a mortal version of Apollo, Lord of Reason, then where is Saturn, after all?"

"I don't know, ask him."

"All right, I shall. Oh Saturn, Lord of Limits, show yourself to me, I plead of you."

"I am there always, but you do not listen. Limit on limitation is your aim...Listen to the cells glowing and moving. Listen to the elves working in their caves. Listen to the ordered earth work. Listen."

"I listen...or try...But again it stops. I shall listen to the centers, to the signals. Then, perhaps, will order reign, will disturbance reduce. Screaming, yes, pain expressed, breathing, too. And listen to the Centers, listen to the signs. That I will do."

SESSION 17: JANUARY 19, 1972

Today Regardie spoke first of my horoscope. The period of the negative Saturn, proper to this month, and indeed, the heavy structure of the last fourteen years which this month repeats, ends in ten days, and will be followed by a warm and loving movement. But, he added, beginning shortly, a new 14 year cycle of deep spiritual development is in store for me.

"That's what I have been doing for the last 14 years," said I, "through pain and suffering largely, but growth all the same."

"Yes," he agreed, but this new cycle would be "slow and insidious" and the "triune Neptune..." would show itself in a remarkable way. Just as I have had a heavy and painful process for the last fourteen, and particularly, the last nine years, the next years will be more benevolent and sweet. "From now on, much less pain and suffering." Good, thought I, a new fourteen year cycle!

"A difficult horoscope," reflected the healer, as he had before, and indeed as had other astrologers, because of all those conflicts; yet a large vitality, "but a good one."

Then to work. "Flat-foot Charlie" for a time, as he calls it, in which I was more nimble and less tentative in bouncing around, and in falling forward, less rigid and freer bending. Then he worked on the chiropractic table on my back and neck. Painful areas elicited lion growls from the upper back and tiger growls from the lower. Rage and battle above, pain and whining below. The upper muscles, the wings and such, were particularly painful. "The last to yield," he remarked professionally, knowing that we would be back at that place many, many times.

And then on the couch. The usual breathing, sighing, as he worked on my belly, diaphragm, and chest. At one point, he asked me to stop moistening my lips and then I had difficulty swallowing. After a time, when I found I could still breathe with my mouth full of spittle, my diaphragm began a reflex. It repeated many times. Thinking this was a good thing, a relief, I stayed with this. He forced air out of my lungs and chest as I breathed and worked, and this too, seemed to free something there. Often sounds came out of me, sometimes like moans, sometimes like death rattles, sometimes like growls. It did so spontaneously. "Did that frighten you?" he asked later on, during the observation period. "Not at all," said I, "it was interesting."

In addition to the diaphragm reflex, however, during the observation period, when the usual flowing and tingling occurred, I found my lips pursing as if in a whistle, and then a sucking reflex began of its own. He let this go a little and then stopped it, by massage of the lips. "next time," he said, "This will be evoked much more easily."

The session ended in a quiet, good place, even though my back seemed to hurt more. There was definite progress each time, I felt. He remarked that the throat, gagging, swallowing, and diaphragm were related embryologically, but no one knows very much about it.

I had let the belly reflex go, I said, thinking it a good thing though I had the need that he work more on my chest at one point. "Tell me, next time," he said.

Afterwards we chatted a little, and I mentioned that I was experiencing the Centers more and more, belly, diaphragm, heart. Yes, he thought that would increase as the tension and rigidity lessened. He also noticed a golden sheen on the back of my hair. He asked what color my hair was as a child, and I responded that I was a little blond or light brown haired, and it darkened as I grew older. He noted that there was a better luster, that I continued to look younger also, after last week. We ended on a jovial note, as I left.

Yet I am still in the negative Saturn. Still another male patient, a priest, wants to stop now. Not getting enough and inconvenient, he said. Just the one who is slow to develop, is still rather boyish. Hard to deal with this archetypal place, though perhaps he will stay and work it out. Negative child: demanding and demanding, leaving when not getting enough. Negative father: not giving and just with the structure. Hard place, inside and out. In spite of my work with the Regulator, I overate once more.

"So then, eat," comes the word from the Figure, and I do. Ate my pear and three little laughing cow cheeses slowly and with relish. A cup of tea to round it off and, hopefully, the ravenous night appetite will be lessened and I'll be more human!

SESSION 18: JANUARY 26, 1972

The past week seemed an even further regression for me: my back went out, much pain, bent over, needing to stretch and pull, less energy for exercises, experiencing the Judge. The healer found my back indeed out, and we spent much of the session getting chiropractic help rather than body work. Pain, getting things back in line, lower back, upper back, neck. He was generous enough to say that he wished that I had called him rather than go through the week, he could fit me in somewhere. Indeed, if I continued hurting the next few days, to call him and we would mange it somehow. I was grateful for that offer.

But he reminded me that this was the Saturn month, when the Judge was giving his last gasp, after all! A repeat of those fourteen years, in spades. Only a few days more, and it will be better, no doubt. Soon Saturn will remove his great weight from my neck and shoulders and back. Do not try fighting it so much, after all.

JANUARY 31, 1972

End of the negative Saturn era, is it? End of oppression, the Judge, guilt? The broken back, the aches, interminable conflict? Well, maybe, but it is still going on today, was going on all weekend, and is harder than ever. Perhaps the end is the hardest, repeating all the fourteen years. Perhaps this last thrust of the Judge is the worst, it is hitting hard.

Oh, dear God, I speak of you. I tell the rabbi that you have spoken to me, that I hear your voice, but I lie. I lie because you have not spoken to me for so long. Yes, I know. You speak to me even now—in the pain and broken back, in the worry and fear, in all of the darkness. But you speak to me, too, in the support of friends, and love from my wife, in the continuity of my struggle which shows the light now and then. You speak to me in all my life, I know. But that is old stuff, is it not? I have accepted that long ago. Even if pain is an act of your love, just as that new nun patient thinks. God loves Jesus most of all, his "only-begotten son," and punished him the most, let him rot and be humiliated and abandoned, let him be a scapegoat for God's own sins. A fine father, eh? So says nun and Church...and so think I, too, in a strange way. For indeed, it would be easier for me to be ruined and humiliated and to die than for me to sacrifice my son! It would be much harder on me, really, though I would imagine that my son would have a thing or two to say about that! Let a person be his own sacrifice rather than send another, eh? And yet, Father and Son are One, are they not?

So, Lord, machinations, plots, reflections, questions, and doubts aside, I have heard and seen you in all my life, all my pain, and all my love and joy, but lately, I have not heard you directly. I have not heard this new You, this new image of unified conscience and desire, of regulation and freedom. Still there is fear and guilt. Perfect love casteth out fear, they say. Well, then, my love—and yours, too—are not perfect then. So, speak, Oh Lord, speak, I pray you. Speak and tell me, on this last day of...what is it in Hebrew, Sivan? Tishrei? I do not know in Your tongue. (Though I know perfectly well that you speak in Sanskrit and Latin and Greek as well, and, surely in Ashanti and Urdu and English, too). So, then, let me silence my tongue, and ask you to speak.

I look up into that Cloud of God. I look up into that greying, blackness-whiteness where the Lord doth dwell. I look up into the ambiguity where child was found and ox, Mercurius the Trickster, himself. I look up into it, and know that the Eye was there, and the Wand, and all of the goodness-badness of my Judge-pain, heart-love, and expectation. I look and pray that the One God, (Shema...Echad!), shall be there and speak to me, gently, lovingly, and in whole-harmony-ecstasy-touch when I shall know that the Lord my God has relented, has allowed His servant to unbend his back, to come off his knees. Speak, Lord!

Or are these very words yours? Yes, they come to me and flow. They speak themselves through me. I speak, it is true, and implore the Lord. My words cry out unto Him. And yet I can not speak, unless He speak in me. I can not cry out, unless He allows me to cry out unto Him. The Lord speaketh unto Himself. I am the Lord. So says the text, the Torah, and the Lord speaks. Rabbis proclaim it...not a jot or tittle to be changed. But Moses wrote it, and others. So the Lord spoke in them, did He not? The Lord speaks to Himself through men. And he speaks here, now.

...But Lord let the words of my lips, which are Yours, speak to the words of Your lips. Let the union take place! Let evil be relinquished. Let the right and left hands come together in a loving, praying, motion. Let there be a rest from this fourteen-year struggle of the oppression of Saturn, of the preponderance of Din, of Gevurah, of your Severity over against your Mercy. Lord, Adonai, God of my Fathers, who both sent the law and repealed it; You, who both gave me the law and gave me the pressure to overcome it, help me!

"A pretty picture. Prayers from the arrogant one! Self-abnegation, prayers and fine words!"

"Is it you, Mercurius? Is it you, oh devil-man? Or is it the Judge there once more? Is he there with his never-ending put-down, sneering at me? Is he there, or are you and he the same?"

"No matter; it is the same! Can you speak with me, match me? Can you gather your strength and your glory? Can you, with miserable ego and vanity, with hope and prayer, with pride and fear, come together in a final affirmation of yourself, your life, your love, and your God? Can you do that and face me, face all the sneering and acrimony and petty spittle? Can you do that?"

"No, I can not. I can not do it with you. I am not a Jesus. Yes, I am a God-man, I accept that. But, there are God-men and God men, after all! We know that. Jesus incarnated only one time and left, did he not? And I have incarnated so many times. Besides, I do not think that the sacrifice theme, self-immolation and torture are of this age. But, no matter, you speak, Mercurius, and sneer. Yet I know that you love me truly. You love me enough to want to strengthen me against your own assault. You love me enough to make me strong that I will not collapse under such attack. I know this."

"So, you know this. Do you know, too, that I can shift and change and become all things? Just as your Magician does? For I am he as potential-actual of you."

"Yes. But, sir, can you heal those sad eyes of my wife? Can you reward her loving, devoted and blissful nature? Can you show me how to love more deeply, and not betray God or my nature? Can you, Mercurius, fool of God, messenger of the Him who dwells afar? I ask you, can you?"

"No, no, no, no, no, no! A double trinity of no's. And of knows. A double trinity is also a hexagon, and the David-Solomon-star-seal. No, no, no. Which is to say, that I can not. But you can. You, mere mortal, fully human, cat and dog, fully human tree of life, fully human fragile thing. You can. For has not the Lord chosen you, and sent me? I am he who has ever come to you, now this way and that, now male and female, cat and dog, in all forms. I am also a fragile and agile magician, imperturbable and changeable. Have I not spoken to you in many languages?"

"Yes. And I have answered. I have met the challenge, fulfilled the claims! I have been alchemist, loving to the death his *sorror mystica*. I have been faithful Jew, loving to the death his beautiful wife. I have been faithful friend."

"And unfaithful."

"Yes, and unfaithful."

"And now, pray tell. What is it you want of the Lord? You have done His bidding, have lived His life. You have heard me and reckoned with me. This you have done."

"I have."

"And yet, you have no trust. You have no faith that His love for you will triumph over evil. You have no trust that His love for your wife, or for your family, or for your other loved ones will triumph. You have no trust."

"Just like Him, His son. Trust flies out at last. Trust flies away, as soon as the fears and pains and horrors become too great. Nor does it require even a Holocaust for you to lose trust. Only the ordinary trials of being the man that you are. Only that."

"Only that! Are you my friend and companion? If so, you will know that my pains have not been just 'ordinary.' I need not tell you that, I hope. Others, occupied with their own pains and not understanding my particular struggle, that I can understand. But you, Angel, Guardian Angel Mercurius, surely you know and understand. You should not accuse me of having 'little faith.' Surely not you!"

"True, my son and brother. True. I should not accuse you of that, but I do. I judge, and now you stand up to me."

"And I feel the echoing fall of my certainty. I hear the whisper of 'self-deception.' I hear the judgment of 'no change,' that the 'Lord has abandoned you' and that He will do it again. No chosen one am I, in the end. The Lord flits about from soul to soul, to do as He wishes, to choose whom he wishes."

"The Lord is your shepherd."

"I shall not weep?"

"You shall not weep."

"Shall I sing the praises of the Lord?

Shall I proclaim Him?

Shall I call out to

        Him-who-cannot-be-apprehended?

Shall I affirm Him who has also hounded me?

And hurt me?

And...yes...abandoned me?

Shall I sing unto Him?

Yes I shall!

Not because I am good or devoted.

Not because I am true.

For I am also bad and unfaithful.

And a liar.

And so is He. So is He!

The Lord is my shepherd."

"The Lord is your shepherd, it is true. And, like most shepherds, He is often not too bright. He is often unthinking. And like most sheep, you are often too gullible and trusting!"

"You change your tune."

"I change my tune. As you change, so do I. Hence my name, Mercurius. Curious and Mercurial, am I."

"And so am I...But where, in truth, has my effort after strength and trust gone?"

"Abandon, and stand. Let the Lord of Love and Power come through. Just as now."

"Is it so?"

"It is so."

"Must it be?"

"It will be."

SESSION 19: FEBRUARY 2, 1972

Today, the beginning of my "no-longer-oppressive-Saturn-period," did indeed bring me to a new place. Today I felt relaxation in my chest, greater than ever, with fuller and more relaxed breathing. True, I soon regressed back into the older place, but it happened. I also experienced, for the first time, a stiffness and pain in my thighs. In fact, as the "layers of the onion" are peeled, there emerges both the awareness of the tension that was there underneath, and the need to release it. It is a back and forth development which is experienced as freedom followed by restriction, along with the realization of the need for greater freedom.

Even more important than these openings, I had a clear perception of different regions of tension and pressure. There emerged, during the work, a clear separation of belly, solar plexus, just below the chest (two sides), chest, throat, and forehead. Each center was separate and each carried a different experience of tension and blockage, release and tension again. This came after we worked on a new method, the "Mussolini Growl," in which one thrusts out the lower jaw, growls like a dog, lets the head come down toward the chest and then, when the air is gone, thrusts the head back and breathes deeply. That is aimed at releasing the throat region, and was effective.

I noticed that Regardie worked with the centers in pairs, the way the Qabalistic centers are described. When I mentioned this to him, he acknowledged it. He worked on the muscles, but only to free them and to get at the centers underneath. I was thrilled by this realization, greater awareness of the centers, physically. I was looking for a union of concepts with the body, not just body alone, nor mind alone! He agreed, but at the moment he was more interested in getting my chest to relax more...As I write this, I sense a tightness in my chest; I breathe more freely and relax it. A strange battle: to both free the tension and to relax.

I spoke to Regardie about the awareness of the centers, as pain or tension, in my work with patients. I said I was working with this to a larger degree now. He nodded again, and suggested that I do the gag reflex exercise every morning before my other exercises, and swim. This would help free the solar plexus center. I was excited about that too, saying, "the power center." He said to "let it happen." Experience, of course, was more convincing than theory. But why, I wondered, did not others who had undergone Reichian therapy discover the centers too? They had experienced "streamings," the flow of pleasurable energy through their system, as I had. They had also seen the orgone energy "in the sky," which I had not. Why had they not experienced or reported this experience of the centers?

Regardie responded that they worked from Reich's anti-mysticism stance. They had experienced the energy, but they were not open to the further perception of the centers; that was even more frightening than the flow. Reich himself did not realize that he had discovered a region where mysticism and empiricism could be united. He was stuck in his anti-religious, anti-mystical, perspective and most of those that followed accepted that prejudice. It was puzzling to me. If, indeed, it is all based upon experience, not suggestion, then experience should demonstrate it. But perhaps one has to be open to certain kinds of sensation, have some sort of conceptual tool to embrace the new experience. I do not know. Neither, at this point, do I want to hastily read and theorize more. I want to stay with the concrete as it happens, as far as Reich and the body work is concerned, and to take up the magical work, oh so slowly! But I felt it: it happened! I made a step in differentiating the centers in myself!

FEBRUARY 9, 1972

Dreams with which to deal. In one, an extraverted, intellectual, unrelated man goes to UCLA, with a group in which there are many of us. I follow, mindlessly, until I see that it leads nowhere. In another dream, I am with a man with a too mystical bent, along with women and children, cramped in a parking lot, dirt. The point, as I awaken from the dream, is that I am just following, going along; I have to think and see what I really want, what is good for me. In short, use better judgment!

One night later, I dream: my daughter tells me that she made a mistake when she was "little." She tried to teach the members of her class, who were mostly Chinese, English and grammar, but she should have allowed them to teach her Chinese! I argue with her about it, but acknowledge she has a point. And then, I sit in that same room, but it is somewhere in the Holy Land, and look out the window to a cloudy evening. The room is in half-light. In the neighboring room, I see a large Turk or Arab, in a windowless, opulent setting. He has rugs and gongs all around. He is tall and powerful and arrogant, and, no doubt, is something of a magician. Into the room in which I sit comes a very swarthy Jewish man. He speaks to me first in Yiddish and then in faultless English. He is a New Yorker, sophisticated, clever, also arrogant, and partakes of all the Mediterranean and Near Eastern wiliness. I think of the two men. End of dream.

I reflect on my arrogance, the pride of my inward, magical, way, the passion and pride of the Arab. I think, too, of my wily, "adapted" persona, making my way in a hostile world to which I do not belong, clever but in exile.

It is from my dark room that I look out. The room of my inner darkness, which is sometimes depressed, sometimes rich, sometimes wily and deceitful, sometimes clever and reflective. I look out on the dim world with its half-light. So it is. But my daughter, my lovely joy and sweet thing who is gentle and true, just like my wife, is as kind and thoughtful as can be. She is growing up, speaks words of wisdom. Look, she says, it is better to adapt and learn from the strange new worlds, rather than to teach what one already knows, n'est ce pas? Oui, I say, mai ouis!

So, then, perhaps it is better to respect this dark Turk-Arab and his inner power. Sometimes he is arrogant, it is true, not "nice," but I can trust and enjoy him, as brother of the clever, sophisticated, wily, and adapting Jew. Can they be friends? Can Arab and Jew be brothers, really? I suppose they can, in me at least. As long as the Arab remains in the dark inner world of creative fantasy, instead of projecting all his nonsense outside, paranoidly, on other people or the world! And the Jew can survive via his cleverness, find his way around in a hostile world. But their arrogance, ugh! Contempt for the goy and heathen. Contempt for each other! Contempt and judging, again. How to protect these valuable functions from judging and rejecting the other?

Is it feeling that is involved? Is it the judging function? Is it my sweet daughter, full of feeling, who needs to learn, rather than teach? Is it my feeling that needs to take a cue from the Chinese, those who have pride and history and culture, but also bide their time, follow the new Utopian vision? Perhaps. In any case, the Chinese theme comes back again and again, as years go by. And one does not know what it means in the end. But, no hurry, one can learn. I must learn, first, to keep my rich fantasy in the inner room, and be on better terms with the wily one. But arrogance?

"Gentlemen, gentlemen," I say, "No need for arrogance! I love and respect you both, I need you both. Arab, Turk, poet, and friend, you I need and cherish, with your rich fantasy, the sound of your gong, your words which ring and the fabric of your fantasy. I love it and you and treasure you. I wish that I could bring your rich thought to the world! And you, wily Jew, good friend, I hope. I know that you are abused, that you suffer from rootlessness and long for the Promised Land. I know that you are arrogant, but also feel inferior, but you tell me of the world as it really is, tell me the dark secrets of its facts, and your sophisticated experience. I need to know it. Intuition of magic-Arab, sensation of perceptive Jew, both aligned with thought, fine. And feeling daughter, who needs to learn still. Yes.

CHAPTER FOUR

SESSION 20: FEBRUARY 9, 1972

Today we talked a lot, almost half of the session. I had come in battered and bruised and depressed from another painful session with a patient.

Regardie asked how I was and I told him. He checked horoscopes and we talked. The hypochondriac patient was just like his former analyst and his current lady, said Regardie. The hypochondria comes as complaints, body or otherwise, and they just need to get through it, be heard and be compassioned...This was reassuring. He also said that some interpersonal connections are shown in horoscopes as karmic, just as our relationship is. He said that my wife's relation with me, under Uranus, is very original and unique, which pleased me, too. We got closer, Regardie and I, since we also spoke about a friend we both admired. He looked again at my horoscope, noted its complexity, all I had done with its conflicts, and he remarked that I would always be in search.

The physical work was good but brief. There was nothing new to report, except a new exercise of stretching the neck back and pulling up the shoulders, while the hands were joined and pulled down from the lower back. Good stuff for the lower back. Also, he mentioned during the stroking period, that ultimately the stroking would lead, as Reich pointed out, to a general flow of energy, the "orgasmic reflex." But not yet. So far, I had experienced first tickling, then pleasant sensations, and an awareness of some resistance. "The armoring," he said.

He thought, from my chart, that I would be Freudian. "Too narrow," I said. "Sex is central, but I need to consider the religious aspect also." Yes, he agreed, and that, too, was the limitation of Reich.

In the night, I dreamed of a wimpish psychologist. I was trying to help this gentle, glasses-wearing, naive and open fellow, a patient of a former teacher. It was at a hospital I once consulted for. I was trying to make things better for him. This shadow figure is certainly known to me. I was clearly naive at that hospital, not recognizing their power struggle and authority needs. I must still be quite naive when it comes to the collective. A fine thing! But that balances the two men of the previous night's dream: the wily Jew and the fanatic Arab-magician! So many shadows! As if the psyche is trying to keep me in touch with all aspects of my masculinity, particularly the darker sides. Trying? No. It is just reflecting it, is it not? The purpose is not so apparent these days, whether seeking totality, or merely slow growth. No matter, it is as it is.

SESSION 21: FEBRUARY 16, 1972

Today I had a most satisfying session with the healer. After last week's half-hour talk-time, I was eager to spend as much time as possible on the physical work. This we did. He worked hard on my chest and belly, and then on my back, upper and lower. I felt little pain, but much work on my part, shouting all the while. I noted that things that he did before that elicited pain, such as squeezing the "wing" muscles, were now only felt as tension-releasing. Also my thumping brought on lots of perspiration. For the first time, he had to get Kleenex to wipe my brow several times.

At the end, I had a marvellous, full, free feeling, characterized most by the absence of pain from my lower back. No pain! Only once before, during the course of the treatment, did I experience the absence of pain after a session, and that was after a particularly painful and horrendous experience, with pain-free time lasting only a few minutes. Now the pain-free time came without all the horror, and also lasted at least several minutes. Aches returned after a bit, but there was a definite change and improvement. Now I felt the tension in my chest and in my legs. What a wonderful feeling of freedom! Imagine, having that all the time!

Incidentally, I also experienced the oral part once again. I licked my lips, enjoyed my spit, and felt a hope that my orality could be experienced in other than in excessive eating-drinking. So good the experience, so great the hope that I would continue to improve in that way!

SESSION 22: FEBRUARY 23, 1972

The week was fairly uneventful, but today's session found my muscles tense again, and my back out, although I was not aware of it. I reported that I had had an hour pain-free, which was a great deal, but the healer said that we would have to do better than that. He began by trying to align my spine and did some adjusting, but my back was too tense, so he put off the full adjustment until later, after the "work."

During report time, I found the tingling, the energy flow, all the way up from my legs and, for the first time, into my belly and even the solar plexus. It did not, however, include my upper thighs and buttocks or crotch. Does castration anxiety cut off the flow? He had worked a lot on these areas, and now I was aware of pleasurable sensations and flow there, with a concomitant awareness of heightened tension in the upper chest, jaw, and head, as well as neck. "Always there," he said, "only more aware of it now." True, I suppose.

Afterwards, he did a spinal adjustment, and I felt rather good. He remarked that someone had taught me to push my behind in. There was no curve at my buttocks or lower back where there should be one, and my neck had a double curve in compensation! Well, that would have been military instruction, of course: pull your butt in, shoulders back, neck in! All wrong, of course, missing the natural healthy posture of relaxation and normal holding up the body. It would take time to get the muscles trained to the new, natural condition.

Outside, resting up from the dizziness of hyperventilation, I found that my sensations were fuller. Colors were brighter and the world looked better. I could understand Orson Beane's experience, although I saw no "dancing orgones" as he did, at least not yet!

SESSION 23: MARCH 1, 1972

Today my session with Regardie was intense. He worked a lot on my chest and neck. After a time, I began to weep heavily, and then laugh, and scream in pain and agony, even experiencing a reflex action of my belly as if throwing up, vomiting all the times of paradoxical frustration and impotence. The thought that kept coming to me was that "my body is my own" and "my body is to be trusted," and finally, "God is in the flesh." Somewhere, perhaps, I got the idea that my body was not my own, was not to be trusted, and that God was only in the spirit. And now my pain and agony of relaxation, of coming down from those horrible tensions, is bringing me back into the flesh, back into the being which is my own. I am entitled to just be me, in the flesh, perhaps. I add "perhaps," because it is not altogether accomplished. But on the way it was a most moving experience.

SESSION 24:MARCH 8, 1972

With Regardie, it was very good. He started by remarking that he had been thinking about me these last days. I was down a little, but glad of his involvement. He spoke of going to see a true alchemical laboratory one day. Fine.

The work was good as usual. At the end, this time, I felt the flow under my legs as well as on top, and I felt twitching over several places. Improving gradually. He reminded me that there would be three classes of symptoms in the course of the work, related to my "high chest" problem: indigestion, insomnia, and impotence. He called these the three "i's." These would be recurring periodically, as a release of anxiety and tension. All right. Too, there would come the sense of meaninglessness, related to early childhood feelings. I understood, and felt a deep non-verbal connection with him, along with a sense of help. He spoke of his "only son," his cat, and I felt that I might fill something of a place like that. Transference? Of course. But positive, and not too strong, and I could wait a long time to discuss it. That seems a good non-ambivalent place for me at this time.

SESSION 25: MARCH 15, 1972

Somewhat quiet today. Usual work, breathing and release, but quiet. During the observation period, I even fell asleep! That was quite strange, to fall asleep during a therapy session. Regardie said that this was not uncommon: the experience of relaxation leads to sleep if one is not used to it. In time, I would be able to be relaxed and not fall asleep. He was also very nice to me. When I spoke about giving his book on relaxation to a patient of mine, he presented me with a copy of it. He even inscribed it for me. During the end, as we talked about technique, he also offered to lend me his unpublished book on method, which I put off for a time, since I did not feel ready. He is quite encouraging of me, respects my wanting to go slow in the use of the method, but I feel again as I did in the days of my youth, the "heir apparent" syndrome. He is ready to adopt me as his son, is my fantasy, teach me Reich and magic. We will be close friends and colleagues one day. Such is my fantasy.

After the session, I hear of other's pain and trouble. I want to go back to the Cloud. Great Cloud of God, great Mercurius of the morning light, great Angel, can I pray for others, as I asked? Let goodness pass through me and go out of my hands and fingers to help. Let it also go through me and pass into the world to the sore afflicted. This is my prayer.

MARCH 16, 1972

Now after almost every session with the healer, I experience a breakdown. Not right away, but the next morning, with a bitter dream the night before. This time I was broken and despairing in the dream, following a meeting with someone I knew in high school, in the forest, near some large pipes. I said hello, in the dream, that I knew him from school. He did not remember me, said that he was in charge of youth, but then gaily went off with a friend. I was alone, unknown. He, I recall was good-tempered, a Jewish lad who was accepted by the gentiles, an athlete. Ah, that is it: the Jew who fits in, is accepted. I needed that then, both in grammar school and in high school. I never did fit in, those days in school: too smart, or too neurotic, or too different. Only summers did it work well, at camp. And now, again, I do not fit in, but neither with Jews nor gentiles, not with the collective, or the world at all. But maybe that adapted side of my self, that dream figure, can work with youth! Yes, the youngsters I now see seem more alive and accepting of what I am doing as a therapist. Yes, maybe that is the side that can adapt and fit in, as a worker with youth.

SESSION 26: MARCH 22, 1972

Well, the 26th session, the six month period that I had initially contracted for, has come and gone. I feel good about it. The end is not yet in sight, of course, but I do feel that there has been a definite reduction in character armoring, a flow of energy, and that the work has been well worth while. I also believe that I have a good future with the healer, both in regard to Reichian work which I need for myself and will, ultimately, also do with others, and also with regard to magic and the "centers"—chakras.

This session began with a long account by him of my wife's horoscope, which he said was fairly good and trouble free, in that there were no squares (as in mine), but that he felt there were several problems. First, the presence of Mars in Pisces made her aggression get "drowned" he said, so that there is some problem of little energy with her. I, too, have Mars in Pisces, but it is very different, in other signs and aspects. My aggression gets "drowned" too, is impotent in bringing about the effects I desire—whether of revenge, hurt, or protection—but I do have enormous vitality. She, though, also has underlying sadness to her, he thought. I doubted this, since she is usually so much more cheerful than I. But that, he said, is the Gemini ascendant, and is more superficial: her depths are more sad. I saw some of that in her concentration camp dreams (Saturn, he said), and her dark eyes at those times. When I discussed this with her later on, she said that the depression could be there, and was at times, but being married to me helped it a lot. She felt my love and care, and anyway, I am such a dark, deep, one that she doesn't have to be! But she acknowledged the problem about her energy: she has to be careful about too much expenditure of it and does need and enjoy periods of quiet nothingness.

Last night I dreamed I was in Pasadena, in a large area which included stores, public buildings, centers of administration, and the like, but all in a community complex. I wandered about, looking for someone or something, alone. I saw a man and thought it was an old friend. I went up to him and saw he had changed: he looked brown and healthy, taller than I, something like my son. But it was not he, it was someone else who knew me but whom I did not know. But then I saw the real friend, looking dark and only a little friendly. They were in a sensitivity group led by another friend. It seemed strange to see him there. They went off to their group and I was alone again. I wandered around, saw little booths, had some minor fling at what was there, but found myself quite alone at the end.

So, my dream, in contrast to my waking life, finds me alone. I have friends, loved ones, relationships, yet inwardly, I am alone. But, in the sense of Pasadena and the "complex" of a conservative community, I am indeed alone. I can not find my place in it, really, attracted a little, but not very much. I do miss the intimate male friendships I once had. Yes, I have ongoing friendships, but not as I did in my youth.

APRIL 4, 1972

Last night, as I started to re-read Jung's autobiography, I felt a deep nostalgia, a memory of the days of Zürich, and my dream was nostalgic too. Go into the Cloud. The Cloud wherein have dwelt dark child and bull, Mercurius and myself. Jung is there, smoking, sad.

"I know, Marvin," he says, "I know. You have struggled so long, I know. I have been through similar things. Not the same, but similar. And I, too, have come back to the inner life. The outer world has been painful, disappointing. Only when the inner contents have gotten realized has it been meaningful, fruitful. I know where you are."

"I am not sure that you do. I have heard that a lot, and have discovered that people do not really. I feel very much alone, much of the time."

"I know. I have no advice. What I can say is come back to the inner life. Therein, is pleasure and meaning."

"Yes, I know that. I have lived that, lived your way with much pleasure and meaning, but also pain."

"Yes. It is like that with one's best. I always waited a long time before giving it."

APRIL 5, 1972

I breathe, I am free. I sit in my office, on a Wednesday morning, and I feel free. I sit, and but a few hours ago, I dreamed that I was in a federal prison or getting ready to be put behind bars. My wife was there, visiting. Someone else, too. There was a pattern, a kind of floral pattern on the floor of this great hall which was the foyer of this prison. Some prison! Grand and like the Versailles Hall of Mirrors in France. The pattern was like a frame on a picture, and I was about to be put behind bars. I awakened early with the same energy and rage that I had been feeling the previous night. Standing up for myself with patients, giving up the old care-taking role. Standing for the belly, not the heart. That which was angry and intense in me was not the little boy, but an image of an intense, dark-eyed romantic man, in his early thirties perhaps. Is it true? Has the boy come out, at last, from the darkened room and become a man? I will have to see in a moment.

"Oh Cloud of Unknowing, cloud of mystical experience, cloud wherein dwelt the hurt boy, the reduced Ox, and the mysterious Mercury, show me now, I pray you, if, indeed, the lad that was there has grown into a man."

I see, now, in the whirl of thin wisps of cloud, this figure of a dark, shirtless man, intense, dark-eyed. He looks a bit like that man in the Thematic Apperception Test, angry and about to be off, away from the woman holding onto him, away from the clinging. But no, he is no mere picture, he is a man.

"Yes, I am he. I am that lad, that boy. I am he no more, yet I am he. You know. As you accept me, bring me out, stay with me, I am a man, no mere child. But sometimes I am, I hide. You know, for you are me."

"I am thee. So you say. But I am both more and less than you. I am but a man. Potent man, and impotent. Like you, child and adult. Impotent rage, but potent when connected. You are there. I need not speak with you, for yours are not words, are they? Yours is the intensity, being with one's self, wandering in the woods, a Heathcliffe, in a way."

"True. But no Heathcliffe, no picture hero, or hero from books am I. You know me. We have lived."

"But he who lives, speaks, has the words, is the Magician, is he not? Are you not from the Belly center?"

"Yes. Belly it is, and diaphragm. Not just heart."

"But now the words are wrong, and off. It is enough that a fantasy brought me there this A.M. No words now. What would you do?"

"I would wander the woods. I would feel the sun. I would run and play, read poetry. Go to the sea.

"I want to feel free and to go off alone. You have been so cramped up, so in prison with your obligations, your routine. I want to get us out. Don't you see? Your dream says that you have had a nice prison, a foyer that is flower-covered, framed. Where is the freedom? Where are you finally freed of the fear of authority? Where do you say, oh, I made a mistake, I'll pay. Period!"

"But you, lad, were the frightened one! You, when a boy, just days ago, sat in despair and fear, could not stand the light or people."

"Yes, because they wounded me. But, when I stand firm and can wander free, I am fine. Come with me, alone."

"Now?"

"No, not now. It is all right. You have tasks, do them. And then we shall go to the sea, and walk and read and be quiet. I would like that."

"And I too."

SESSION 27: APRIL 5, 1972

I write on the day following the session. The usual hard work and effort was added to this time by a spontaneous screaming which came out of me. He encouraged this, at one point, when we worked on my legs for the first time. I was to raise my legs, one at a time, and bring them down hard, screaming angry words at enemies. I laughed at that—as I did through much of the session—and then got into it. At one point I was banging both legs up and down and screaming hard. A lot of release of tension was in it. At the end, during the usual observation period, I found my back very relaxed. I was even of the opinion that my head was forward, rather than back as it usually feels. The full relaxation was short-lived, but still there was progress. "Three steps forward, one-and-a-half back," said the healer.

When he worked on my forehead, he asked me, when I was opening my eyes wide, to visualize something terrifying and horrible. I did and screamed. What came first was the memory of the dream I had at nine or ten years old when I was about to have intercourse with an aunt and a snake or worm crawled out— horrible. I also visualized a devilish monster threatening me with an axe. These were only partly successful in fear-provocation, but still...

Now, the following day, I suffer from indigestion. One of the "i's" of indigestion, insomnia, impotence. Well, luckily the impotence is well out of the way, for the moment.

I am moody, can quickly go up or down. So, back into the Cloud.

The Cloud is blurry. It lifts and shows someone seated in a chair, bent over, depressed. Is it a man or woman? A woman, I think. Bandana around her head. She lifts her head and shows her face, it is ugly, with a leering quality, sickening. I put my hand to my mouth, fearful of throwing up. Is this woman making me nauseous? This depressed, miserable, old woman, always in need, always down, bitter, and unhappy? Will my old womanish depression die...? She turns back into herself, the leering and false smile are over. I throw up and look at bits of corn in it. Corny, sentimental. I also see worms. Worms of my aunt, who was/is, indeed, a bitter old person. She felt left out, not attended to, always wanting, not giving anything to anybody in her life. Yet, sometimes she was happy to see me.

"So, come now, aunt within me! Depressed woman of my soul, let me hold you in my arms, as you die. Let me rock you and comfort you. Your life has been without fulfillment, you have wasted yourself, been unfulfilled. Now, woman of my soul, old bitter thing, tell me if this is true."

"Not so, fool! And if it were so, would I admit it? Fool!"

"Yes, I am foolish to think that you would. I do not know where you, my depressed soul, have been wasted."

Just now, when someone asked for help, needed to see me, my depression lifted. Perhaps that is it. Meaning comes through helping, just as it did with the Nun. She has always been taking, these last few years. She needs to give, now. Is it so with you, that part of me that has been taking, not giving? Funny, because I have been complaining the other way around, that I give too much, have to attend to others too much, do not get enough myself. It is puzzling. As I start to attend to myself, does that selfish but sad old woman die? I do not understand. Is it compensation, opposite? If I reject the care-taking role, and look out for myself, does the depressed woman die?

I have the feeling that I should not, can not really talk to her. That I must just accept her there, let her die, or be. Stop trying, for heaven's sake! I am always trying. That is me, forever helping, straining, not accepting. If I let her just be, not try to communicate, to heal, to do anything, maybe that is the better death. Or, transformation. Or something. Trust, perhaps. Let me just stay where I am. That is what I am trying to do. For Heaven's sake, let me do that with parts of myself, too...! Good... I feel better already... She looks up and winks, smiling, but looks back down again. A game? Understanding? So be it... Take a little walk.

SESSION 28: APRIL 12, 1972

Before my session, driving over the hill to the healer, I was looking at the sky, unusually a clear and sparkling blue with rare clouds, and at the redness of the hills. I listened, too, to music on the radio, Mozart, when a warm glow swept over me, an emotion of joy and gladness which came as an experience of God's love. I felt it as full and as profound a place as when I had experienced the torment of God, the crucifying pain of being given an opposite message. It was benevolent, redemptive, but the hint was that God's love is also so great that it, too, is hard to contain!

In the session, I felt looser, more flexible. He did not use any pillow for my head today, though he worked hard on my neck, which seems to show the greatest tension these days. At least I am experiencing it there now. He did several chiropractic adjustments on it and I do believe that it may be responding a little to treatment. But there was the usual work on the various armored regions.

During the observation period, I noticed that there was a flow of the energies in my chest region. At one point, I felt the urge to reach up my arms imploringly, and call out "Mother," though this was not accompanied by any pain or anxiety. I told him so and he then worked on my belly a bit more, but no more change. In all, the usual good session, but this time I again felt giddy, as I had not after the last two. I reported that I had felt indigestion, following the last session, for two days and, for the first time, I experienced insomnia, too, just a bit.

So, that is that for the work. Otherwise, I seem to be on the upswing. I had a good talk with a colleague friend, as we worked on the archetype of the judge together. What came out was his power-drive in questioning, probing, and my shifty evasiveness. His and my devil-judge were in the open, acknowledged, and then I felt an eros flow toward him, openness, too, which he remarked about the next day. But our views of openness are different. He thinks of dichotomies, open or closed. He sees that the openness in a relationship can increase in time with greater trust; but what increases is greater duration of openness, before closing. I, on the other hand, see openness as more a continuum, degrees of it. I am open in some areas, not others, for example. Or I am open with where I am in a relation with another person, but not about a third person. So, for me it is more complex. But still, good. And in my work with patients, I could see an open place in feeling and fantasy. I also had greater openness with shifty men. So, my work is okay. Go into the Cloud.

Sleepy. The cloud is a gray, silent, wispy thing that trails off like, like...semen. I think of my talk yesterday with my son about sex and love. A good beginning, a contact with a difficult area and expression, but only a beginning. Not the kind of openness or connection, or love flow and warmth that I would like, but he needs his distance, I think, and that is okay, too. But I am in the Cloud. It is a semen cloud, perhaps.

I do not like it. I am confronted with the bad smelling/tasting semen, my own. Smells are bad, body. Such as many bodies are much of the time. I am confronted with my own bad-smelling semen, however. What is bad about it?

"Because it is creative," the answer comes. "Creative juices are always a bit murky and smelly. Does not a child or a cat or a piglet smell bad when he emerges from the vagina of his mother? So it is with all creation. The odor of creativity demands that others as well as one's own ego stay away until the force is sublimated."

"Who speaks?" I ask. "I, Mercurius, of course. It is always I. I who am Magician and Poet, Teacher and Guide, follower, too. The other!"

"And what do you think about my being so...what is the word...puffy, persnickety, prissy—yes, prissy is the word—prissy about my own semen, my own body smells...and now as you say, about my own creativity."

"Well, aren't you?"

"Yes, I see what you mean. I am doubtful about my own creativity, indeed."

"Just like your semen."

"Well, there is doubt, Mercurius. There is doubt, is there not?"

"Yes."

"What do you think?"

"I, I am just a reflector, am I not? Am I not, as the Existentialists claim, just another mirror of your own thoughts?"

"No, I don't think so...or I am not sure. That, too, is now a bit shaken after talking with L. There, too, I am puzzled, confused, unable to express. God speaks through me, but it is not me, yet it is. Or, I am a partial expression of God...and...you know all that. It is, indeed, wispy, semeny, not clear. No firm child is yet born of my creativity."

"Yes, you are in doubt. Thus the wispy, semeny, funny place."

"Yes, I see it. I guess I accept it, too."

"Good, that is a good thing to do. When the semen gets thicker, when the menstrual blood is thicker, only then does there come a time of deep creativity, and the readiness for conception!"

"But what of the flow? What of the...urge...dribble...silence...wait."

SESSION 29: APRIL 19, 1972

This past weekend I was a star. I gave a talk in San Diego and felt great. I truly felt a sense of being able to be myself—an achievement. I explained, I was helpful, witty, kind, and even had some deep connecting experiences, as well as positive feedback. One woman wrote to me, very movingly, that I had indeed made her aware that she was a vessel of the Spirit. And yet...my dream a day or two later involved going to UCLA (as I will next week to give a talk) and finding a new area, one where the leaders lived. I drove through and came to a place where communion was held (as it was on the San Diego weekend), but it was not satisfying. Finally, I left, since I found the whole institutional setting depressing. So it was for me, really, and so, I suppose, it shall be when I speak next week at UCLA. I need to have my spirit validated, it is true, and that is gratifying, but there is something very depressing about institutions that hits me. It is the old *senex*, the form, Saturn hovering over me. Even if I succeed in being myself, and even being a star, something is still not right. My real life is with individuals and small groups, and alone. Yet I also need public recognition. It is still something of an uncertainty. Perhaps, when I am truly myself, I shall relish those group moments and not pay such a great price.

For that is what I did. When I came to the healer, he found my chest hard as a rock, my spine was out of alignment. He worked like hell on me as he pounded my chest and belly. I broke through with tears and with laughter, without any content or imagery coming through. When he asked how it was that such a re-rigidifying took place, I spoke of my great anxiety in giving my talk. Well, that was it. I no doubt held my breath and kept my chest up. I must be able to breathe, now and then, from the upper chest and reduce anxiety. How about giving up institutions? No, he answered, I have too much dynamism for that. I will need to be able to speak and give out my power and intensity without getting so anxious. Easier said than done, say I, in my not so original way. But now I must prepare more for my upcoming talk.

SESSION 30: APRIL 26, 1972

Today, on the thirtieth session, I also gave the other "big talk" at UCLA. In a theater, no less. But it was not as "big" as I thought it was going to be—200 people rather than 600. The leader of the series anticipated 600 for the series, but only 200 registered. Just as well. I gave my little talk extolling Jung in a more positive way. I showed a film of Jung interviewed, and a friend gave her talk on art therapy as well. Hers was fine. I felt especially effective during the hour-long question-and-answer period. Another step in external validation.

The session with Regardie was also very good. This time, there was much more energy flowing over the whole of me, particularly the left side. Somehow, the right side, other than my arm, did not flow. He had worked a lot on my chest, and I felt the flow up there as well. I even felt a pulsating flow and a circular movement in the left lower back area—not where the pain-trouble was, but to the left of it. It was very pleasant. Regardie added to it by placing one hand on my head and the other on my belly, but it was my own energy. I am definitely well on the way toward having the full flow of energy and, now that these talk obligations are completed, I can soon begin my study of Reich, of magic and Tarot as I had desired.

SESSION 31: MAY 3, 1972

Regardie worked on my inner thigh muscles today. I rather felt the need of it, and he guessed it. When I asked him how he knew, he said that he just followed what came to him, as he pointed to his chest. Well, the session began earlier than usual and lasted longer than usual, as he worked on those ultra tight, ultra painful muscles. At times I would just breathe and let the legs drop; at times he would assist by pushing them down a bit; and at times he pummelled the muscles. The latter was excruciating and I could hardly take much of that. Yet it seemed to work very well. The energy flow was even greater than last week, though again it was mainly on the left side of the body and in the arm and foot on the right side. At one point, the trembling in my lower body (which lasted from the middle of the session onwards), made a leap right through the small of my back, where the most rigidity is. There was intense quivering and jumping there. I felt the energy especially strongly in my hands and feet.

During the observation period, the healer said that the flow in the feet could be felt especially just above the calf, a kind of center is there. He also said that the flow is general and that the breathing regulates it. He said that I would be feeling more and more of it. Today, he said, some block got relieved so that there should be more during the day and during the week. Just sit sometimes and notice it. The flow will be in the hands. Just pose them across from each other and they will jump the gap. One can even see the tendrils of the energy at times, he said. I must experiment with that this week.

Just after the working part of the session is always the best time. There is a flow and wonderful loving feeling. Regardie asked me to describe it, saying there is a typical answer given by everybody at one time or another. I described it as something between the kind of loving I feel when I give from the heart and when I am aroused sexually. It is a feeling, perhaps, of being loved and loving, rather than "chosen." Regardie said that there was another reaction, much as what mystics have always reported. He said that this is almost always so, and I remarked that such a technique, with very definite results of energy flow and healing, could be most useful, indeed. Maybe, I thought, that the Reichian method was more on the healing side, whereas psychotherapy, as I did it, had more to do with consciousness-raising. He felt that consciousness came in the Reichian method also. I am sure it is so. Anyway, my fantasies are now beginning to touch on doing that sort of work: changing my couch into a treatment couch; getting a board and putting a mattress on it. The couch was from my mother, her gift. Appropriate that it also be used for healing and work with the body. I have also been feeling the flow in my hands and wanting to touch or massage patients sometimes. Regardie also remarked about someone I referred to him, saying that he was eager, a bit "dark" and sinister in horoscope, perhaps, but as I saw him, too, as gifted, and in time will go far. He said that I had helped him a lot, which the patient acknowledged. Well, so much to the good.

I have plenty of patients now, and even a clamor, since my "smash hit" talks in San Diego and UCLA, so I don't need to worry so much about finances.

But enough of this reporting. It is no diary but a record of healing...it is...But I want to get into the cloud, the cloud of psyche. I think that the Qabbalah speaks of the cloud, too, does it not? Anyway, my dreams are somewhat sexual again, but I do not understand what they mean, what is happening on the inside. With my friend and colleague, L, its clear that her psyche is registering huge changes in energy distribution, as she waits for change in her life. With me, it is less clear.

I look into the cloud. But now I feel it around my heart, or on the left side of my chest. Pain. It is like a circular, small halo. I yawn and breathe, relax a little. The pain subsides. What was it that smart young girl patient said this morning about the pain and its subsidence? Being true to freedom? I yawn once more and relax. Lately, these days, I want to relax, yawn and breathe, feel the flow of energy, but there is still pain in the small of the back, and now, in my chest too. Yawn. Yawn.

Who is there in the cloud in the chest? Yawn. Sleep. Read or sleep! Dark sleep. Red. Red blood in chest, blue veins, arteries. Nothing to say.

But surely there is. What about my dream of the guru and his guru dog who is a guru for other dogs? What about my being able to deal with the instincts and behavior better?

I am walking about inside the circle-cloud-halo which extends from my chest. It is a light glow. I radiate heat and light. But it is now like a breast, soft and white and then hard...energies...fantasies of the girl patient this A.M. Questions? How to deal with these energies? Yawn. Lie on ground and feel them, concretely, a voice says. All right.

SESSION 32: MAY 10, 1972

Yesterday, I had session number 32. During the week, my back was still out and difficult, so I had to see the healer again briefly for a "re-alignment," a manipulation of the spine that would bring it back into place. He was able to do so in part, but not altogether. Instead, he showed me some "first aid" methods of doing it—standing with my back and head against a door and lifting up my foot and leg to my chest and stretching it. This several times with each foot, careful not to bring my head down, but to bring the leg and knee up. This did help.

But yesterday, the real work began anew, strenuously. The usual work with chest primarily and breathing, some with belly, with throat and just a little with my thighs this time—I could not take too much. But still, heavy. He also worked once again (he hadn't for a long time) on my back and that did both hurt and feel good. Oh, the "masochism" of it! Oh, the feeling of needing those hard muscles and armor to be beaten, pushed in and so, at last, comes relaxation, an absence of pain and stiffness. This work is just the way to learn to relax, I am convinced. So we worked, sweated, breathed. After the observation period, when I again felt the streamings, he was able to press upon my lower back, since I could not endure it earlier.

Observations this time included a strange feeling of alternately great heat and great cold in my toes, particularly the two smallest ones of my right foot. That, plus the heavy streamings at times, though not as strong as last time, and the highly pleasurable feelings when he stroked my legs, chest, sides, enough to bring out a kind of pleasant moan in me: these were the main things of the session. We also chatted a bit about people we knew in common. Chummier. We, no doubt, will become closer in time.

Afterward, I felt good, but somewhat tired and weak. In the evening, my wife and I took a long swim. That night, I had again a "wipe-out" dream, as I often do after a session. My colleague, L, experiences this after her sessions also. That, plus waking up with a headache this morning, suggests that the energies are really being "pushed around," that work is taking place.

In the dream I am being held captive by a number of young men in a house which is also like a shop with many things for sale. They start to abuse me, but are interrupted by a member of their crowd bringing in a wounded person. The person has blood on him and also a kind of substance which is like the white of an egg, messy and semi-solid. It is something from "inside." This stuff on him gets on me and I don't like it. As they put this on me, I get angry and now refuse to take any more of their abuse or being captured and I simply run away. They do not follow.

I wander about and see some of this semi-solid-fluid substance in the streets. Some elegantly dressed ladies walk through it without recognizing what it is. I then urinate around the side of a tree. I walk on and then I see my father. We go on together and come to a bus stop which we recognize as a place to go home. We get in the bus line which is just starting. The line gets longer and longer behind us. Just behind us is a friend of colleague. Glad to see him. But then, it is getting quite warm, so I take off all my clothes except for my underwear. It is comfortable, although unusual for the other people. But now there is some pressure to get dressed and get my things together as the bus is coming. I try to get dressed but have great difficulty. I seem to have ski pants instead of my regular ones. Well, that is OK, but how come I have those on? Still, trouble getting them on. As I gather up my stuff, I see that some of it seems to belong to my friend. OK. At last, I seem to have my stuff and pants on, while a woman on the bus worries about me. Anyway, it seems to be too late and the bus goes off without me. End of dream.

Some dream. A fuck-up dream. Yes, the egg-white "insides," and my squeamishness about such stuff, smells, greasies, semenies, and so on. The wounded man? Probably my wounds from rejection. Captured by young men and abused? Don't understand. Youthful impulses have me cornered and bother me? Yes, they still do, I suppose. But my squeamishness frees me, as well as the "wounded one," who is youthful also. I find the *prima materia* in the streets, and the elegant ladies walk through. Well, that is an improvement: the "elegant ladies" (my squeamishness, prissiness) can now walk through such "ickies" without being aware of it, even. And I can urinate, relieve myself. Then, I go on with the Father. In the world, I can find my way with the Father better. Yes, I have a kind of father now, in the healer, and I am also in a somewhat better relation to the world and the "Fathers," although that jerk from the Temple, pompous ass that he is, bugged me silly. But I simply said "no" to his demand-request, and there is nothing that he can do to hurt me. He can't hurt my son, either, since even if we are kicked out, it is the learning that counts, and he can have his Bar-Mitzvah ritual elsewhere. Besides, I would make a huge stink with the Rabbi, my friend. So, I can stand up better to the negative father in the world. But I find a collective bus, and then foolishly disrobe to be comfortable! Fool! I meet my colleague there, too, a "wounded healer," like myself, but I am too exposed, and this time, getting my clothes on, even ski things (late development for me), also my need for grace and such keeps me from joining the crowd. Apparently, I am left alone. Well, OK. Another bus will be along after a while! Don't panic.

But what does that dream say about energies? I am still with the youthful wound, still squeamish—although improving, and still poor in persona, though improving there, too. All right. Youth—hoodlum capture is as bad as negative-father capture. I know. I surely need my introversion, and I am working towards repair. Perhaps these same youths are trying to care for the wounded one. It seems like it. Well, enough. We shall see what my friend, L, has to say about it.

MAY 13, 1972

Several things have happened. First, my friend gave a very helpful interpretation of the dream, one that really got to the point. The fluid "insides" are what I have been wounded by with people so much, they projecting on me, blaming me, etc. That is why I run. This young man has had the same wound, probably, as I. The wound is not that the "insides" are from within him, but that they come from outside him! Yes, other people's "insides" and blood, touching me, have wounded me, make me run. That may be a good place to be "squeamish."

Going home, I experienced an inpouring of love, while listening to music, Bach. It was almost too much. I felt, yes, I have been "chosen" by God, but not loved so much by Him or the universe. Loved by people, yes, not by God. Well, it seemed to be pouring in impersonally. I tried to let it flow out it that night to my wife and children.

SESSION 33: MAY 18, 1972

Yesterday, my 33rd session, was marked by a very high level of streamings. They began even during the preliminary stages of the work and, by the time the observation period began, they were very strong indeed. Now they spread into my chest. The streamings were intense and I experienced them as covering a rectangular area, just below my nipples and above until the upper chest. Regardie said that the streamings were just in the area of the chest armoring. They flowed under and were blocked by the armoring. The chest is the most difficult place, even though I feel my pain mostly in belly and lower back. He worked some on my lower jaw, which hurt a lot. Oh, how tight my armoring must be there, shown in jaw-clenching! He also did another technique, which involved having me follow a light around with my eyes. He held a pen-light above and around them for some time. He said that Baker, in New York, did this a lot, but he did not. Besides, for me, the main difficulty was the chest, I had good movement around the eyes. Later, though, I wondered if vision could not be improved by freeing of the armoring there.

The streamings were variously intense on my feet and legs, but not on the soles. Those were very cold indeed. Curiously, I also felt great cold in my anus. Later, when I sat up, the streamings became deeply throbbing in my legs, so much so that I thought I could hardly move them. I also felt the streamings in my back and chest and up into my face. Until then, I had felt warmth or wetness on the face, where he had worked, but the streamings had not come through. It was like the area of the chest before the streamings started. Now the energy was great and I felt a large circular spot at the top of my head which was warm. It was like a monk's tonsure. I thought of Kether, in Kabbalah, or Sahasrara, but I said nothing. When I stood up, I was dizzy, being hyper-ventilated. Regardie said that the streamings would last longer now, and get more intense. He suggested that I do a "sniffing" exercise. When I walked (as I do, to and from the gym, every day at noon, for fifteen minutes each way), that I should sniff rapidly with each step. The breathing is what controls the streamings, he said...Well, today I tried it. I got hyperventilated a bit, experimenting with the rapidity and depth of the sniffing, but I did not feel an increase in streamings. It seems to occur largely at his place, after the treatment begins...I experiment now with sniffing and holding my fingers apart. Yes, I feel the heat, but not the streamings. Well, I am in no hurry for a change! Let it go at its own rate.

SESSION 33: MAY 24, 1972

Yesterday, I was under the weather, broken down. It was, I thought, because of the previous evening's overeating and drinking. I was, in short, "hung over." I went to the session in this headachy, weakened condition, even though I did not think that I had drank or eaten so much in actuality. Was it that I had fasted the previous day and had drunk too soon? Was it age? I did not know.

The healer worked on me chiropractically a longer time than usual, to get through the "grosser tensions," as he put it, and this helped. The treatment, as usual, helped a lot, too, but I had less of the "streamings" than usual. This was due, I suppose, to my weakened condition, my hangover. Regardie said that this was so, that my chest was depressed, and that it was a good idea to break a fast more gently. He also recommended the gag-reflex and throwing up. He was hardly against alcohol, or even drugs—they can be very helpful and valuable at the right time. When you need to get rid of it, though, then do so right away. He gave an example of a fairly recent visit with a psychiatrist friend of his, where a chemically made kind of marijuana was tried. He liked it, but on the way home, he got ill and promptly went to the side of the road and threw up. Get rid of it. Good. He is right. Curious, though, as I now reflect, how the healer-patient archetype gets constellated. I am "patient," he "healer." He looks well and happy usually. I know that I am like that with my patients, mostly. But I know it and accept that I need to be a "patient" for now also.

SESSION 35: MAY 31, 1972

Before I get to the session yesterday, I have to write a word about the couple I just saw for their appointment. The lady, a nurse's assistant, and her boy-friend, a policeman. He was very honest with his feelings, open, direct, intense eyes, with a straight gaze. His struggle was about returning to his ex-wife after the nurse-assistant had more or less said that he wasn't enough for her. Well, never mind the details. I also struggle with what is morally right. Inner morality is the answer, of course, but how hard to find that, how hard to live it. His lady was a bit tricky: looking for money, position, etc. When I told him, "whatever you do is wrong," he understood. I felt that a simple person, a cop, as was this man, was more to be valued and trusted than the rich man's morality: take care of yourself, and don't get caught. But all of these collective nostrums seem hurtful to me, just as my own nostrums are. My own critic says the same things. Even though the old morality and values are dead, they are still alive and kicking in the psyche as the severe critic. Mine is a morality of struggle!

And that brings me to the session. My morality of struggle may be just part of my own armoring, my own inability to relax, enjoy life, feel happy. This time the healer felt like chatting a little at first. He asked how I was, and I wondered if my own symptom of high chest was intractable. He asked if I had noticed any changes over the 35 sessions. I answered that I felt that I was on the right track, that I was more optimistic, that I had less of the early morning depression. He said that the high chest was very difficult and that he had thought about me as like English boys, with high chest and feet apart. He thought that the depression was much as I had experienced as a child, in fear of my mother's dark feelings. I must have felt cut-off, alone, despairing and frightened every morning, but still had to put up a big front, chest and all. My anguish and rage must be still blocked off there. I agreed that there may be some, but I felt that I had worked so much of it out, after more than twenty years in the field. He said that I was more Jungian than Freudian, not reductive, but that my dreams might show some of this also (I had remarked that my dreams did not seem to show the effect too much in content, but the structural, energy changes were showing). I smiled and wanted to embrace him on this, feeling actually, that the Freudian view had some possibility but was rather simple. He said that he had been a patient on the couch all the time from 1925 to 1950! So, there it was.

We went to work on the chest. He showed me a way to stretch my chest by myself, by using an ottoman or small stool and arching my back on it so that only my toes and tips of my fingers were touching. That would stretch the chest and help the back too. I did it and it felt good, particularly when I did—as he said—continue the breathing. My tendency, always, is to hold my breath, tense up. But, after a few minutes of this, I felt a big change in my chest and tension reduction. Similarly, later on, on the couch, he showed me a way to push my shoulders back when I was lying down: arms close-in and pressing down with my shoulders toward the mattress. This ached my back and arms, but also had the effect of stretching the chest. I had to breathe. I can only hold these things for a short time, too much pain. He suggested holding it, continuing breathing, until a cramp begins, but I can not do that yet.

Today, I practiced at the gym with these two exercises and I think that I will use them. Perhaps I can facilitate the treatment with them. I hope so. I am breathing better, yawning too (relaxation).

But what of the content? What of the psyche? I seem to be short-changing that.

I feel the cloud in my chest, and I sink into it. I look and see a little boy sitting on a curb. It is like the painting of my artist friend, Martin, when he was 10 years old. A boy, lonely, reflecting, sad. I think, too, of my own photo at three or four: serious, deep, dark eyes like the policeman, sensitive, sad...Yes, the boy who was myself. Can one speak to one's own boyhood? Can one speak to a picture of one's self? Why not? I have spoken to historical figures, archetypes, images, why not the boy that I was? All right. The cloud becomes the picture of the boy that was.

"Marvin," I say, "little boy that I was, at three or four, is that you?"

He looks at me intently, and nods. Then he smiles, sparkling.

"But you were depressed and sad, little boy, were you not? Did you not fear your mother, her dark feelings?"

He grows sad again, or serious. I feel that he smiled because he was glad of my attention, but grew dark at the mention of those topics. He either can not or will not speak. Maybe he can not speak because it would be betrayal of something or someone...I hold the picture close to me and I hug it to my chest. I breathe deeply, sigh and weep.

"Oh, little boy, lonely and deep little boy. You look very beautiful in that picture. Serious and dark, but handsome all the same." I seem to remember how I felt when that picture was taken. I remember. My mother took me down for a picture but I was ashamed, awkward, and clumsy. I did not know how to sit. I think that I did not feel manly. I held my legs like that so that I would seem manly, and also hide my penis area. Yes, I was afraid that I might have urinated in my pants and that it would show. Later on, in adolescence, I was afraid that my penis would show as erected, but at four and five and six I was worried about urinating. How late was it that I wet the bed? Very late. It was expressing rage at my mother, I suppose, and also fear perhaps, but I do not remember fear. And what about the stuttering? I stuttered as a child, too. The same thing: fear and rage.

"So, now, Marvin, sitting there in the picture, feeling not manly or secure, I see you."

Interrupted by an ex-patient coming in, bearing gifts and asking for help with Blue Cross. Phone, frustration, but it worked...! I could help him. Maybe this is synchronistic with the boy that I was. Helpless against higher powers, the world, mother, and also unable to express his own rage and frustration.

JUNE 5, 1972

Funny. I started out this morning feeling out of myself, absent, needing to connect with my own innards. And now, as I sit down to write, to connect, I am feeling less out of sorts. The weekend was OK. Sensory awareness seminar—interesting. Many things before and after. Yet, they did not nourish sustainingly. After a day, it was like the proverbial Chinese food: one was hungry again. Let me return to the child that I was.

I see him, sitting there, hand on his knee, dark-eyed, intense, deep, serious. He smiles once more, and I return to myself as of now: older face, lined, serious, but smiling and funny too. A bit pudgy, I think, not handsome. Funny, other people seem to find me good-looking, well-built, deep-eyed and intense. Only the latter do I see, and not that much. My critic looks out at me from the mirror, making me feel oldish, fat, hard and unloving. It is the critic himself, of course, that is reflected there.

But the boy, Marvin, is smiling. As I type my name, I get sentimental, want to cry a little. Was Marvin ever a boy, or only a serious little old man? Perhaps that is why I am short with children and their incessant demand for attention. My own child gets so little. Thoughts of the workshop leader and what my colleague said about her week-end in Essalen; about the grey-haired, chicken-legged lady whose own inner kid was screaming.

OK, Marvin, I am with you. You smile. We now look together toward trees. We sit in the park on Santa Monica, the cactus park. He and I on a bench. I sense the warmth of the day, smell the dust. And I remember a time in that resort that my mother went to in Ontario; Paradise it was called, or Monte Vista. I see myself in jeans, looking happy, too. And smelling good dust. And that old man who was a vegetarian and a wise man. He ate only salad and lived in a hut, like an old Indian. He was dark...I pause...wander off.

"Marvin, are you there?"

"Yes."

"Tell me, are you sad or lonely?"

"Sometimes."

"Speak to me."

"I live in the afterglow of a world apart. I live in a memory which is impaled upon the thorns of imagination. I live, yet I do not."

With these very words, which hardly belong to a boy and certainly not to me as a child, I try to bring him close and feel his body. He is tense, and I am aware of a smell. It is fresh sometimes, and youthful, but also rancid and smelly: from pants with urine in them, or faeces. Pew! I take off the pants and take a wet towel to clean him up. He smiles, looks at me with big eyes. Like my sister when she was an infant. Images of sister as a child, in sunshine, feeling good. I lie down on the floor and am with wordless fantasy.

...I lay for some time, with sensory impressions, with quiet, with nothing. Body. Energy flow. Pain and obstruction at times. Peace. It is well.

JUNE 6, 1972

Experience with L, in deep meditation together, was profound. Feeling so loved by her and so loved by my wife. Loved by women, despised by God. What God is this who despises me? What God is this who pushes me into painful places, into both yielding and containing, into huge potency and impotence of spirit, soul, and flesh? I felt the pain of the boy in the back-room, the boy in the cloud. Pain in the genitals, pain and sadness in the soul. Speak, if you can...

I draw the cloud down. I hold it as a large balloon and bring it down from the upper to the lower centers. I bring it to my lower belly, to the spot just in front of where the back pain is. I see the lad, sitting in darkness. I go into this darkness. "Lad, Lad," I say, "such pain have you. Yet you are loved"...The boy looks as if it is hard to believe. He is not sure it is true...I think of a friend and her love for her daughter. Affection is always there, she says; sometimes it stops me from being firm with her when I need to be...Yes...Down, quiet. Sleep.

JUNE 7, 1972

Woke up this morning with terrible anxiety of free-floating kind. Is the exercise working? Is the stretching of back and chest that I am doing finally bringing forward the anxiety that the healer says is there behind that high chest? Anxiety and depression. Wanted to stay cuddled up with my wife...Look at pictures on my desk. My children and my wife. How happy she looked when my son was an infant! That was more than twelve years ago! What has happened since? I weep. Yes, we have two delightful children, our house, my work, and our health. But what struggle over that time. More for me than for her, of course.

I read over more than a year's worth of dreams. I find that some of the themes are the same: no clothes, anxiety, depression, UCLA, sex, etc. Also "good" dreams, such as stone slab and astrology coming together, Jewish symbols and earth, sense of beauty in nature. Shadow things, urination, pain, etc. continue. Maybe, at last, I can get at this in the body way, and feel the "stone" of the Self therein, the reality of it! Yes, I have hope once again.

CHAPTER FIVE

SESSION 36: JUNE 7, 1972

A sad week, difficult, as I wrote earlier. But the session was not so notable. We worked very hard on the usual, chest and such. And I emphasized my pleasure at being able to pursue exercises during the interim. I really feel the effect of the stretching of the back and the falling. In the mornings now, the new exercises take a longer time, so that I must get up earlier. He also mentioned that the breathing was essential, no tension exercise. I rather need to relax than the reverse. We will, ultimately, get into the use of a halter, to stretch my neck. And I am trying to get one at the YMCA gym, as well.

SESSION 37: JUNE 14, 1972

Session much as usual. I am doing more of the exercises alone now, during the week, such as stretching my back, leaning over an ottoman, pushing my arms down, and breathing also, for fifty each plus the Flat-Foot Charlie as well. In other words, an attempt to help things along. Can't tell the effect yet. Also practiced the gagging and screaming reflex. So, not much more to report.

On the psychological level, my dreams have been involved with the Judge once again. One night he was upbraiding me for betraying him, for lying to him, he hated me deeply. Another night it was a former analyst talking to me, hard, with no insight at all that he had hurt me. So, these two judges, both having no connection with my feelings, my views, the reasons I did things, how I am hurt by them, continue haranguing. Maybe I must do as H. has done when she had a similar dream of the Judge; just have her own judgment and reject that of the other. Yes, if I could. But I seem to be still dependent upon the Judge. I am so fatigued. Sleep.

JUNE 19, 1972

This A.M. I awakened in despair, even with suicidal thoughts. And this, after a nice weekend! My son graduated from Hebrew school with honors, my sister had a nice Father's day for the family. Despair's content had to do with not being able to express anymore, and not to be in touch with my introversion, plus my feeling with my Father yesterday, during the family celebration, that I can't express my love to him, he can't take it in. My sister says that I am too serious. I am. No words... Feel I can't breathe, am choked. But I don't want to try the gag reflex, throw up. Can't write.

SESSION 38: JUNE 21, 1972

Yesterday I had my 38th session and it was a relief. I had been so despairing, with dark dreams of negative judges and old relations. The healer said, well, of course, as the armor breaks down around the chest, the repressed affect will re-emerge also. But I had worked so much with depression in the past, I maintained. Yes, of course, but there was even more. It will happen, more and more. Repressed affects will re-emerge as the armor breaks down. The thing to do, he said, is when I awaken so down in the morning, to crawl to the bathroom and do the gag reflex as much as possible, until I can see my anus coming through my mouth! The point is to upchuck all the heavy, dark depression and relax the belly, after which all will relax.

It made sense. Particularly since I told him about a dream I had about him, during all of these dark, negative Saturn dreams, where I am impotent. In this dream, which seemed quite sensorially concrete, he and I were on a journey with my car (my "vehicle," my body, I think) and we stopped for gas (in my depression, did I need energy!). I felt a warm sense of affection from Regardie in the dream, and was aware of a positive smell. That is particularly notable since one of my prissy symptoms is my sensitivity to smell. Well, here was a good smell. We then entered a room, while waiting for the gasoline, where there were small sculptures by my wife, little heads and things. They were beautiful and delicate. I associate that with her artistic creativity. Perhaps that is associated also with my own anima - creativity which needs to be worked with. I think so.

Well, the session went very well, with the usual exercises on my part and work on his part. At the end, I was able to watch the streamings and attend to the sensations of my body without closing my eyes and "going off." He thought this an important and necessary thing, to stay with sensory consciousness at this time. He also suggested that I start the Middle Pillar meditation with L. I mentioned about our energy work as different, of course.

I came out feeling relaxed and good spirited! I walked about a little, still groggy and "drunk" from the hyper-ventilation, but fundamentally optimistic.

SESSION 39: JUNE 28, 1972

Yesterday, my 39th session, began with my telling Regardie of the recurring depression and the changeover accomplished by having breakfast. He assented strongly, suggesting that I did, probably, have low blood sugar, and should indeed have many little meals a day, with much protein. Sweets, alcohol, even fruit are merely temporary pick-me-ups which enhance the sugar curve but drop quickly and leave the organism depleted, depressed, etc. He gave me a book called "Body, Mind, and Sugar" on the topic.

Anyway, the session was excellent. I felt the effect of my own exercises and the gradual softening and stretching of the tense, tight muscles. The end of the session found me most relaxed, loose, and aware. The tension was largely not in the small of the back, where it usually is, but in upper back and neck!

Chiropractic adjustment of the neck seemed to help a lot. I noticed, during the session, how the healer seemed to flow with me. While working with belly and solar plexus, he shifted to my legs and thighs when I made a movement there; and then to eyes and forehead when that happened. I can see that the "transference" or relationship requires a heightened sensitivity to movements, as well as to a sense or intuition of what is going on with the other.

I felt good for a long time afterward, but in the evening, the usual exhaustion took over, need for sleep. My back ached terribly, more than ever. What was this? I asked my wife to massage me a little, which she did, but she was tired too, and could do so only briefly. I then exercised, in my exhaustion, following the need of each muscle by stretching, lying, since I could not reach them myself. At last I took a long swim, and this seemed to relax them a little. I then read (Dion Fortune and *Moon Magic,* which I love) and fell off.

Now, let me look, once again, into the Cloud of the Cave, and see how the Boy and the Ox are doing.

I look into the Cave, which is formed behind the Cloud, and see neither Boy nor Ox, but Mercurius Himself, in a sneering, devilish guise.

"Ho, Mercury, My Lord, what wilt thou do with me," say I, in a kind of English way, not knowing why this style comes up.

"I am here, my Lad, to smile at you, and to deflate certain things."

"Deflate away," say I. "You could not do worse, I imagine, than the Critic Himself, who comes in all the time to say I am unworthy, or boring, or a sex-pot, or greedy, or impotent, or a liar, or what have you."

"Yes, all of these are you. And the sooner you accept the whole mess, the better it will be for both of us!"

"Accept that I lie, mostly by omission, leaving out what I don't want known?"

"Yes."

"Accept that I am unworthy, that I am fundamentally not entitled to what I wish: freedom, wholeness, health, good relations with those I love, fame? Not worthy of these?"

"Yes."

"Agree that I am boring?"

"Especially."

"And that I am a sex-pot and impotent, both?"

"Relatively easy."

"Well, I can guess what you might mean. If I accept these things, then I am on the way to accepting myself, since it is easy to accept my virtues, isn't it? And in accepting all these vices, perhaps I can really be whole."

"Of course I mean that."

"And I suppose that you mean if I can accept that I am unworthy, then the good Lord will be good to me in spite of it, a good old Christian view."

"Yes, and not to be sneezed at, in my opinion. As an Angel of the Almighty, I suggest that you accept such a view!"

"It seems equally mercenary to me, I must say, Angel Mercury. Accepting one's bad aspects, in order that God is seen as a 'goody,' and then he gives one the 'goods.' I am afraid that I can not buy it, in good conscience. I know too well that there is tragedy, injustice, and that God is not only good."

"Yes, you know that of God. How about yourself? You can accept God as less than perfect. Do you expect more from yourself?"

"I wonder, Mercurius, my friend. I wonder. I think of Jung's *Answer to Job.* Job, victim of God's injustice, saw more than God did, in one instance, saw God's behind really, his dark side, and this led to the incarnation. Job was, indeed, superior to God in his goodness at one point. Am I, indeed, embracing a Job position...? I do not think so. I keep on trying to transform myself and accept myself, both. Where is the new image of God, then, in me? I am aware of the Tree, as it now lives, the energies and centers in me, as I pursue them. The Old Eye of God and Phallus of God, that were the quarreling opposites in me, have now become several centers of God, loci of energies and gods within me. And I still worship and adore and bow to the God ever-beyond-all-imaginings. So, I feel at home with it. But, what about self-acceptance and what about God's goodness and evil and my own right now? I seem to have no clear idea at this point."

"That is true, my son. Just as your son is loved by you as a father, just do I, angel of God love you, too. But you guess that he, too, is a God, creative, sensitive, and poetic. And you know that I belong to the upper centers, flying and hovering and 'going to and fro,' for I am both 'devil' and messenger, as you know."

"You, then, Mercurius, are really part of God Himself, and my Self, too, I know that, old friend... But to accept being those specific things...aye, there's the rub, as Hamlet—who could only think obsessively before he killed the 'Old King,' the usurper, the ruler of consciousness who did not belong there—said. Liar am I, yes. I accept it, but it is painful.

"Sex-pot and impotent am I, yes. Yes, I am over-energized and depleted, a greedy Pan and weak old man, I accept it. But I struggle with it don't I? I must add that, I guess. Now I laugh a little, aware that I do, indeed, try to 'be good,' though I fail.

"Boring am I, and greedy, too? Yes. Wanting to be famous? Yes, I accept that, even if when I call it 'vanity' I know full well that I mean acceptance of the Self that I am, and not just the ego.

"Yes, but boring too. Someone said that the bore is the person who has no sense of humor. And I suppose I am like that at times, particularly in the places of my wounds. I think of the lad in the Cloud Cave. Not much humor in him, with those deep, dark eyes, and that pain and quiet. Nor is that ox particularly funny. But I do laugh, and I do tell my puns. There is a level of clever humor in me. But I am so serious and, therefore, a bit of a bore.

"Finally, 'unworthy?' Yes, I suppose so. I have hurt those I have loved. But how is God unworthy these days? Tell me, friend and father, Mercurius. Tell me, how is God unworthy these days?"

"Do you mean God or the Self?"

"I don't know. I mean both, I suppose. That God who dwells within me and guides my being, and the God of Everyman, of this Universe, who transcends me, transcends us all, and has His being both within us and among us and beyond us."

"You spoke a prayer, my friend and son. In so praying and speaking, you defined your God, and spoke truly of Him."

"I think, Angel, of that man in the class who responded to my reading of the 'dialogue' with Jung: 'Jung should have told him not to read his paper,' he said. That hurt, Angel. The possibility of self-deception is very painful."

"I know."

"Even you are not necessarily the all-knowing."

"We both know that, do we not?"

"Yes, we do... And so I remain confused. I remain uncertain, human, I suppose. For I am not all-knowing, all clear, all loving, all good. But then, neither is God—at least not all the time. No, I do not even know how God is. For He is beyond all my understanding. I can only confess my inability and my limits. I can not even understand myself, let alone God. Yet I need to. I need to understand and accept as much as I need to eat, sleep, and make love. We both know this, Angel Mercurius. Tell me, Angel, help me in my dilemma."

"There is little more to say. Accept limitation, accept darkness, accept unworthiness, greed, loneliness. Accept these in you, in God, in the Universe."

"Why is my acceptance needed?"

"Accept in order to achieve."

"Accept bargaining? Quid pro quo? Accept business?"

"Accept bargaining."

"God bargained with the Devil?"

"God bargained with the Devil."

"God wagered with his own dark side, and took the consequences, becoming human and suffering with us?"

"God did."

"God is a Jewish businessman?"

"God is a Jewish businessman." Laughter.

Long laughter. The worst thing of all, it appears, is to be a Jewish businessman! How strange it is for a nice, deep Jewish person like myself to reject the Jewish businessman! Is not my father a Jewish businessman? Is he not also honorable and very caring for the poor? Is he not a most loving person? He is. It is not that 'father' who has to be killed or overcome. Far from it. He is not the King of Hamlet.

"Rather, I must accept the Jewish businessman. As does God, now. No longer must the money-changers be driven from the temple. No longer must one eschew all the 'things of this world;' no longer must one be anti-matter, anti-pleasure, anti-body. God is also a Jewish businessman... Yes. Have I not pursued those who owe me? Have I not been overcome with rage at the injustice of being used and fooled by them? And have I not, embracing this demand from within me, achieved a certain result with it? The one man who evaded me for a year now, is, on his own free will, a patient of mine. Another promises, and another delivers a little. I have accepted my mercenary side...no it is not that. It is like God, to achieve justice for myself, as well. So, then, as with the Shylock, the Jewish businessman. He is out for justice for himself, not to be cheated. Do not some cheat? They do. Do I not cheat? Not in money, usually, I think.

"But I must accept not only my dark mercenary side, seeking goodies for itself, but justice too. I must also accept my 'gambling' side. And, wonder of wonders, is not my own father a great gambler? Different from me? But no; I too am a gambler. But I do not gamble much with money. Rather I gamble with my reputation, my life! Well, if God can gamble with the Devil at the expense of poor old Job, I can gamble with my own good, patient, long enduring side who trusts and has faith. And I gamble even that perhaps my whole life is one vast self-deception! Who was it hinted that Christ Himself might have realized, on the cross, when he said, 'Eli Eli, My God why hast Thou forsaken me,' that he might have been full of self-deception in thinking that he was chosen of God, God's son. Yes, even God deceives Himself! So then, the last thing to accept is the possibility of my own self-deception. I can wake up, at the end, just as I often do in the mornings, in despair, in the realization that all my thoughts, aims, beliefs, central ideas and experiences, even, were mere illusion, self-deception. So, then, to accept the 'gamble' and the 'self-deception' too. All these. Well, if God is in these, why not? Why not, then, accept God in me, the totality? But not just the totality of everything, but the totality of the particularity of me. Of me the particular liar, greedy one, unworthy one, the particular gambler and self-deceiver. The God of the Universe, the totality of everything, is over and beyond... So, do I think, Mercurius, so do I conclude this monologue."

"And so, my son, do I. I weep for you and with you. For I am that God-Self who loves you and needs you. Just as the lad of the Cloud needs you. I, your ruler, your Mercurial representative and Angel who flies among and within, who reaches up into the heaven and down into the hell of life, and even to the reaches of the God who is ever transcendent, even so, it is I who love you and embrace you."

SESSION 40: JULY 5, 1972

Yesterday, my fortieth session, was much like the others. As in the past, there was definite relaxation, feeling good, but intoxication at the end. He worked on my back a bit, and I noticed that he could squeeze those muscles without my experiencing huge pain. Indeed, I did not have to scream at all. So, although it is slow, there is progress.

But today, I am sad and down, as so often. Patients quitting, sense of not being able to hold up my practice, talking with a colleague who is also despairing—all of that. My friend, like me, is cut off from colleagues, so he thinks that is a source of the problem: no one to support, to share, etc. We have also gotten far away from each other in the work area as well as in other ways. All we share now is our pain and despair, it seems. I think it helps both of us to talk about it, but still...

My own aloneness... Not only is it the uncertainty of my practice, whether I will get new patients, whether I can continue in the way I have, whether what I do is effective—I have had all these concerns ever since I started analytic practice almost thirteen years ago!—but also being dependent upon patients, having to adapt to them. Always something. Yet depressed by nature, perhaps. And, if the Reichian work is going to cure it, it is going to take longer than one year!

I was looking forward to coming back from the gym today, to get into myself. To think about Jung and his wonderful autobiography which I read again with joy and admiration, and to get deep into a place where I can converse with God.

My thoughts were that God must either be sending the depression and sadness, or be it Himself. And this, on the basis that the most powerful thing in the psyche must be God. In my Cloud, however, there are only the sad-eyed boy and the sad-eyed Ox. Mercurius, perhaps, not sad-eyed, can answer it.

But I long to ask God Himself, directly. Oh, Lord, my saviour, who does not save me, my Chooser who does not choose me, is it you who send me this depression? Is it you? Are you the author, or are you depressed yourself? Must I give up my chosenness, as I have hinted to myself? Tell me, Oh Lord.

The Lord is my Shepherd, I shall not want. He maketh me to lie down in green pastures…where there are worms and bees, and bugs and all manner of stinging insects. These stinging insects bite me and harass me and drive me mad or depressed. The Lord does this.

So, I sit in a large green field—beautiful, but the insects sting. The lad is there with me, quiet, thoughtful. The ox sits also, like a dog, some few feet away. The field and hill are beautiful, but nature is rife with the stinging, paining, irritants of man.

"Did the Lord not create moths? Did he not create sting-rays? Are these not as much the province of God as mortal man, who thinks himself Lord of Creation?"

"Who speaks?" I ask.

"It is I, the agent of the Lord. It is I, the insurer and defrauder, himself."

"Mercurius, you again. Of course… Yes, I know that the Lord created all those things…I know. And I have thought that I must give up that ancient idea I had of being chosen by God, among men, perhaps, and surely, among insects. But now I see that it is all the same to the God of Nature. All His creatures are equally valuable to him. And so, if I am stung by life, if I find little creatures who deprive me of my 'true value,' if I find that what I think is important is not important to others—insect, animal, or man,—well, then, so much the worse for me. Perhaps my depression is merely the other side of my vaunted ambition and conceit. For, if I were just to enjoy life like some others, then I would not expect so much from myself and others… I say 'I' now. It is I expecting much from me, now, not the Lord choosing me and expecting things from me. I have taken on the responsibility for this self-demand, I see. All right. If it is, indeed, just the other half of conceit…maybe I must, indeed…

"I grow sad and tired, and sleepy. Lord, show me… I long to close my eyes. To drift off into a deep, resting place where God shows Himself to me in pleasure and glory, and with good tidings. I long for that. I long for the energy of old…but then, I had depression then, too, did I not…? I take some protein pills. For energy… I ate too much last night and the night before, and, of course, up went the weight. Today, I expect to eat not at all...is that, too, unrealistic? Another defeat for ego or plan?

"O Lord! Show me a place where I can rest. Show me a plan. Your servant Jung followed you resolutely, intelligently, and with devotion. I would do the same. I have, O Lord. I have. Mercurius! Angel of God! Convey this to the Lord for me, tell Him that I have done so. I beg of you."

"What God should I inform? Is it a God who is bifurcated, bisexed, and bisected?"

"I don't know... It is the God of depressions. It is the God who either sends them or has them... Yes, I remember the God who made rivers and seas with his tears, and deserts with his depressions. I remember that. Is that the Lord with whom I must deal?"

I can not...eyes close... I slept for a time, perhaps as much as an hour. I awaken refreshed, not so depressed. But still, my sadness and depression are surely not a question of diet, of rest, of energy expended and not renewed... My God... I look at the bookcase and see "The Healing Gods of Ancient Civilizations." Should I approach them? Want to read, meditate. Nothing more to say. Mercurius? Lad? Ox...? All is still.

The Lord is my Shepherd, I shall not want...

I shall not want, my Lord, but what do you want? Show me your form, or face, or speak a word unto me...

"Have you considered my servant Job?"

I have, Oh Lord, I have. I know that he was loved by you, gambled by you, used by you, and through him, you came unto men, and became a man.

"Have you considered my servant Job?"

I have, I have. But what would you have me consider, Oh Lord? What is it further that you would wish me to reflect upon?

"I would...that you would..."

"What, Oh Lord, do not be modest with me, I beg you, nor faltering. Speak unto me that I may hear you. Speak unto me so that I may obey."

"The man speaks as if he is as one of us..."

"I know, Oh Lord. I know. What more...should I merely fall on my face? Say, and I shall do."

"Fall unto your face."

"Unto my face?"

"The face that was there ere creation began."

"The face before...?"

"The pristine face..."

I look and peer. I imagine that I look into a mirror. In this imaginary mirror, I see a youthful face, it is the face of me at six, as is shown in the photograph. But that is not the pristine face.

"No, not that face. The Face before you were born."

"Ah yes, that face. The face before I was born is the face of the Self, I suppose. Is that a Buddha thought? I seem to remember it...the face before I was born...I see a kindly face, of an old man. It seems like the face of God Himself.

A kindly old man, smiling…is that the face before I was born? Is that the face of myself before I was born in this life? This man, smiling, wears a suit, I think, of the style of the thirties, so it is hardly the face of the man I was before I was born. Who are you sir?"

"I am he that answers questions of those who put them."

"And who might that be?"

"A figment of imagination. A creation of the soul. A vague memory, combined with bits of images. A creation of creations."

"That you are. And yet with your own life. One who can speak and answer questions, and put them, autonomously."

"Of course, you know that. Ask and it is answered. It is merely a routine of speech… I could shift and be a flower, or a peach, or anything else. Whatever fantasy creates, there it is. An old principle of magic and of the world, is it not so?"

"Yes, I think so. But it used to mean more to me. It used to be, that the magical figure in me was something special. When it was beautiful and alive and put me in touch with the divine. Now it seems only illusion, and a kindly old man. By your own statement sir, you are 'merely a figment'."

"Yes, but a figment is something after all. Although everyone could produce such a figment, should they but desire, not everyone tries, is willing to risk, or takes themselves seriously enough to produce it. In that you are special."

"Please don't speak to me of 'specialness.' I am so crushed, so pulled down from any height of specialness…"

"Yes."

"Yes? Is that all you have to say?"

"Yes. The machine wears down. The fantasy becomes thin. The magical part, a circle made of tacks, wears loose on its hinges."

I am near tears. Let me ask I Ching, my old friend. I have not consulted I Ching for many a year. My good old Japanese friend, Mokusen, would not enquire of it unless it was a life and death matter…

I sink further down…my belly aches… I call the patient who had called. She wants to leave L.A., go back home. This is a Saturn never-never land for her. I understand. To return to parents, to make something of her life. Good. I suggested that she go ahead with her plan, but wait, too, to see if a dream comes that says something else… There goes another patient hour. Scary. Will I get a dream showing the way? Lord, you no longer speak to me in dreams or in fantasy. Or, if you do, it does not sustain me. I do not trust. I am fearing…and losses come…phone rings. Another person cancels, one who put her own vulnerability and unhappiness on me. She felt 'kicked out' and blames me for it. I spoke up, at least, and said my own feelings too. I am glad that I did… Now I am angry. She is upset and vulnerable, crying, and says that I 'booted' her out. That really makes me angry… Lord, Lord. I am sick of being a scapegoat. Sick of having people expect me to just take care of them. Sick of them putting their expectations and persecutions on me. Sick of it! Yet, I need to earn my living, need to get approval. Need lots of things… Bad day for me. Bad.

Trust? Can I trust? For me? I don't know... I am ill. Feel like throwing up. Throwing up and off all that having to take care of people. Throwing off their expectations, and my own as well... So what happens? Have to crawl some more...? Lord send me a dream. I beg of you... I call back to the patient, thinking that there was anger in her, needing to get it out. Offering to work it through. She responds that there is probably anger, but...and she twists my offer! Then I really get angry. Lord I am sick of this, sick. I await your message.

JULY 12, 1972

Well, there was no message from the Lord...at least any that I could notice. I am feeling better. I woke up this morning feeling sleepy, but after some exercise and watering the plants, I felt okay. What was it? The fact of making love last night? Yes, probably, much of it. If my connection with my wife is good, in deep trust, then I can take on a lot. It is absolutely central for me. But it is not everything, either. There is the fact that there is always something...

Lord, I spoke to you before, asked for a message about my own pain and grief, about my own practice falling off, about being a scapegoat for people's stinking projections. I asked for a message, and didn't get any. Yet maybe the fact of recovery, of gradually feeling better, is the message.

I now see Mercurius in the Cloud. The kindly old man this time. He nods and smiles, as if what I say is true. The feeling better is the answer to the prayer, not words or dreams. All right, I can accept that, even if it is delusion, self-deception. If it works, causes no harm, why question it...? for Truth, of course, which is also important.

Lord, then, I appeal to you once more. What is this pain and tragedy in human life...? I see the same kindly face, like Robert Donat in "Goodbye Mr. Chips." How I loved that film as a lad! That fine school-teacher, who loved his wife and lost her. What tragedy. And the generations of children coming to him. How I wept then... Funny, I start to weep now. I am that same lad of twelve who leaves the theater in tears. "Goodbye Mr. Chips, Goodbye!" says that little boy, third or fourth generation of pupils, father to son. Yes, there is such an ache in the place of beauty, appreciation, love, and the loss of love. Life is just too beautiful and too painful. One feels too much, perhaps. Yet I think of a certain sentimentality, as if a young person who has not experienced so much (as I was when I saw that film) weeps, and does not know that all the pain and beauty are ahead of him! And yet he knew, and wept... But no. Surely I knew that from my own life of those first twelve years, or from other lives. How many times is one born into birth and death, love and pain, beauty and ugliness! Buddha knows how long!

Well, Lord, is that your answer? That of birth and death, rebirth and re-death...? Nothing. But quiet. The Cloud gathers into a fine mist. It slips into my chest, as a kind of subtle body. But now I feel the ache there. I feel the ache of tears and the pain of that boy. My high chest, in ache and pain, in rigid form. But as I attend to it, the pain reduces a little. The Cloud is now the subtle body! The Cloud is now my soul itself. The Cloud, which I have looked at and followed, for a year now, with its boy and ox and Mercurius, is now, I think, an air-solid, liquid-vapor thing of subtle body, of soul-mass. And it is in my chest and aching.

I see the Cloud moving about within that same chest cavity. It can not be free. Now I feel an ache in my back and neck. The bearing of the burden—of pain and disappointment, of tragedy and disillusion—is too much for the back, behind the weeping chest. The neck goes forward, too, in Jewish despair! The burden of sadness and pain in life is too much.

Yes, Lord, I can see it. I can feel it. I am that lad of twelve, who is like my own beautiful son, who is also twelve. But I was already bent over then, already saddened and alone. Praise God, my own son is not in such poor shape. He is handsome, strong, and far happier than I was. He is even a good student, which I was, but he has other things too!

"He also has a different father," says Mercurius. Yes, Mercury-Angel, it is true. I am more connected with him, but my own father loved me, too, in his way. He did not, could not, understand me, but he loved me and was gentle with me. Far gentler, really, than I am with my own son!"

"True, my son, true. But give yourself credit for being a good father, too, won't you? Can you not love yourself a bit, too? Recognize yourself, too? You long for recognition, and you give yourself so little."

"Yes. I recognize that I am a caring and loving father, but I am also hard at times, and even unjust, though I correct it when I see it."

"So, let it be," says the Angel.

Now I feel the Cloud reaching about like an amoeba. It reaches up, but is blocked at my neck. It reaches down, but is blocked from flowing to the solar plexus... There it remains... All right. I yawn. The sign of relaxation. I yawn again. Deeper. I stretch my neck and take a deep breath. I yawn again. Good.

SESSION 41: JULY 12, 1972

Regardie worked on my legs yesterday, most of the time. I lay on the couch, face up, legs slightly apart, knees up. The task was merely to let them flop to the side, then raise them up slowly while I inhaled. I did this for some time, and he would occasionally force them a bit lower as they flopped. The tightness of my thighs was great. Once he poked me there and I yelped. Castration anxiety? I don't know, but I could scream all right. But once he continued with the leg-flop assistance, it was much better. It was a relief to have some aid in stretching out those muscles...it seemed to reduce the tension in my lower back. The session was good as ever, and I felt the streamings pretty well during the observation period. We talked a bit about the depressions, which seem to be lifting some, and I felt good at the end. Indeed, I am convinced that the slow, steady progress is gradually going to clear up the pain, reduce the armor and bring a successful conclusion...In working on my legs, he asked about my sex life, had it improved lately. I remarked that it was variable with my wife, but that I felt better when I was in a good connection with her. But not always. Depression, though could focus on practice, or something. Anyway, he thought that I might be too hurried with the sex, since I seem to increase the rhythm when working with the legs. I said that I thought this was because I felt the greater effect on the small of my back. Anyway, he said that sex would improve, and that the quality would change, too. Not so much thrusting, more pleasure in the slower movements. Strangely, I did not feel very communicative about sex, though not upset: I mentioned about the use of the energies, which he seemed to understand, but I am not sure. I surely have worked on sex as much as anyone I know, but no doubt the armoring is there and there will be changes.

But I hate to be "reporting" again. That is not what this is all about, is it? It should be hegira of the wounded physician. The healing of the healer. Like just now, having to call up an insurance organization about the fee of a patient. They arbitrarily set the fee lower for psychologists than psychiatrists. The patient suffers for it, unless I reduce my own fee. And to talk to people at organizations! Well! She could not understand that I was objecting to the discrimination; "the rule is the rule" is all such types can deal with. So, I try to get to her superior. I doubt whether that will help, but I must try at least. The patient doesn't seem to mind about it, paying the extra dollars, but I do... My usual Don Quixote efforts at the world, without much effect.

But neither can I talk about the deep work with a priest. Sharing the agony of his process, and our trust that the Spirit will show the way. I can not talk about that, either. What then?

What then? Why, back to the Cloud, of course...but torn. Maybe read. Maybe nothing. Well, read a little, and see.

I read a little, about "self-esteem." I took this test the man gave, and found a very low self-esteem. He is a layman, but it is true. I vacillate between high independence, self-worth (son of God!), and low self-esteem. He is right. He gives several ways of improvement: awareness, re-conditioning, action. Maybe I will pursue it more. But even reading it makes me feel inferior! How is that?

And yes, with all that low self-esteem, I can really connect and be close with people who are undergoing great conflict, agony, suffering, a discrepancy between spirit and flesh, expectation and achievement.

Talked to my son. What a wonderful boy he is! He readily forgave me for my shortness this A.M., and also told me about how he blew up at his sister for being a slob, as I do at him. We talked it over, and I thought that he might be emulating some of my worst qualities (yelling), and maybe, though he was right in his idea, he could apologize for screaming at her. He agreed. He told about getting a bad grade in school, but recovered so well in talking about how he was working on a flower scientifically, in the same class. He was full of joy, appreciation, interest, and real pleasure, just as he was when he was little. He was so beautiful then! And still is. I can not be such a bad person, with low self-esteem, when I have such a beautiful son, and a beautiful daughter. Not that I can take credit for their achievements or live through them, but I do see that I am having an effect, as I am, good and bad, and that they come out pretty well, after all. Good "self-esteem," but also able to be self-critical, joyful and serious, traditional and innovative. OK. Lord, I accept that as something that I have contributed to!

JULY 18, 1972

Now I feel sleepy, want to get deep into my fantasy. All right Lad, I will start with you.

"Lad, go deep with me. Show me the way into the deep inner darkness which is beyond the darkness of us, you and me, and reaches the places of which we speak and struggle, the magical places where desire becomes incarnated, but where negative prayer, worry, also incarnates itself against out desire and will."

The boy looks long at me, and now turns his eyes back in upon himself. His eyes look at the back of his head. They shine onto a moonscape, like two flashlights or searchlights. A rocky, dusty place right in the night, illuminated only by a far-off earth-light in the sky.

"This is my home," the lad says. "No darkness here. Only a darkness of the absence of light, not a darkness of its own. Here it is peaceful, quiet. Here it is the same as the Cave, here it is the same as the Cloud."

"Yes, quiet," say I. "Away from the pain of my Japanese friend who is suffering unspeakable sorrow and agony with his sick daughter. My own pains are as nothing compared to that. And he is so…"

Phone rings. Young man wanting me to supervise him, so he can work in private practice. Don't know about him. Also wonder about malpractice insurance…And about whether I can supervise when he is not working with me. How else? Only trust him to do what he needs to do.

SESSION 42: JULY 19, 1972

Today, the day after my 42nd session, I seem to be very tired. Took a nap a few minutes ago which helped a little. Could it be because I got up 15 minutes earlier? Doubt it. Did not go to bed later. I think it might be the effect of the treatment. I am getting more relaxed, I think. Evidence: today I had a massage, after not having had one in about four weeks. My muscles were notably less tense, said the masseur, though lower back and regions around the upper back were still tight, sore. So, maybe the relaxation taking place is a result of the treatment.

The session itself was fine. We worked at first on the various exercises that I have been using. They seem to be good for the condition. Particularly to be remembered is the need to keep breathing, not hold the breath. Inhale upon coming up in sit-ups, for example, and exhale coming down. OK. After the session, I felt particularly relaxed, and was pain-free. I walked about a little and noted how my body was relaxed, how the small of the back was without pain or tension. This lasted for quite a while. Well, not quite: the great change I experience immediately at the end of a session changed within a few minutes, but it takes almost a half-hour, say, to return to the older condition. "It took a lifetime to get that way," says Regardie, so obviously it will take some time to change the habits of muscle control. Yes, I am aware of that and can appreciate it. That's the end of the session, and now I turn to the fantasy.

I sink, no climb up into the Cloud. Now it is on a platform far above the earth. It floats in the air. No, in point of fact it goes around the earth like a satellite, even though it is larger than an ordinary size room. Clouds swirl around it, but it goes up, in its voyage, in ever higher arcs, and is now far, far, above the earth. It lands on the moon. The moon is dark and cold; lights of stars in the sky, as well as the earth in its beauty. I look around for the Boy, or the Ox, or Mercurius. But I am alone. None of them is present just now.

I sit quietly on the moon, next to this platform, and am peaceful. I notice my breathing is deeper and I am less harassed. I feel tears near the surface, but they do not come. It is just peaceful. I do not weep out of pain or sorrow, or even happiness, which one might expect that I would have with so much going well for me. No, I sit peacefully. I feel the coolness around me. But I also feel a kind of air, a cold and pleasant air, as if on a mountain top. I know, intellectually, that the moon is practically without atmosphere, it is almost a vacuum. Yet there it is. I sit and breathe. I am on a fantasy moon, on the moon of my own feelings, yet it is most real, related deeply to that concrete moon which shines in the night sky and upon which astronauts have, for the first time in history, set foot.

I sit peacefully upon the moon. Now, I notice the lad sitting too. He has been here all along, but invisible. He smiles at me. He smiles because I have discovered that which he has always known. To sit peacefully, without words, in the cold clear air of the moon, far from the earth, with a view of it and the stars—ah, that is most serene. It is like Buddha beneath the Bo tree.

I put my arm around the lad, but he shrinks a bit. No touch here. Only open, alone, and let the breeze play upon us. It is enough that we are here together. We touch in the sense of mutual presence, presence of God. Physical touch only makes for a humanness, a warmth which, though good in itself, detracts from this experience. Or why even come to this psychic moon? This is his thought, which I can sense telepathically. He is right.

So, I sit peacefully. I think of what Regardie said, that he now hates writing. He has written so many books, and is also bringing out several more, but he detests it. A chore. He has said what he has to say. I can understand it. Once one has had his say, why write more? Surely, there are lots of motives for writing: expression, fame, or a way (like me) of expressing and validating one's spirit when there seems to be no other way. Yes, all of these. And yet, I can also see that I could, at some time, no longer even want to write, I will have said what I had to say! So be it.

JULY 26, 1972

Feeling low again, although this morning was fine. I long to sink into myself, into the God-level and there be nourished. I re-read my nun friend's letter. It is so beautiful; all my nun-anima could desire: she calls me dearest, says how much my being means to her (and I now believe it to be true), and describes her experience in the convent, praying, meditating, dancing before the altar—all of this fills in my religious, Christian anima who longs to be deeply connected with nature as well. I am gifted in the people around me, in deep friendships, why must I feel bad?

But let me examine my dream of last night, which had to do with that. I was at the beach with a young black boy. He was worldly and told me about the place. One could walk or bicycle down Lincoln Blvd. all the way, vertically toward the beach; even though, in reality, it runs parallel to it; a kind of cross is made by the dream. The boy said that going down that long street would be hard on the left foot! After that, we see several other black youths, and they are suspicious of me. They go under a tunnel, know about the area. Then I acknowledge that I know very little about the area, indeed, about how to get on in the hard world, they lose their suspicion. End of dream.

The dream brings me in touch with an extraverting side, I think. This black boy understands the outer world, also they are at home with the long haul. The left side (introversion), gets hurt in all that long travel, though. And his friends understand the tunnel, the ways of manipulating, getting on in the uncaring world. I suppose they, being poor and black, have had to learn this... The dream reminds me of another that I had some time ago, with another black young man who really knew the criminal element and how to deal with it. This lad and his friends, though not that old or in touch with the criminal side, are also savvy. I surely need that kind of information, I think, because I am always getting hurt in that area. This black lad seems to be opposite to my Lad with the dark eyes, my introverted, non-verbal, Moon friend. All right. Let me address this dark skinned lad and see what he says.

"Lad, of my dream, I think that you know about the outer world more than I. I think that you are more clever, having had to claw your way around, and that you might help me or teach me about it."

"No problem, big boy, no problem. You already know, you just don't listen. I tell you lots of times about people and situations but you don't listen!"

"You are probably right. Lots of times, I don't listen to the dark-eyed boy of the Cave-Cloud either. I am sure that I don't hear you. I didn't even know that I had you in here."

"You sure enough do. You remember that southern lady psychologist you treated?"

"Yes."

"Well, in the very beginning I told you that she was not to be trusted. And it took you a long time to find that out! You really got it from her! And you could have avoided that if you had listened to me."

"I suppose so. It is hard to trust these 'dark' perceptions, though. Sometimes they could be wrong."

"Why sure. I am not always right either. But just listen, hey?"

"Yes. But why are you nice to me? And your friends? After all, I am 'white,' and I am no friend of yours."

"Yes you are. You are not stuck-up, you are not arrogant, you are a pretty good guy. Besides, you need us... Take that little kid of yours, in the Cave-Cloud. We know about him. He sits all alone, doesn't say a word. Isn't he lonely for companions? For friends?"

"I don't know. But I doubt it. He seems to like to sit alone in a cave or on a cloud or on the Moon. He loves the cool air, the stars, the shape of the glowing earth, and to be alone with himself."

"Well, I suppose so. But he doesn't say much to you either, does he?"

"No, not very often. Mostly he lives in some of my body places and quiet places... Where do you live in me?"

"In your head, of course! What a question... Well, maybe in your nose, too. You can smell dark things too, can't you?"

"Indeed I can. Even though I get funny about that, as you might know."

"Yes, I know."

"Come with me to the Cloud. The Lad of the Cave may listen to you."

"All right."

We go up a ladder, all the way to the Cloud. It is dark, as usual, and the boy sits inside it, in its form of the Cave. The black lad peers at him with his own dark eyes and speaks.

"Hi! How come you just sit there quiet?"

The Lad of the Cave looks at him, silently.

"Ain't you gonna talk?" he says, and I wonder why the black boy now slips into a kind of dialect and slang when he didn't speak that way to me. But I wait before speaking.

"Ain't you gonna talk," black boy repeats. Quiet lad shakes his head.

"All right," says Black-boy, "Then don't you say nuthin.' Just sit there and feel sad and sorry for yourself. Sit there and say 'nobody cares for me.' Sit there and say you are just afraid of the niggers and kikes and all the hoodlums. Just sit there and enjoy the smell of your own feces and urine and sweat..." (and now the black-boy's language changes back into the way he spoke with me). But this also has no effect on the lad.

I speak to Black-Boy. "How is it," I say, "that you spoke in slang with him and not with me, and then changed in the middle, even with him?"

"I don't know," he replies. Sometimes I talk 'black,' sometimes white, sometimes not at all. I talk the way it comes to me. If I feel somebody is prejudiced, I oblige him and talk 'black.' That makes him the fool. I changed with your dark-eyed boy because I wanted to confront him, to have him see me straight. Of course he thinks that I belong to the frauds, to the miserables of the world. The world itself is awful for him, unless he sees it from the moon! Isn't that so?"

"Yes," I had to admit.

"And I could be his brother, if he would let me. I am not against his needing to be alone, to see the great vision of the whole earth. I am just against his arrogance, which is based on fear, in my opinion."

"My, you are using big words, indeed. Hardly like some little darkie!"

He laughs. "You are not so free of prejudice either, daddy-oh!" says Black-Boy. And I nod, having to sadly agree.

Now I take the hand of the black boy and the lad and make them join their other hands with each other. We can make a threesome, alone and seeing the world as it is in its darkness. I see the need for both... But where is the fourth? And I am still not certain that the Lad accepts Black-boy. Is the Ox the fourth? So many males. Except for Mercurius, who has both male and female in him, these are all masculine. Am I so identified with the feminine that I need such heavy male compensation? Or am I so old that I need young lads to compensate? I think the latter. The former is not true, although I am closer to women than men, mostly... I think about male friends, they are there, too. Once again, I grow sleepy. As if my dialogue has lost its validity or appeal. Once again I remain in the upper image centers and lose the concreteness... OK, close eyes, sink down.

I am back with the lad, alone on the Moon.

"That fellow is not real," quiet lad tells me. He speaks freely now that I am alone with him. "That fellow is just a figment of imagination! I am real because I am with the true world of being, an experience which you know of. That fellow is just conjecture on your part. What do you really know of the hard outer world? Very little I dare say."

I am surprised that he speaks, but I answer. "Well, I have lived a fair amount and know some. I have smelled 'rats' and things, and he can link up with that."

"That is true, too, of course..." And now the lad is silent once more, as if he is taking in what I have said.

I feel a heaviness once again. My eyes are sandy, and the lids come down as I yawn. Silly words come to me, "git yawn-tiff" and so on. But I feel the lad is trying to get me to feel the reality of this moon-place, and its airs. I lie down to take it in... Now I feel the lad is dancing on my chest like a little gremlin or figure from Defoe. He and the black boy are now tiny creatures who dance on my chest. I motion them to dance higher on my chest. I want them to dance upon the place of my armoring.

"Dance" I call out, "Dance! Dance away the constrictions and narrowness of my chest, lads, Dance it away! Dance upon my concrete inner life! Dance your deep awareness of the world and how it really is! Dance you two and help me to free myself from the old constrictions where I could not breathe! Dance upon me and bring to me a depth of solid inwardness and sensible awareness of the outer world. Dance and bring me renewal!"

They dance and thump about my chest. I want them to break up its constriction. I pause... I think of my new friend. There is the possibility of spending some days in a cloistered convent. Prayer, gardening, a cloistered life even for a few days, how I would love it!

"I would love it, too," says the lad. And he would. For there would be the quiet inner life plus other religious people too! But the black boy would not be happy there, I think.

"Not unless there was a lot of nookie," says he. And I nod. Got to have the flesh, relationship, involvement, passion in a material form, too.

But I have left these lads jumping on my chest. Phone interruption and mail. Good Lord, no wonder only males inside, all those ladies outside with both requests and offers of connection! I take the lads on my chest and realize that they are not doing much, really, to change its rigidity. Fantasy, yes. Truth, yes. But not effective on armor, not at this point, anyway. I tell them this. They both look sad. The moon-lad looks at me disgustedly and I know he thinks that I am foolish. We both know that what I have just said is not true. The Inner Reality is the True Reality, says he, and effective at some level. Black-Boy looks at me, and reminds me of the story I wrote as a young boy, called "Blue-Black" in which the Black boy suicided. That sensitive extraversion is always getting killed, he implies. Now he, Black-Boy, is silent! Yet he makes me very much aware of his sensitivity. I have rejected, suicided, my extraverted sensitivity to people and situations, particularly when it is hurtful or frustrating or dark. Now I must appreciate and accept it. Not having to reject, in turn, of course, but just notice.

SESSION 43: JULY 26, 1972

Today's session brought a comment from Regardie which said, in effect, that the depressions should be over by now. That, in itself is interesting. I have, indeed, been having less of it lately, but during the day it returned, sadly. But first about the session.

Not only was the depression ready to lift, but we should begin the harness for the neck soon, and it is also fine to take the month off, as I had planned. That will be after the 45th session, I believe, and I look forward to seeing how I will do during that month period.

Notably today, however, was the experience of being relaxed and falling off to sleep—almost. I mentioned that I felt the need to reduce consciousness in the head, but to stay awake, and let the relaxation go down the body. It is as if I want the energy to move down from head and throat and heart into the lower centers, particularly into my hands. I almost wept when I spoke of the energies moving into my hands, since my image was that the energies would go into healing with the hands! I wanted to be more "substantial," less airy and heady, and the healing, too, to be more physical and less verbal. Part of the need for the magical work, I thought. Regardie said that this was more of the "other place" (occult), rather than Reichian itself. He suggested that when I found myself falling asleep, that I keep up an observational view of myself, along with a running commentary. This would keep it going, he thought. I might also find, he said, that my body would go to sleep, even snore, while I was still aware! I must try that when it happens. He also thought that I could induce it by just starting from a memory of that place—just lying down and getting myself into that frame of mind. It reminds me of his little paper-pamphlet on relaxation.

Okay, I am already relaxing. I am drifting into fantasies of the orgastic reflex, of being free, of my wife having Reichian work.

I am growing sleepy. I am...rather, I see myself lying down and attending to my body. I yawn. Eyes close. I feel wind in the belly. Flatus. Eyes open. Think of that horrible lady who was a mother to a patient of mine. He was horrible, too. Why? Both rejected me! Hah, that is horrible. OK, self-rejection, too. Yawn. Energy, energy, where are you going? You are sinking down out of my head, out of my head and eyes, down in the yawning mouth, down beneath the mouth. I yawn. I sink, or try to let the energies sink down into the throat. Deep yawn, and large sigh. Now they sink, but into my nose, nose is full. Hay fever, memory. But not now. Just fluid in the nose. Feel the energy in neck and shoulders. Yawn. Feel a flow in...my fingers. The fingers are moving, typing, feeling. They are alive and I am dead. Who then is doing the typing? Is it a disembodied brain? Down, yawn. Down. Head falls over, neck is stretched. Again.

Move now from typewriter, says a voice. Who is this? Mercurius, I think. But I say no, because Mercurius is too happy with the upper centers, the questioner, talkier, ruler of Gemini, We must get down, my friend and Lord, say I. We must get down where the pains are, in back and belly, in body. Yawn, deep, sigh. "All right" says Mercurius, "for I can fly within as well as without, in shells and bells, in limbs and lymphs." "I know," say I. Yawn, a deep one.

Energy in bottom part of body. All right. Do not type or lie down just yet. But let the energy flow down and wait, quietly, expectantly.

Now lie down, say the words.

...I found that I could not talk aloud—too embarrassed, at this point, with the prospect of somebody coming in to get a book. But, conceivably, I could in the future. I kept my consciousness, however, and noticed that, after a bit, there was a kind of pulse or heart-beat which ran up my spine from the very spot of the pain at the base! It seemed to relax the area. I watched this for a bit, then felt the need to stretch and put my arms behind my neck. I found that I could do this with less effort than usual. Relaxation was happening. All right. For some fifteen or twenty minutes I lay there. Maybe I went out for a minute, I don't know. But now I am back at needing to do the bills.

I have done so. Now, will I just read, or work on the "Judge?" Read.

Want to go home and see my lovely wife. Have a swim, a drink, and go to the mediumistic class. OK. No struggle with Judge today!

CHAPTER SIX

SESSION 44: AUGUST 2, 1972

This past week has brought me a great deal of back pain, as much or more as in the early days, the days when I could hardly stand it. I would exercise more and more, in order to get the relief that came briefly just afterwards, and then had more pain again. I know that I had this the previous week, and I know that it was aggravated by this past long week-end, in which I was tense indeed.

So, coming to the session with Regardie, I spoke of the bad back and he noted that it was, indeed, way out of line. He did not know why, perhaps the exercises. I think that I worsened it by continuing with the exercises excessively. He could not get it back in, however, until we had done the whole session of work. The bulk of the session was with the inner thighs. I flopped, he pushed, and he squeezed and hammered, more than before. I screamed loud and with great pain, but the tension did reduce. This, plus the work on belly, and particularly, solar plexus, helped a lot.

At one point, he plucked or hit my solar plexus, which felt like a great sock, even though it is a mere tap, and I doubled up in a reflex of pain and sorrow. I began to weep, but he did not permit me to indulge it but continued to work. It was right. I felt the words "Mother" come to me, as if I were calling to her not to leave me. Sadness and pain.

During the observation period, the currents were especially strong in my arms and hands, practically beating away. This, I think, because of the return to the screaming and yelling, the heavy breathing. Regardie felt this, too. The session reduced a lot of the tension and after the work, he could realign my spine more easily and I felt much better.

We are still working on getting a head-halter for me, which I hope to use during the month holiday, when I will be away at the mountains and the sea.

I sink down, into the Cloud, which is now the Cave. The dark lad is there. Silent, arms on knees, legs drawn up. Long-haired, thoughtful... I look at him, and he at me. He seems compassionate to me. He understands and knows where I am, without words. That is nice. He is compassionate to me. Usually it is the other way. Yes, I am hurting, and have no words.

"I feel your compassion my son. I feel your love and understanding of me. I know that you merely retreat here in the Cave. But, let us bring our pain to a higher place. Let us bring..." I speak, but I can not. I can not even say the words "God" or "Divine Being." I feel I can not do that. Too easy and too hard. Too easy in that I always have brought such grief and frustrations to God, and too hard in that I have no faith in the adequate answer any more. So then, I shall sit with my son.

My inner son, my lad and I sit and are silent. I sit as he does, but I put an arm on his shoulder, and then around him. He snuggles up to me. He is loved by me, understood by me. And I hold him, lovingly, warmly, as if he were my biological son. Now I start to weep, there is a release. A love from father to son, son to father. And I suffer from lack of the love from my Father God in Heaven with his hard, guilt-making Eye and frustration of my needs. I suffer from that. Why is not my Father in Heaven a more kindly father? Why is He not as kindly a father, even, as I am? It is said that the Father in Heaven is ever so much more merciful and loving. Yet I do not sense it. My pain and frustration are so little compared to the suffering of many men and women and children, with violence, meaninglessness in their lives. Yes, I do not deserve to complain, O Lord, compared to others. But I do not deserve to suffer as much pain either, as far as I can see.

"The Lord makes a suffering a treasure and delight for those who love Him."

These words come. I wonder if they come from Mercurius. There is no face or person who manifests with them. But I ask anyway, "How is it that the Lord makes a suffering a treasure and a delight for those who love Him?"

"By the grace of Being," comes the answer. "By the grace of feeling and knowing that one is alive and struggling and seeking. By knowing that the Lord is present, summoned or not, and that there is not just an emptiness or voidness."

"And yet, the Void is the great God, too, say the Hindus."

"Yes, it is so."

"But you say the grace of Being is knowing that God is present in the suffering, therefore it is a treasure... All right. Then show how God is present in the suffering."

The image of Christ appears, on the cross. And I know it well. I do not reject it. I wish, however, for another image, another word, another help to cope with this apparently senseless continuity of pain.

"When the image is outgrown, then will Love appear," says the voice.

"When the image is outgrown, then will Love appear." So He says. Does that mean that the image will be faded and dead, or that the reality of acceptance is there, or Resurrection? I wonder.

"With the end of image becomes the beginning of life. In the beginning was the Word, and the Word became Image, and the Image became Flesh. With flesh is life, the rest is soul and spirit, as you well know."

"Yes, I know it. But this does not add much. I look, rather, to a benevolent God in Heaven. I look to a Heavenly Father who is kind and helpful. I hold my inner son and my outer son, and I call out to my Father in Heaven.

"Oh, God, my Father! You must know what it means to be a father. How one aches to love one's son, and see him happy. How one rejoices in the union and closeness. How one longs to see the son's Self and his capacities fulfilled. And here I sit with my own sons and treasure them. Where are You, O Lord...for me?"

"Pray and it shall be answered you," come the words. "Pray."

"I pray, and have prayed, Oh Father in Heaven. I pray once more, even though my prayers have been acts and deeds, meditations and writings, rather than requests. Lord, I have need. I need surcease from my back-pain. I need recognition for my spirit in this world, and from you. I was once a chosen one of yours. When I was but three, you came to me and told me that your symbol of Sun, above, was like that of Sun inside my chest, in my heart. You showed me a competence, a beingness in the World, on my tricycle, and I was yours. I feared Mother, I feared the little girl. And now, Oh Lord, the women are kinder to me than you are. I fear hurting them, and I fear their hurt, but they are kinder and more loyal to me and understanding than you, O Lord.

"Oh, Lord God, Author of my being, Guider of my destiny and wielder of the forces which have both pained me and formed me, Lord who has whipped me with the Tree of Life, grant me now the capacity to have that Tree inside and not be so whipped by it. Grant me..."

The words stop. Feelings come intensely, but suddenly there is a stop to words. I remember the previous words told me, about suffering being a grace. I do not truly understand it or accept it. I see only that it goes on.

"Lord, I do not understand! I am silent... I think that perhaps I am too selfish. I should pray for others, not for myself. Surely that is true."

Now my thoughts turn from the Lord. I think of Yogananda's sweet book, his autobiography. I think of his Saints, who make perfumes, who levitate, who meditate endlessly. Everyone has a path to the Lord, all different. Once, Lord... I had a path and now I seem to have none. Only endless struggle with opposites. And yet, in these statements, I despise myself for complaining."

I lie down on the floor. Resting. Letting the energies go where they will. A picture. A porch with sunlight on it. Memory. A little boy, a photo of me, with white sailor suit and black tie on. Harassed, standing on this porch. To whom did it belong? Age of three or four. Harassed, sad. All right...no exit...I call home. Talk to my son. He just sat around this afternoon, after summer school. Felt frustrated at the lab, so just watched a movie, read a bit. I understand. Frustrated, like me. Can't get the vibes going. But he feels better. God is in action, doing something. And in relationship. All right. Read, too.

I read in the paper my artist friend gave me, on Koheleth, who is the Solomon of Ecclesiastes. I looked at the Bible, in Psalms. David sings, calls out to God too for surcease. Let my tongue not cleave, but let it also speak of need.

Lord, let me, like thy son, David, dwell in thy temple.

Let my heart know thee continuously.

Let not skepticism and barrenness bring me far from You.

I know that it is better to know You in suffering than not at all.

I know that this is what You meant, some moments ago, when You spoke of the grace of suffering.

Now I understand it, comprehend it.

Better to be suffering and in Your presence, Your temple, than to be at peace and outside it. For, to be outside is death... I understand.

Lord, I do not seek suffering, but I accept it, if it is in Your presence.

Lord, I accept it as the realization of You...and me.

But Lord, let me also rejoice in You. Let me also feel your tender touch. Let me feel the kind Father and the gentle Mother. Let the sweet milk fall pleasantly upon my mouth. Let it happen, Oh Lord.

SESSION 45: AUGUST 9, 1972

During the week, I had a conversation with my mother on the phone which echoed previous pains. She could not see how she hurts me with her questions and her—to me—uncaring third degree and guilt-making. She is sure it is loving or she is entitled to her opinion. I guess it is only connected with her own pain. Mine goes by the board. Well, it is futile to try to change her, but I still am unable to protect myself from such things without having to blow up, become rejecting, and hurt her. Pathetic for a man of 46 to still be in such a place! And after so many years of working on it! Well, but I must not be so hard on myself, since she is unable to deal with any aspect of the relationship herself. Must be a Karmic tie. We hurt each other, have such different temperaments! But I must try and be more tolerant and accepting.

Anyway, the session with the healer, the last for the year before starting on my holiday, was all right. He was kind enough to have purchased the neck-halter for me and showed me how to put it on. I am so awkward with mechanical things. Last night, as I tried to put it on, my wife helped me, and I was most clumsy indeed. Anyway, I hope that I can truly stretch those neck muscles with this traction and aid in the process.

The session itself was much as before. We worked a lot, on the thigh muscles and I screamed and yelled. I was able to keep open better than before, but I surely screamed. I ended up quite drunk on air, and this was good.

During the observation, there was much relaxation, and I almost fell asleep three or four times. I am falling into that deeper place of relaxation, and would try to keep it without falling asleep. But thus far, I can not... At any rate, I finish the first year of Reichian work, 45 sessions, and am ready for a full rest. Normally, I go off on holiday with lots of plans. Now, I really want to rest, follow the spirit of easy, dreamy life. I long to get back in touch with my passive dream life. I am so active in it that the flow and nourishment have gone away... I look forward to a peaceful, meditative, reflective and joyful time, alone, and with my wife and children.

Shall I look now into the Cloud? Shall I sing a song of appreciation to the Lord, for he did answer my prayer a little. Shall I call back the Persian lady who so much appreciated my helping her to calm her fears, and find her way back to the Moslem God?

Let me do all of them. First I shall look into the Cloud. I shall ask of Boy, of Ox, of Mercurius where they are now, at the end of a year. And I shall give thanks to God that I am privileged to be alive, though often in pain, that I am getting better slowly, that I could attend a Bar Mitzvah with my son. I thank the Lord for my wife, my children, and the others who love me and whom I love. So many am I gifted with, so much! Dear Lord, I thank you for all of it, and I unashamedly ask you for more love, for my pain to be reduced. All this I ask. And I ask that you equally bless my loved ones. Bring them that which they need and want. At the end of this year of work, and before my holiday, let me ask a blessing for them. Lord, I shall call on you enough when the High Holy Days come, when my son's *aliyah* comes.

And now, the Cloud. The Boy is there, but vague. He seems older, perhaps like my own son, 12 or so. The Ox seems more like a cat, like our own cat, Rada. Mercurius is not to be seen.

"Where are you all, after a year," I say. "What have you to say?"

The Boy is silent. He smiles and seems long-legged. The Ox, now become a cat, is also silent, but rubs his hairy face on my hand. All is silent. After one year, silence, but benevolent. So, close eyes, and be silent.

SEPTEMBER 13, 1972

It has been a month since I have written. A month of holiday, away from my own patients, away from the healer, too. How has it been? Well, not good. Depression. Much sadness and awakening with pain. Yet, good times too. That walk with my son in the high mountains, in which we spoke of his early memories, was a lovely time. The beauty of the week in the cabin in those same mountains, plus the week at the beach with the children gave great pleasure. The additional week with my wife, alone, travelling and being quiet together, dinners and just loving each other, that too was very beautiful. But the depressions were also very much there, along with back pain, as bad as ever. I tried to do exercises, but the help was only minimal. Now that I am back in the routine of seeing patients, I feel somewhat better. But today, when I will also be seeing my own healer, I am depressed. I had hoped to be able to write here, to take care of letters and such, but I have done very little. During the holiday, I had my dreams, tried to re-connect with myself as I had desired, but the dreams were mostly old stories, old conflicts and not nourishing. The depression did not lift. And so, today, I will write here again.

The old, boring, painful dreams are about psychologists, being rejected, just as it used to be. I just looked through some of what I wrote last year at this time and see that then, too, there was sadness. I began, then, too, to explore the dark cloud of my depression. I have spent a year of work and healing effort on it, but I am surely no better. Is it the darkness of the time before healing? Perhaps. It was so, indeed, during my first analysis. As I got deeper, I got darker, finally, though, there was light and joy. Would that this were so for me now. But I shall look at the dark Cloud once again.

The Cloud, dark and dreary, has the same form of demon-face, or jaw-extended angry man which I have drawn. Tough guy.

The depression is an angry man, though. Where is the sad-eyed lad and the ox? And Mercurius? Only the drawing of the angry-jawed man is there. Angry at being depressed, at no change. And sick. I feel sick in the stomach, nauseous. The headache returns. Probably need to shriek it all out, throw it up, get rid of it. Today, perhaps, as I breathe and scream and curse, I shall throw some of it off.

But now, I am not content with a mere cartoon of my depression. I am not content that it is just a drawing of an angry, tough man. It does not reach the feeling, or the depth of it. Nor does it change anything. I am eager to change it. I am eager to pray, to contact my God. I pray, Oh God, for the poor patient of mine who is dying rapidly of cancer. I regret that I saw him only a few times and was unable to help prepare him for death, to meet you. A sweet and good man, an honest businessman, one that I admire, as I admire few businessmen. Yet an atheist; and to die so is sad. I feel for him, but can do nothing, since when I returned from my holiday, he was already in a coma and sinking. Bless him, Lord.

But who am I to speak to the Lord? Who am I? I who once felt chosen and special? I who once felt that even the anger and pain and condemnation of God upon me were all right because I was stronger than others, had a direct connection with God, needed no intermediary. Now I am weaker, more confused. I look to others and need their mediation. Yet a part of me still speaks to the Lord. My own Lord has abandoned me, it seems, but perhaps will not abandon those others.

So, I must go deeper... The black cloud is now not above, but below. It is like an asphalt pit, both tar-like and a great dark hole. It goes from one image to the other. The hot tar, I can hold in my hands, mold, as I once did. I can shape it into the sad-eyed ox. But I leap into the great pit instead, and fall down, down. As I fall, I breathe and sigh. A weight is lifted, because I abandon myself to God. Lord, you no longer know me, support me, love me, or give me what I want or what I think I need, but I still abandon myself to You. I do so because that is what must be done. I must love and trust the Lord, even when there is no sense to do so. When it seems like, I, too, should "curse God and die." But no. I do not curse God now. Instead, I fall into the pit, and felt myself breathing more freely. I can let go and relax. Let God carry me. I feel strings crossed beneath my back. It is a minimal net, the ends of which are carried by four dark birds. They are black and have big beaks. But these dark birds are not raven-like in meaning. They are dark, but not malevolent. They almost smile as they fly and carry me. I am carried out of this pit of darkness which may, after all, have no bottom at all. I am carried up and up, once again, and now I fly. I fly over a sunlit countryside, full of beauty. The dark cloud has become four dark birds and a dark, single-stranded net, crossed. The birds deposit me upon a high hillside, beautiful, like the mountains where I was on holiday, and yet like a Swiss meadow, too. I am alone and at peace in the sunny, cool, wind-blown place. I sit on the hill and reflect upon the meaning of the dark cloud becoming the cross of a net and four birds. A mandala, to be sure. A cross of the spirit and peace. This occurs when I "take the leap," abandon myself to God, to trust Him even when there seemed to be no basis for trust. When I did so, the cloud changed into that which could support me, even a kind of intuitive bird-spirit which looks dark but is light and helpful and brings me to my aloneness in a good, peaceful, way. I am at once in the mountains of my holiday, where I was at one with my son, and in the Swiss mountains, symbol of my individuation, and my previous spiritual journey.

It is good to be quiet. I do not question, now. I do not mourn or weep, but I sit quietly and trust. It is a very good feeling, indeed, to rest so. How can a dark cloud of sadness, despair, and meaninglessness change into a mandala of bird-carried support? Yes, in the beginning the cloud was also a bed, as I recall. It is my aloneness. The depression is my aloneness, dark and negative, unrecognized, rejected (including self-rejecting), and a failure. But the depression changes to a positive, peaceful aloneness as soon as I take the leap and trust in God.

In what do I trust? In a good God? Not necessarily. Not since Job, and since I learned my Jungian psychology. But in a God of development, aiming at wholeness. I trust that.

And now? Shall I sit upon this peaceful mountain and just smell the flowers, and look at those which are beautiful and smell not? Or shall I...? I need to be quiet and write no more now.

SESSION 46: SEPTEMBER 13, 1972

Yesterday I had my 46th session. I returned after a month of holiday, as I have written. I greeted poor Regardie with the statement that I had been depressed during the holiday and that my back had been bad also. I say "poor," because he took it rather hard. His face was dark and he said that this was unexpected, a symptom that was quite unusual to occur. By now, he thought, the depression should have lifted. And then the back. He thought we had better get pictures of that back. He gave me the name of another healer and I shall, at last, have X-rays of what that back is about. Perhaps another tack has to be taken.

But why the depression, he wondered? Well, I told him I thought it was endogenous, grabbed real difficulties and disappointments and turned them sour, neglecting all the good and happy and loving things in my life. Today I saw a patient, a priest, who had come out of his depression during the holiday, had found his vocation again after several years of dryness, gradual death. It was a miracle. It seemed that this transpired through the hope and expectation that his prayers would come true. Before he prayed in despair, and now he prays in gladness and thanksgiving.

The session was light. Regardie was gentle. I remarked about it and he just laughed. "I can be gentle, too." Of course. But he was just gradually getting back into the work. We agreed that perhaps a new layer of feeling and armoring was being touched. He acknowledged that my chest was very difficult, did not respond very much, but we shall continue.

Strange, to read his Magic book on holiday and be so impressed, yet to find him somewhat different in his office. We are not so much with magic in his office, perhaps a different kind—a magic of healing the soul by working with the body. Just the reverse of all that I have done in my own work.

Now that I am back with my own patients, it seems all right. Despite my regression, I seem to be able to stay connected with patients, indeed, be even more open when indicated. One person, who had experienced me so "elevated" before, was glad to know about my fear, inadequacies, doubts.

So, hope builds anew. The prayer of yesterday, and the work with the fantasy, trusting my leap into the void, helped. This morning, early, I felt it again, which was strange, because my dream had no such quality.

I dreamt that an older Jewish man, a father, was expressing his gratitude to me for having helped him and his sons. The eldest son, about 30, was there and thanking me also. He was a physician, looking older than his age, a bit shy and, I thought, not very bright looking. The second son, a mathematician, was also there, also grateful. The third son, 17 or 18, was not there. The youngest was the most gifted, and also wanted to be a healer. I had done something for all of them. End of dream.

What had I done for these people? During the day, I had, with my fantasy of peace on the mountain, been at peace with the son (my own), and the father (Jung, Swiss Alps), and with God as Father, but now the dream was presenting these very human, Jewish father and sons. These are not Christian God-The-Father and God-the-Son images, and I do not understand what is meant. So, I shall dream the dream onwards, and ask. I shall welcome the father and the sons into the Cloud. But my thoughts shift to the Doctor who is to take the X-rays of my back, and I wonder what he will find. It is a relief, at last, to do this thing, but it is also a sadness that it must be done. I seem to have no fear, however... So, let me return to my dream.

"Welcome, sir, to my Cloud and Castle. I am pleased that I have done something for you and your sons, but I must confess that I do not know what I have done for you."

"You do not know? Maybe you are not the doctor who has helped. Are you not the orthopaedic surgeon?"

"No, I am not. I often get calls from his patients. But I am not he. That saddens me. Apparently I got mixed up with him, even in my dream!"

"No, sir. Do not fret. I only said that to test you. To show you that you are in need of thanks and gratitude, and that it hurts when one does not receive it. I also show you that you do not even know that you deserve it. Don't you know that you are doing much for the healer image? Don't you know that with every effort, every devotion, every paper, that you are advancing the art and science of healing? I, too, am a healer and I know. At thirty you were a healer, and went deeper. And you will go deeper yet, I know."

"You seem to know much about me."

"Yes, I do. It is no mystery. I inhabit your psyche, not some other. I inhabit your world, and I know."

"All right. I accept it. But it seems so much like those dialogues of the past, which speak but are not convincing."

My mind wanders to concrete tasks and to other things. Yes, let it wander. Other things to do.

SEPTEMBER 20, 1972

Today would have been my 47th session with Regardie, but he is out of town. Instead, I have things to report which are not too pleasant—as if the recent things have been!

Last night, as arranged, I underwent extensive X-ray examination of my back. The young man, cool and efficient in his manner, was technically perfect as he spent more than an hour and a half on the process. He left me in the cold, instrumented room, with the suggestion that he would have to take more pictures. I tried to keep warm with stretching, meditation, and some yoga exercises, as I lay on that hard surface in my underwear. But I could have dressed, of course.

The main thing was his description to me of his findings, along with his graphic portrayal of it in the X-rays. He said that I had extensive deterioration of the discs between the vertebrae, particularly in the upper back and neck! In the lower back, where I experience the most pain, there was a wearing away between two vertebrae, something, he said, like "kissing bones," but this was not as serious as the above. Indeed, he said, without very much sensitivity or eros, mine was the worst case he had seen for someone my age. My upper back was like that of a man of 60, and my neck like that of a man of 70! The only reassurance was that in the lower back, and hips, I was more like 30! These ages were startling and painful, particularly since he said that it was deteriorating and could get much worse. He was reluctant to suggest any therapy, leaving that, of course, to Regardie to talk over with me, but he said that it could be quite serious if I were hit from behind. I had already done remarkably well with that picture, probably because I was in such good shape. I had a kind of arthritis, deteriorating, and that was that.

The news sank in only gradually, and I felt its dark truth. Yes, an old man, perhaps all my life I had been so, in that round-shouldered forward-head way. In the perpetual burdens I carry, I am surely an old man. Well, now it is in the bones, so to speak. Saturn above and below, in a youthful body. Well, that is how it was. I was comforted by my wife, of course, and by a friend too, who showed me the foolishness and coldness of such diagnostic labels, but the image of the Old Man in the bones has really had me. I have wept and felt better. I have fantasied that continued work in meditation and magic would bring about a miracle cure. I would be renewed, reborn, and it would even show in the X-rays! And I have also had despair that Reichian therapy would be very limited for me, that I would have to be satisfied with meager results, that only my continued massage and exercise would keep the process from deteriorating too rapidly, and that an early death was probable. How many years had I, I wondered, before I would be crippled or unable to move about? I could still do psychotherapy, I comforted myself, sitting at home, and perhaps earn enough to support my family. Rather dark thoughts, and before I really know what can be done.

Nay, Lord, the old Saturn is not *on* my back, he *is* my back! My back is old and Saturnine, and is in pain. But the image I have is of my carrying an old man piggyback upon my upper back. He has a long ear, is irritable and irascible. He kicks me like a horse and pushes me. He never lets me go. I try to throw him off, but he climbs back on again. I sit down and weep, and he gets off for a moment, but only a moment, climbing right back on again.

"Oh Saturn, why do you dog me so? Why do you bring me such pain of soul and body? Why?"

He only laughs, this old man. He says no words, so he is like the silent Scorpio boy, but the boy, as in L.'s dream, is a beautiful, hurt one, full of ideals and hopes and aspirations, unlike this one.

As I look at him, though, he seems merely an old man, like an actor in a movie I saw. He was a person who had mined for gold all his life and was continually frustrated and disappointed. He finally found it, but through human cupidity and the meanness of others, it was grabbed after by others. Finally, the wind blew the gold dust away and the actor laughed uproariously at the foolishness of life. Are you such a one, old man?

"I am, but am not. I am sad and serious, but have compassion for you, my man. I have seen much, known much. I am your experience itself. You have seen a lot, are no longer quite the young man that you were. I am that other half, having lived much, but I'm not so bad-looking after all, and have a sense of humor. To have me on your back is not so terrible. It could be a worse sort of fellow."

"I agree, actor. But I would rather face you than have you ride painfully upon my back."

"You do not understand. The pain, disillusion and age, are in the very experience of it. If you can laugh like me, dance like me, then you will, indeed, have faced me, been me. It is not getting rid of the pain, it is bearing it rightly that matters!"

Yes, old man, I shall reflect, and be back. Tomorrow.

SEPTEMBER 21, 1972

I have reflected some and been in pain. Oh, I am always getting in pain! The hurts of relationship, of need, of misunderstanding, are always there. I am sick of it.

I think of Anais Nin and her diary. I think of a colleague's criticism that she writes there and does not come out with people, in relationship, does not show her true feelings: she makes her judgments in her little book. But then I think of her with her analysts, and how her book got started, despite the fact that the analysts wanted her to give it up. She, the little girl, was writing a letter to her father! Lonely little girl, cut off from father, writing to him. So, a fifty-year letter to a man who, she later found out, was merely self-centered, vain, and incapable of love. As I think of that little girl, I think of my own daughter and weep with the idea that she should be alone and miss me! I could not bear it! So, I'll have to give up the idea of suicide! Right.

All right, some few tears shed. Back to the old man, the actor. The actor's name is Walter, but I know that he is an inner man, derived from a film and story, so I shall address him as Walter, the Saturn-Man.

"You, sir, as a positive old man, I need your wit and wisdom and humor. I am so sad, and get hurt so easily. I am like a woman, really. And, its true that I get along better with women than with men."

"Yes, one can see that…"

Phone rings, lose track. Mind wanders. Feel sad again. On edge of panic. Memory of such days in my office. Hopes and…Same old man, or one like him, in a dream that time when I felt that my intuitive circling of the earth was at an end. I look at my "trophies" on the shelf. Lots of people I have helped, but there also those not helped, too. Sadness.

Into the cloud I go. The sad Lad is there, Scorpio dark.

"I have met a man, my son, who is an actor. He is an old man but wise and happy. He can laugh at himself, laugh at life, and laugh at limitations, pain, even. Not from outside but from inside, from a place of experience."

Scorpio nods.

"This man," I continue, "Advises me to learn from him, and I wish I could. But I see you, too, with disappointments, hurts, and I can not do it. Old Jung was always teaching his friends in his cloud. But I am forever learning, encountering, confronting. You, soul-eyed Lad, need my help and I can not give it. Perhaps the Old Man can...Can you, Saturn-Man, help this Scorpio lad, so sad and quiet? His hopes and illusions and ideals are crushed all the time, so he is hurt and hides."

"I know such lads: I know how they are. My own lad was such a one. So was I at one time. How do you suppose I could get to the philosophical place that I am in without having undergone such suffering, too? I really have, you know."

"Can you help him?"

"I don't know. Perhaps I can help you, and you can help him."

"Why, is that easier?"

"Not easier, just more natural to me. Since I am a ghost, I find it easier to speak to people like yourself, rather than other beings and ghosts from other levels of existence."

"You say you are a ghost. But I have assumed that you are the old actor man in me."

"Have it your way, it does not matter. I am here to help and win brownie points for being helpful, so it does not matter to me how you see me."

"All right. Show me how to help this sad lad, how to cope with the repeated pains and disappointments, the repeated hurts and disillusionments. Usually there are tears, maybe anger, lashing out, withdrawal."

"Yes, I see. I'll have to think about it. All right? Go and read or something. I'll return to you, soon."

"All right."

SEPTEMBER 27, 1972

The days have gone by, and I have not felt depressed. For the first time in perhaps two months, I have not been depressed at all. Yesterday, I awakened with a dream about my son's Bar Mitzvah, which I discussed with L. After that, I felt so good. My connection with her and with others gets deeper and more whole. The bigs and littles of us come in, there is an even greater spiritual connection, with both a union in similarity and in individual differences.

But I am back with myself and with my God. The dream I had yesterday was a clear one. At first I was in the synagogue, and saw Mrs. B. She, the prim and proper German-Jungian, sees me and we nod. But I notice that I have no white shirt on. I have my pants and a dark jacket (for me a great improvement over my

frequent nakedness!), but no white shirt. There is intermission, however, and
time for me to get it. I rush out and go into my car, but am then lost in my own
dream-world and fantasy. Suddenly, I wake up and realize that I do not have the
white shirt, so I rush to get it. The place to go is a room of the synagogue.
There is a drawer in a bureau there in which there are shirts. The room,
incidentally, is long and narrow, and I associate it with a priest's robing room in
a church. I find the drawer of shirts, but the collars on them are stained with dark
spots. I look up and see that these stains have come from a rent in the ceiling of
the temple, through which have come raindrops mixed with dust. So, the shirts
are not usable. I look at another drawer, with shirts in it of the father of one of
my son's friends. He is a member of the temple whose son recently was Bar
Mitzvah. I see that his shirts have a design on them which is not mine at all,
does not suit me. I could not wear them (could not follow his pattern in being an
increasingly ritual and law-observing Jew). I now see the rabbi in the room,
together with an unknown woman. We have a connection. It seems that the stain
on the shirt is not my fault but that of the temple, and we both know it. The
rent in the fabric of the ceiling is the difficulty. We nod. But now, my son is
busy completing his Bar Mitzvah on his own and I am not there. I am relieved
that he can go through it all right, saddened that I am not there, but somewhat
relieved, too, because of my uncertainty with the ritual. End of dream.

It was clear, this dream. My lack of proper behavior, knowing the ritual (white
shirt), and, of course, the very criticism once put on me by the Mrs. B types
("bad manners"), is at issue. I realize my lack and try to repair it, but get lost in
my own inner life (car and fantasy). When I do get to a remedy, it is stained,
because the temple itself has a crack in it. The ceiling (mind, spirit) is cracked.
When I was 13, I took to a freer intellectual development, then a mystical one,
so I did not learn the ritual and the doctrine so well. That, I am assured, is the
fault of the synagogue and its lack of repair. All right. Even the rabbi is with me
in this. For he, in actuality, as I know, feels encumbered by the "administrative"
aspect of synagogue life, would love to go and live in Israel and be truly
religious. But rabbis there are a drug on the market! My son goes through the
ceremony and is all right. My inner son is being initiated, apparently, as well as
my outer one. And it is all right. Is that the Scorpio boy?

Last night, in actuality, I saw the rabbi, and also had an interchange with the
treasurer of the temple, who confronted me with not having renewed
membership. I answered that my son would choose his own religious direction at
13. I was strong in it, but the poor man, as the rabbi later said, was merely
trying to keep members, get money for the temple, and keep prestigious names.
I understood. I even told the rabbi my dream and gave my interpretation. I think
he understood, in part. But we got on to the practical matters of honors,
placement, etc,—all of which helped me to get some sort of "white shirt" for my
actual son's Bar Mitzvah.

Now, I am here with my writing and my God. Yesterday, I received a lovely
letter from my oldest friend, Martin, the painter. We had such a memorable
evening, the other night, with our wives, renewing our connection. He has such

a modesty and a philosophical attitude now, about his work and recognition in the world, a far cry from the pain of his youth. I hope that his fire is still there, and that his—and mine—are not crushed by the disappointments and frustrations of life. Yes, I am lucky in my friends and relationships, so much love and care come to me! It is almost shocking that I have been depressed.

But, my depression is in relation to God. Yesterday, I went back and read some poems I had written, and found them good. I was reassured. The connection with God and gods is there. But why must I punish myself, if it is I; or why does God punish me, if it is He?

Lord, are you there? Are You there in the cloud? Is it my own Scorpio son who is being initiated, coming into his own? Will I get more healing, or be able to live better with that old back, the Old Saturn thereon?

The question sounds like a soap opera. Tune in again for the continuing saga and never-ending problems. My life is really like a soap opera all right, inside and out. Perhaps other people have it like that, too. Surely my patients do. But I am really able to help them, connect with them.

Well, then, Lord, what shall it be? Will you come?

In the stillness, the Lord emerges.

"Love is in the asking. Love is in the act."

A poem starts, but does not continue... No, the poem is in the quiet. It is not spoken. "Be still my son," says my Lord. "Be still," says He, "And know that I am alive." I am still.

SEPTEMBER 28, 1972

Yesterday was to have been my 47th session with Regardie—and it was, in a way, though he refused to charge me. Rather, he went over the X-rays and report that he had received from the roentgenologist with me. He thought that it would be wise to stop the Reichian treatment for a time, and heal my neck particularly. He was not as dark and pessimistic about the back as the X-ray man had been, but felt that the severity of the neck degeneration would require straight orthopaedic treatment for a time, because the Reichian work might do damage to it. I was disappointed by that, naturally, sensing that termination was really being mentioned, that there was no hope for me and my aching back.

But no, he did not want that. He telephoned that "Toad-like colleague" in my presence, and told him what he desired—that the orthopaedic man treat my neck for a time, before returning me to the Reichian work. That was somewhat reassuring, but I was sad anyway: not knowing whether to trust regular physicians, who despise chiropractors, whether to see another man for a second opinion, to follow Regardie's recommendation, or what. I thought that I would get another opinion of the films from an M.D., and Regardie agreed. So, I will try to find the least rigid and open of the orthodox M.D.'s. Funny, my own rigid back and neck and my struggle with that rigidity and orthodoxy both within me and outside. Should it be healed by further orthodoxy or not? Similarly for the religious, guilt-place: can it be healed by maintaining an outer connection with orthodox religion? Apparently the answer is yes and no. I must keep a connection with orthodoxy, somehow, but also be free. Like keeping a stiff back, but being flexible. But, God, who will help me?

I was very depressed last night and awakened early with the oh-so-frequent gloom, insomnia, nausea-indigestion. I went to the bathroom, mobilized the gag-reflex several times, took two aspirins and went back to sleep. I awakened again at the regular time—though I had felt the flow of some energy in my head—and immediately did my exercises and swimming, which always make me feel better. I had also used the gag-reflex to loosen up my belly. I seem to be able to do that now more easily. I guess when it is absolutely essential, I can do it...but what a loss to give up the Reichian work now! More and more I feel its importance—the value of working with the body armor and energies. Once again, I am thrown into confusion about my back and pain.

This morning, I saw a patient who is doing very well. She keeps on reporting the enormous changes in a person like herself who is so difficult. She is very able, many-sided, herself a healer and the lover of a healer whom I once treated. Nobody, except her lover, has been so deeply into her soul she says, and the effects are showing. I report this, not to demonstrate to myself that I am indeed a healer, but because she suggested I work with my neck and body with auto-suggestion, hypnosis. The subconscious—as distinct from the unconscious—is sensitive to that. I should get myself into a trance state several times a day, and give that level of my psyche instructions that the "negativity is gone out of my back, harmlessly." If I would do that, along with meditation, then I should be as healthy as she, who is never ill. I think she may be right. She is, indeed, very intelligent, has worked with magic, is not out to convert me to something. What I have to contribute to her is the capacity to connect deeply with the unconscious—also with her patients. This she has already begun to discover. What I need, apparently, and she has given to me, is a way to connect with the less deep but potent subconscious and its automaticity. Naturally, I have happened on this idea in other places—the Occult, Tarot, etc. I must now try and do this myself.

Perhaps this is what is needed, Lord, "helping myself" as she says, rather than calling out to You for help. I shall try. That, along with the magical meditation I do with my friend, L, may carry me further on the way.

OCTOBER 2, 1972

This morning, I again awakened with depression. Back, many doctors and which doctor, weight, fear of financial insecurity after hearing about the heart attack of a friend, all those things. Many people fear such things—health, security, appearance, validation, yet I become so down with it. But after exercises and swimming, I am much better.

A friend calls with a suggestion to contact a Chinese information service for a licensed acupuncturist. All possibilities: self-hypnosis, physiatrist, chiropractic orthopedist, acupuncture, medical orthopedist...

But I am alone with myself. And with God, who does not answer. What was that story? A man says that he is God. How does he know? Well, when he talks with God, he finds that he is talking to himself! Yes, the Self, the Bigger self, is surely inside. What is Self and not self? Ego and non-ego? Enough. To my cloud!

The cloud is there, and I am in it. But I want to go higher. I want to go higher and higher up. I want to speak with the Angel or with God Himself. Where is the one who can speak for me?

Lord. You are not there. Please speak to me, in my lonely silence.

Silence...But, if the Lord will not speak, I can at least go back to my cloud. Or can I? Once I wrote easily. Now it does not come so easily. Empty...I remember other times of dryness, emptiness. Feeling fat, depressed, down...I close my eyes. The Scorpio boy, now tall and almost thirteen, like my son, sits on the cold stone floor. He is quiet in this lightest room. His eyes look at me, sad. He looks away. As I did once before, I look into his eyes and see the blue sky, high up. The eyes open up to the vastness of the universe. In which, God...Nothing. Empty. Fill up, with food. Oh, how I must have been depressed as a child, yearning for something, and stuffing myself with cheese sandwiches, peanut butter, milk, cookies, and reading Sunday comics. Fill me, Lord, I did not say. I was just lonely, and yet loved to be alone.

And now? There is nothing for me to say or do.

OCTOBER 4, 1972

Today, a Wednesday, would have been another session with Regardie, but of course, I am not having one. Instead, I saw an M.D. this morning for another opinion about my back and am to see an orthopaedic chiropractor this afternoon, for a similar reason.

This morning began not too promisingly. The doctor was half-an-hour late, did not apologize for it, and in the course of his history taking, I had the impression that he was like the usual M.D.: authoritative, provincial, technical. But he did know about acupuncture, said his brother was an analyst in New York (Freudian). In any case I told him as much of the story as possible, Reichian therapy, chiropractor, etc., fearful that he would put down chiropractors. He examined me thoroughly and read the X-rays. To my surprise and pleasure, he did not think that my back was particularly abnormal or diseased, certainly not that of a 60 or 70 year old man. On the contrary, a 70 year-old man has osteoarthritis and bones falling away, mine were firm and well calcified. He saw some slight diminution of the tissue between the bones, and indeed, there was a little curvature. The spurs were not serious, he said, and the bones growing together were probably cogenital. Most importantly, he said that my natural, genetic condition, typical of Polish and Russian people, is to have tight muscles and ligaments. That is not tension or anything else, it is a genetic condition. Indeed, the tightness is a compensation against the tendency to too much looseness. My initial pain was probably from a jerking or lifting something, and the lower back is all right. He was careful to say that the X-rays were not so bad and that, generally, they are only good in conjunction with clinical findings which, in my case, were far from seriously pathological.

Last night, I dreamed of a flabby and old, puffy-eyed, weak, yet dangerous man. He was annoyed with me, could even kill me, or do something bad at the

Bar Mitzvah of my son. I had to "banish" him when I awakened, with a ritual or sign-of-the-cross. Yes, it feels right to banish this demon rather than argue with him, try to convince him, or absorb him. I cannot, it is too destructive to me.

And today, the fact that the physician said that I was not so severely ill, that my back was all right, may be a clue to it. It is an ordinary condition, having once sprained it in some sport or in some other way, being of a certain genetic make-up and living accordingly. Yes, I need not submit to the "judge," or to the need of someone to get their "feelings out" at my expense. I need no longer be victim or the abused one—transference, healer, or no.

In short, I proclaim that as a healer, I no longer need or wish to be the "carrier," the tree upon which the diseased bandage is cast, as one who can absorb it. I am no longer "chosen." All right, then.

OCTOBER 5, 1972

My time at the orthopedist began fretfully. His office was filled, and I had to wait another half-hour. Physical doctors are funny, I think. We soul-doctors are always on time, operate by the clock—have to. Body doctors are always late, it seems. I wonder what that means. Perhaps the soul, because of its evanescence and subtlety, defies time, hence requires structure, whereas the body, with its concreteness, asks for flexible time. But it merely made me annoyed. Beside that, it was the nurse who had to apologize for the lateness, not the doctor! I must tell him about that, and about the lack of eros of his X-ray specialist some time!

Anyway, he finally examined the X-rays and me, the former carefully, the latter—it seemed to me—a bit pompously. Still, he seemed to know what he was doing, and spoke fairly straight to me. He felt, too, that clinical findings had to be compared with films; oftentimes people have terrible films with little symptomatology, and vice-versa. He felt, however, that my neck was, indeed, a very sore point. There was clear evidence of there having been a wound and that there was spasm and much reduced movement in it. When I told him that I had seen a physiatrist who said that it was essentially normal and that the limited movement was genetic and inherited, he asked, "Dr. R.?" I said, "Yes." And he said, "We get lots of his patients." And then began the usual competition among the "doctors." He felt that the physiatrists did not have experience or knowledge of backs or X-rays, just as the physiatrist did not respect the knowledge of chiropractors—did not know that they were specializing now. Well, I did not want to get into that struggle, but I did a little. I mentioned about my physician and friend's remark about "broken necks" done by chiropractors as he had seen at the hospital. This chap said that he had investigated many such stories, had even been on national television about such claims and had been able to find only one such case. And that should have been a malpractice suit! If a doctor says that, then malpractice should be instituted! I thought he was right and resolved to talk to my friend about it.

Well, I went home and felt somewhat down with it, but was heartened by the fact that the orthopedic man felt that I could be helped with treatment in two to four weeks, three times per week, consisting of manipulation, traction, mechanical use of a vibrator, etc. That seemed reasonable to me. When he said that I could resume Reichian therapy in two to four weeks, well, I felt much better. I thought that I would probably institute the therapy.

Today I agreed to begin the course of treatment for the neck and hope that it will end in two weeks, as he suggested. All is moving faster these days and I feel better. Where there was utter despair, from the X-ray man a week or so ago, now there is hope and buoyancy.

CHAPTER SEVEN

OCTOBER 18, 1972

A week since I last wrote. The Bar Mitzvah: what a day it was! Early in the morning, my son and I arose and went to the temple. The previous Thursday had also been a beautiful one at the same temple. But then we went into the small Bais Medresh—the little room for a small "minyan," where we both put on phylacteries and read together from the book of morning services and the Torah. My son was summoned to the Torah, to say the blessings, and I said the prayer thanking You, Oh God, for bringing me to this day and of now handing over my son to You directly. No more am I responsible for him. Lord, oh Lord, treat him well and fairly. Love him and guide him in Your way. He was so beautiful that morning, carefully wearing the fine prayer shawl and *yarmelke* that we had bought the previous Sunday. I, too, was feeling fine in my own new *tallith*, along with the little velvet bag to contain it.

But Saturday, the Bar Mitzvah time, was a great day. We came early, he and I, and soon began deep prayers. Others gradually arrived. There was a row of priests next to me, my friends. First my father, who swelled with joy and finally wept near the end, thinking of how his father would have loved to have been there. Then there was Jim, ex-Roman Catholic priest, then Mokusen, my deep and beautiful friend who is a Buddhist priest, then Sam, who is both a priest of Quakers and of the Edgar Cayce sect, and finally, Tom, who is a Roman Catholic priest. Funny, that it should have been a row of priests. And, in front of me, B. and O., both doctors and healers like myself, and Martin, my artist friend. Behind me, H., who chanted and sang and knew all the orthodox prayers and procedure so well. He was a help, when the time came, to lift the Torah from the ark. And the women: first, my wife, so lovely, and daughter, Tamar, sitting big-eyed and like the beautiful angel she is; then my "gemini-twin," Sister Lucia, looking at me with such appreciative eyes, and then sister-in law, Beulah, who had come early, and soft-eyed Helen, looking so loving at me, too, and Lawrene, with her spirit-smile. Then came my mother, so proud, and my aunts, and my sister Teri. All of them, so many who loved me and whom I love.

The service went well. My brother-in-law, Morrey, was called to the Torah after me, then his son, Rick. They, like me, made mistakes. It was funny. But all my family were blood close, blood-speaking to You, Oh Lord! And then came my son, tall and proud and handsome. He prayed and chanted and the walls were enflamed with love of You, Oh Lord, and Your love of us. I weep now as I recall it, and think of it—and You. My son, my boy, he cried out, joyfully, and prayerfully, full of happiness. He chanted his *maftir* like a great rabbi or cantor, his final prayers of blessing caused a great opening in the sky. The dark day, a day of Noah according to the Torah text, cleared and the spirit of the Lord went up and came down, from Lord to Lord, from son to father, and father to son.

Then the rabbi spoke. His strange sermon, about escape, was pathetic almost. But he tried hard, I think to please me and the healers present. But he did not understand us. But when he spoke to my son, congratulated him, reminded everyone of what a good student he was, and of how he, the rabbi, and I had had so many long talks of a Sunday, reading the texts of Talmud and of Torah, and of mysticism, he recalled all these things and spoke with deep appreciation and devotion. For this is the man that he is, devoted and religious. Not brilliant, alas, for he would like to be, but true and deep to You, oh Lord, following in Your commandments and following in all the ancient ways of Your people. How fine he is!

And then it was over. Another doctor chanted beautifully, children sang, and it was over. Down we went into the basement to drink a toast and bless the bread. My son blessed the bread in Your name, oh Lord, and we celebrated. In the afternoon, we all went to our home, so beautifully prepared and festooned and garlanded with all manner of flowers by my beautiful wife. A small Israeli group made music with zip and fire. We drank and we danced. Martin and I danced our Russian dance, just as we did thirty years ago, and Bob and I did so also, as we did fifteen years ago. All our friends were there and family, close and far. It was so beautiful! M. was charmingly drunk and told palm fortunes, danced and embarrassed everyone, in a delightful way, unexpected from Japanese. We all danced and ate fine food. A great day!

My healing by the orthopaedic man continues and he is very hopeful. I shall be free of pain, he says, in just a couple of weeks. Perhaps I shall need to return once a month after that, for support, but I shall be all right, and be able to resume the Reichian work.

But I must come back, and go into myself, touch the wound which is always so easily hit.

I call upon the Cloud, and I see it at once. Now it is small, like a small disc or circle, which alternates as solid and as smoke. It is a milky ether, rising and coming down into me from above, as if I were doing a Middle Pillar ritual, as I have been doing so nicely with L. I miss it, the Middle Pillar meditation with her, not doing it at all last week, while she was busy in saving a life. But now the Cloud comes down through my head. Down my neck and chest, expanding to the edges of the body. It goes down my middle and to the waist, but pauses at the lower back, where there is pain. But it pushes itself and goes down further, through legs and feet. It spins and comes back up again. It rises and comes up to the top of the head, and spurts out like the Fountain of the Middle Pillar. I break wind and it is no disgrace. For it is an expression from below, as I want to call out the name of God from above. I call out *Yehovoh Elohim*, and there is a certain peace.

What is this? Has the cloud become the energy of the Middle Pillar? Has the cloud depopulated itself and become the energy with which I engage and hope to deal with magically? Has fantasy gone away? If so, where has my struggle with

Judge and pain gone...? I feel a throbbing once again. Should I, then, do a Middle Pillar?

I did so. In the middle of it, an old summer camp mate called me. She is now working with a colleague, and spoke of me and old camp days to him. She got my name from him and phoned me. She spoke of how strange it was that the "loner" from camp days should become an analyst! She spoke, too, of how she ran away from camp when her father died. Now she is trying to find her way. She is divorced, has done many black-white encounter groups for several years. Camp days call me. Those summers were wonderful, the only time, apart from Zürich, when I was truly in harmony with the world.

But what of the Cloud?

The Lord is my Shepherd...
The Lord is my Lamb...
The Lord is my offspring...
The Lord is "I AM"
Eheieh. Eheieh.
I Am.
Eheieh. Eheieh.
Will be.

I hold the Cloud, now. It is like a ring. It is small and compact and round, and I feel it on my fourth finger, just around my wedding ring. What is it? I am wed to the Lord. I am pledged and wed to the Lord, in the Cloud, in the state of I AM.

Amen.

NOVEMBER 22, 1972

Weeks since I have written, and then only a little. But some things have looked up. I have been much healed since my last words. The chiropractor, true to his word, did bring me much improvement in my back and neck during those six weeks. I did, indeed, achieve more mobility of neck, less pain of back. There is still pain, it is true, but reduced. And now, my visit frequency is also reduced, to two times a week, for a few weeks, and then once a week. Soon, I shall resume my Reichian work which I lost and which promised a union with flesh, a breakdown of the armor. I slipped and wrote "amor" instead of "armor." How funny! One letter, deleted from armor, becomes love!

Love, family love. A family meeting the other day. In the struggle with the Judge archetype, with my wife's suffering with our son, my own awareness of how the Judge is behind us, and how the tyrant emerges in all of us. Yet we were all so human in dealing with it. And I saw that as my wife treats our son authoritarianly, so does he treat my daughter, and she reacts with the passive-aggressive manner that he does with my wife! And, I, biggest tyrant of all, am also the most volatile and easiest to deal with, since I, unlike my wife, do not withdraw. My son, like me, can not bear the withdrawal! But we all struggled hard, and it was good. But now my son hangs up a picture of a huge policeman bending down nicely to talk with a little boy, lovingly. Oh, that makes me weep too! How my son seems to need that! My own inner son needs it as well! And yet, my wife and I fear that we can be the policeman, not loving, but just authoritarians...

And, as I write this, my beautiful wife calls. She calls, and I am in the midst of tears. I tell her about how I have read her poems, and how sad I am to hurt the one I love most, and she too, is so loving of me. We talk, of flowers, getting and buying, and the Thanksgiving at our house tomorrow, with relatives and others coming from far places, Israel, Mexico, and of family grouping. Thanksgiving, indeed, the annual family feast at our house. Family love, from the blood and sinews! It is good.

Oh, Lord, I weep once more! There is so much from You in love! There are my family, my friends, so much in love! So much in pain, so much in love. Perhaps the nun is right, we must welcome suffering as a way of growth in love! But Lord, we have done that! We have known crucifixions, is there not a growth of love from love? From gentle tenderness? From passionate union? From understanding...? Another call comes. From the struggling black lady who stood me up so long ago, and only wanted "things." But we will speak again. Understanding there? I must understand. Yes.

But now, Lord, I want to turn to the dream. Begin, as always, with the dream. Begin with a message from God. Or is it? Did the dying business man, having dreams, feel them as messages from God? His dreams portrayed death as an initiation, a mere change in identity. But not all dreams are sent by God, just as the ancients thought. Some are mere desire and wish-fulfillment as Freud believed. Others are only mirrors of what is happening. Still others are tunings into time and place, like a stellar or astral newspaper. And yet, God speaks therein all the same. So then, let me begin with a dream. For I am a healer, after all, and this book is meant to be one of a healer in search of healing, is it not? So, the dream.

I am speaking to an unknown, paranoid man, trying to help him. He seems to have blond straight hair, not well-kempt, a thin and tight face with strong jaw. He is at once like a Swede and like an American, sometimes young, in his twenties, and sometimes a tie-wearing businessman, in his forties. But he is frightened and, seemingly, paranoid. He tells me about the things that he sees and they terrify him. Others do not see these things. And what are they, I ask? Well, he says...and he grows terribly frightened. "There it is now" he calls out loudly, looking behind me. I instinctively turn around and myself see a kind of transparent screen, some three inches in depth, upon which are appearing a kaleidoscopic run of images, people doing things, flowers, motion, a whole scene of life. I look and see this, and note that this is what the paranoid man is afraid of. I muse that if I see it, too, then he is not paranoid, that it is really there! He is not mad and alone in it. I tell him this and reassure him, also saying that I am not sure what this is. Is it the astral level? Is it some mutually experienced fantasy? Yet it does seem quite concretely real all right. The man is reassured. And now he seems to fade away as I look myself at this dimension of existence in the midst of ordinary existence. Now, as I look, I see a kind of frightening figure emerge from this dimension. I can not see his head, but he is a large man in a suit who is coming out of the dimension in a threatening, aggressive way. I grow frightened, just as the paranoid man did. I notice that he comes toward me as I inhale and that he recedes as I exhale. The control of it has to do with the breath and breathing. Frightened, I try to do a Banishing Ritual from magic, but do not remember it. I try and make a magical sign of the cross, but fumble with it. I awaken in fear. End of dream.

Now resistance comes to me. A heaviness. I do not want to write. I am afraid again? Want to lie down and sleep. Perhaps to see this dimension again. Do I want to write it as an active fantasy? The old way of introversion? There are letters waiting to be written. Want to run. Sleep, retreat. Help! Help! Shudder. Wait. Write a letter. Now, pain and needing to defecate. Fear centers operating. Sleep. Lower centers. Yawn. Do nothing. All voices. I am paranoid like my dream patient. Taking over the illness. Yes. What then, Lord...? Sleep, a few minutes.

I sleep, awaken. No working on this dream, yet. Letters first.

NOVEMBER 29, 1972

I sit in my office and hear a terrible racket of a cement-making machine outside. Constructing that huge building next door, the racket has come and gone, but this terrible machine, now in its third day, is absolutely sickening. Last night, I was exhausted, but it took a patient to tell me why. I had been hearing that incessant pounding all day long. And now, feeling sick anyway, I sit here in it. I want to work on the two shadows, to begin the "healing of the paranoid man." And I should be writing letters, too. But this racket is terrible. Partly, I want to just go outside and sit in that little corner park and read. And maybe I shall in a little while. Beverly Hills has parks, thank goodness.

But I am sick... Now, blessedly, the machine has stopped its heavy blast and there is only a low hum, followed by occasional jack-hammer blows... Can't stand it, I have to get out of here!

SESSION 48: DECEMBER 6, 1972

Yesterday was the 48th session. So long since I had Reichian therapy. Regardie was very nice to me, and I was aware of my heavy transference with him. Feeling the need for reassurance, I wondered aloud if I would one day have the "full result," the orgastic reflex, and fearing that I might not, because of age and back condition. He was rather agreeing with me at first, which made me feel worse. But then, we had to leave it open. Our work went fairly well, as I breathed and worked on the legs and effecting the lower back. He did notice a considerable change as a result of the chiropractic work. My neck is far better, no need of a pillow now, and he noticed that I was breathing "through" my chest! A real improvement. So, there is still hope.

My thoughts wandered off to my colleagues who are also in Reichian therapy, as I discovered the other night at Laing's lecture. It was surprising and strangely unhappy-making. I guess I cherished the idea that I was "alone" in it, the secret traveller along these dark pathways, just my friend L. and I. But no, others are coming there, too. It is a feeling of loss and a challenge to keep my true individuality, I suppose. Anyway, they are not with the great Regardie!

He also suggested that I begin doing the Middle Pillar meditation every day. He was pleased that L. and I have been doing it together weekly, and he nodded when I reported that we usually get some sort of para-psychological effect, telepathy mostly. It is easier with company. He thought that he might do it with me once, in a session, and that if I continued every day, the energies would rise from within and break up the armor more. That, with his work on the outside, would help a lot. Good, I am ready to do that. But so much: needing to read, write, meditate, have relationships, family, work. Time, time, time. And yet, need to do nothing, too, let time just float!

DECEMBER 13, 1972

Last night, my meditation group looked like it was going to fall apart. M. said that he no longer felt like a member of it, since last year's horrible group weekend. L. felt it not a work place for her anymore. Others were dissatisfied, too. I had planned to discuss it more after the New Year, but S. brought it up anyway. M. really felt bad about new people coming in, we can not deal with Koans and such with such different levels all the time. True. L. can not deal with any of these people in the magic place, with the exception of me, I suppose. T. and L. would like other things, such as Christian prayer. My wife prefers the straight Zen meditation, and the newer people want to share, but offer rather little so far.

So, I awakened with a sadness and further dismemberment. The season is fragmenting, of course. But I feel the process, which began six years ago, the separation for me from the Jungians, still continues: group life and connection continues to be fraught with failure and dissatisfaction. When I said "failure" last night, people jumped on me. Also "end." But it seems to be true to me. All those people "outside" who seem to carry pieces of my "inside," do not get integrated out there. Less, even, do they get integrated inside myself. So, I am left with an uncertainty about how to proceed.

It is difficult to fulfill needs with the limited time that I have. I want to connect with each of the people close to me and with whom I have a spiritual or working relationship, but my efforts to bring this about in a group have been only partially successful. It looks as if there is a centrifugal force afoot now.

I can continue with my individual connections as they are, for example, go back to meditating with Mokusen. That might be nice, indeed. He and I meditating alone, as we used to, and then working on our Ox-Herding book or Koans.

But for whom am I writing this? For myself? For the "record?" A statement of the unhealed healer and where he was at such and such a time? I feel like a foolish Nixon or Johnson, wondering and trying to preserve a place in history… Phone rings. Patient wants to put off starting with me until after the holidays. True, what a fragmenting, sad time. She needs to be with family, loved ones; can not live on one hour a week of therapy with me. Okay.

But what of my needs? I get a little teary. I think that maybe I am really only nourished by my one-to-one relationships! All these group efforts lead to frustration. The only thing working so far is the group that I lead! And there it is good because I am earning my living and getting experience by working at being a leader and myself. No, my needs for earning a living and a work place are already met. In groups outside, there is less personal connection with those I love and less work, too!

Can I really accept that? Maybe, what is called for is to realize the direction things are going, to keep my individual connections and let the groups go.

I call up Mokusen and re-connect. He is beautiful. It "didn't matter." The group wants to continue, so new group-old group, it is all right, he feels. I also told him that I wanted to continue our personal connection, meditating and writing, if we could. So, he wants to come see me next week, "see my face." But he spoke so nicely about letting things happen, letting things grow into "nothing" if they need to. Feeling of detachment necessary, not struggle so much. Yes, it is right. A Buddhist priest speaks!

SESSION 49: DECEMBER 13, 1972

Yesterday was the 49th session. We worked well, especially on the legs again. My chest is more mobile, too. I felt, as I did the last time, that strange pain in the arm and forearm, plus paralysis. Again I was reminded of my broken arm as a child of 10 but, as I informed Regardie, it is the right arm which was broken, whereas I felt the pain and paralysis in the left arm! This happens, he reassured me. There is a memory in the arm, so to speak, but there is also transposition or sympathetic pain as well. The pain left only when I exercised and moved the arm, not when he massaged it.

After the observation period, Regardie made a very distinctive point about doing the Middle Pillar meditation. Ultimately, he said, it becomes automatic. One awakes and finds the energy circulating, the God-names being said. Then it is working properly. After that is achieved, one can begin to work at such powerful things as Kundalini Yoga, but only then. I understood the importance of this Middle Pillar meditation: it really awakens and circulates the energies. He reminded me of Jung's Golden Flower book and suggested that I re-read the part about the Circulation of the Light, which is very instructive in regard to the Middle Pillar.

Regardie also suggested that I use a certain substance, called "Heet," in my meditation. It is used for arthritis, but its function is to put heat at a Center and to make a sensation there as well as the fantasy image. It was exciting to be dealing with these things. I felt that perhaps I was connecting with why L was feeling alone in these things: her energies were already operating more strongly, and her need was to keep them going: to make "real" the flow and reach the Center of *Yesod* on the Tree, having moved up and been on the Path from *Malkuth*.

SESSION 50: DECEMBER 20, 1972

Yesterday, the 50th session, was like the last few: work on legs, trembling occurring: ultimately, the trembling should spread up into thighs and back, resulting in reduction of armoring. That, along with the most important Middle Pillar work, would bring about the desired result. It was as exciting at the end as before. I was thrilled, strangely, at the hope and prospect of both getting more free and doing this magical work also. He responded that he hoped that I would be more touched by Middle Pillar work, rather than by what he said. Very good. "A good man," and the transference is in full swing. Funny, how I am now "hooked," just as my patients are "hooked" on my work. We are both sincere and dedicated, plus also being intelligent and creative. Mild approbation, what? He is with the body, I with the soul, both with the spirit. It is with his spirit, connected with Magic and Qabalah, that I am also apprenticed. Funny, to be both a beginning, slow, dull-witted apprentice and an achieving, respected, professional at the same time! I accept this paradox, as I have so many others. This one, at least, is quite easily resolved: it is easy to be excellent in one area and a beginner in another. So, I felt well.

Now I return to a dream that I had, which is important I think, for where I am. In my dream, I wandered about a meeting of psychologists, not feeling at home at all. At one place, the sea came up, which interested me, but the others just got their feet wet. I thought, either I go in or not at all! Then I heard a lecture, boring. I did not want to hurt my host but I excused myself anyway. I called someone, hoping to make a connection, but that person was involved in her own troubles, and I had to listen patiently and caringly; there was no point in bringing up my own. At last I went back to the Registrar of this group, to at least keep my name in it, even though I felt cut-off and left out. As I did so, I noticed that inside the building, in front of the Registrar, were many former colleagues, and also my Aunt—a closed, self-seeking, stupid woman. Seeing all that together, I said, the hell with it, and took off.

Immediately, in a second dream, I saw A., the beautiful and entrancing girl from my youth. I had been so attracted to her, but she wed another. Here she is, asleep, and very beautiful. Now her hair is grey, but her face is youthful. Shall I wake her, I wonder?

During both dreams, I am also at another level, continuing a kind of discipline or task of the Middle Pillar meditation. I am very slow. I can come down from the higher centers of *Kether* and the throat, but can not get down below the Heart Center. It is so difficult, and I am a long way from the Circulation of the Light altogether.

I awaken from this dream, and it seems clear. The first part shows my frustration and inability to really find my place in the professional world, and my sadness in lack of connection to it. The second, of course, is the old anima who rejected me so long ago, she of the world, the *Anima Mundi*, the Tarot Card of the Saturn Lady. She is old, as am I, but still youthful. Shall I awaken my old needs for fame and fortune, for excitement and life and prestige and adventure in the world? She, this anima, has not been in a dream of mine, I think, for many years. When I was 25, I think. I dreamt, then, that I kicked her downstairs, for she hurt me so! Many women had suffered from me, because of her rejection, too. And now, here she is again, but asleep. Do I awaken this *Anima mundi*, this lower Center creature? This worldly one of the flesh and concreteness? And if I do, do I suffer once again and become disillusioned and deceived, as I have so often?

I take my troubles and uncertainty into the cloud. Shall I share my dilemma with my friends? You, my friends, Scorpio Lad, Mercurius, and Ox, all masculine, are you not? The feminine, the anima, has not been there with you and me in that cloud, all this year. I, who had written poems to the Goddess and was on first-hand terms with the Muses, who is so enamored by and with women, I have spent this whole year of the healing work and the cloud experience without a feminine being at all! Should I wake her and ask her to join us here, my friends?

You, Scorpio Lad, you nod, as does Mercurius, with his smile, and ox, too. Yes, perhaps you, like me, have grown bored with our continual talk and swing about, no worldliness, no outside care to deal with. A silence of the night and inside, clouds. No world. But, if awakened, will she come in? And, is she both the girl and woman of my youth and the *Anima Mundi*? If I awaken her, is it magic, dealing with a living soul? She was so important an anima, and she has been "downstairs" and asleep, indeed, for a whole maturity, for twenty-one years!

I hesitate to awaken her, even here. Do I delude myself again? Do I raise hopes and needs, only to be dashed? My sense is not to do it today. Wait.

But I will pray to this Goddess, who is both woman and genii. I will speak to her asleep, and to what is behind her, the dark and mysterious force of the world, the *Anima Mundi*. Oh, Goddess, oh woman, I long to awaken you and have you engage me, love me and I, you. But I feel the fool, having tried before in other forms. I feel the fool, too, in that our leftover pains—or mine, at least—of the past are here to haunt me. I feel the strain and pain, and I shiver for my beloved wife. Not again an assault on her from me... No, I will stare at you and adore you, and be frightened of you for a season. I will not awaken you. I shall let you awaken of yourself.

DECEMBER 28, 1972

So, then, shall I begin? And, if I do, is it A, as she is in the dream? Or is she *Anima Mundi*, as I surmise? And would it not be best to call her, unpointedly, Anima? I think so.

Yet, I think of her as that girl of long ago whom I loved and shivered to, also. But, let her speak for herself, after all. Yes, I shall risk it now...

A ...? I touch her gently. She opens her eyes and smiles. For a second I see in it the beautiful face of my mother, in her youth, but this fades quickly. She smiles, with high and rounded cheeks. Her blue-green eyes look at me. The image of a Knight's lady fades in and out. Her eyes are bright... I hold her hands... A, is it really you...? She continues to smile, saying nothing. A tear forms in her eye and falls, but she still says nothing. Again my thoughts wander, to other ladies. My inner anima says nothing, so I wander elsewhere for nourishment, ideas, involvement. She says nothing, I think, because I have neglected her.

"Right," the word comes to me, but not from her, for she is still silent. The "Right" comes from an automatic old anima place, which she, in her judgmentalness and cruelty and petulance, would say to me whenever I would mention it. She, in Hera-like grievousness, would always manage to find me at fault. But this old pattern must stop. "A," this anima, does not say "Right": not at all. Nor did she blame me those years ago. She hurt me, but she did not blame me. Even when I told her she must wait for me, she only cried. She said nothing. So, she had something of a heart even then. I must remember that my last encounter with her, in dream, was over twenty-one years ago, and then I screamed at her, "You have ruined my life," and kicked her downstairs. Well, here she is, speechless, through that curse at her, long ago. She who hurt and rejected me, the worldly one whom I rejected also, here she is. Is she silent because I have not appreciated her...? A, is it you? Speak to me, please I beg you... But she speaks not. I must wait.

What words, then, beautiful lady? Shall I, then, tell words to you? Shall I sing to you, tell you stories and poems? Shall I woo you back to me, to love me when you would not...? Perhaps I should just be a story teller and woo this lady of the soul, this Anima Mundi who will not speak to me. Yet, here, in my vision, she looks at me lovingly, she looks at me with a tear in her eye, she seems to think well of me. Perhaps she cannot speak, it is not willful. And perhaps it is true that whatever she says, I will take it amiss. I think that is it. She wants me to speak to *her*, to tell *her*. Somehow, I think that just as a dream had to do with my trying to heal a man of paranoia and saw his own vision, now I may need to speak to the Anima and tell her stories.

And yet, I am uncertain of this... But I think, lady of the World, you are of the world, the World itself. I have been rejected by you and rejected you. How can I woo you? How can I get fame and fortune to smile upon me?

But that will be my tale, will it not? My tale will be that of the poor healer, who longs to get approval and words of love and appreciation from *Anima Mundi*...Oh, I grow somewhat weary with the prospect. I am tired. Where are the words that will please her? Where is the tale to which she will respond? Where is that true soul in me which will produce this, because that is what I need—to be myself and my own soul, and find the world responding... I am tired. I have talked too much, and it is all only propaedeutic. Let me nod.

SESSION 52: JANUARY 18, 1973

Time goes by. Sessions missed, changed, but the Reichian work goes on. I am encouraged by it. Little by little I feel the armor is reducing. Today, for example, as he labored hard upon my thigh adductors, as well as the high chest, the armor moved up. Each time there was a freeing from below, the next level—belly, diaphragm, chest, throat—would appear and feel armored. I am becoming more aware of both the armor and the lack of it. There is itching and twitching of various parts of the body. A freeing is happening, slowly, slowly. So, I think that one day, in one year or two or three, that there will be a dissolution of these rigidities and tightnesses.

The magical work also goes on, slowly. My meditation is improving. I discovered that I could meditate even when I swim, which I do for a quarter-hour in the morning, and for half-hour at the "Y" at mid-day. I continue my usual ritual of "laps," but now I also sub-vocally vibrate the names of God at the centers, and fix upon the Light, both circulating by itself and, later, as a circulation through the body. This addendum to the regular sitting meditation, although not as effective or deep, is at least making this work sink farther into my "sub-conscious," so that automaticity will, in due course, result.

So, on both counts, there is movement, progress. And I grow deeper in my relationships, all of them. I am aware of the flow toward a greater totality of myself in each. The split into this relationship for consciousness, this for intensity, this for nest and tender love, etc., is gradually breaking down—just, perhaps, as my armor is breaking down. I find a need in each to get deeper, not be just one or the other. This is frightening in some ways, and yet the direction is right.

The Book of the Healer, this was meant to be. Well, I am gradually being healed, but...

Is there more to say? Oh, my friends in the cloud, are you there?

I see the cloud swirling. It moves about like a subtle body, airy and wispy, semi-solid, semi-liquid. I see faces through this wispy cloud, not in it. I see the face of Mercurius, smiling yet a little dangerous. I see the large-eyed lad, now a teenager, I think. And I see the dark-eyed face of the bull-ox too, soft and tender. I even see the face of A. there now, doe-eyed and silent. The cloud goes by them, they are solid, but only from the neck up. What does this mean? They abide, are known, but their reality, as totalities, goes beyond the vessel of the cloud, and I do not grasp it yet. Yes, that is the sensible interpretation.

Should I go on with this...? I feel a draft at my ankles, as if a little animal were nibbling at it, and now a cold draft. I lift my sock. Was it a ghost or presence? Who is pulling at me...? It feels like Radha, our cat, or some other little animal. At the feet. *Adonai Ha-aretz*, the earth, the center of *Malkuth* and concrete reality. The animal level, earth, is pulling at me. How to realize it?

Later, I will meditate with L. And then I will have dinner with my wife. I will chat with my children—all very nice. What, then, is gnawing at me from my solitary life? Where is that alone place which also wants to lead into the world and be known? And where, even, is that alone place, just to be alone?

JANUARY 20, 1973

Here is that alone place just to be alone. I am here and need to sense this aloneness. But even as I write, I fear that these typed words, unlike my written words, will be seen by someone. My words when I write in my dream journal are legible only to me! What a blessing! But here, they are typed, and can hurt. Openness is not the only virtue, nor is truth. Sometimes openness and truth and honesty are too painful and destructive and accomplish nothing. But I need not reveal all, even here.

What I want is to get down into the depths, to be alone with myself, to know and heal. All right then. But there is self-deception as well. For example, I am growing to suspect that the shadow of my Mercurius, the mighty Trickster and Clever One, is very slippery and dark. He is intimately connected with the judge and with the projective factor which has been so hurtful to me. But I doubt that he will cooperate with me. I am drawn to the fairy tale, where the hero must approach and save the feminine which is enthralled to the Dark Magician. Let me sink into it.

Mercurius, Lord and Master, Lord of Light, and of Darkness too, I summon you and beseech you. You, Mercurial figure of my soul, please come to me and speak of your nature and your darkness. Tell me of your Being, and how you flow and twist and scheme and...

"I am these, it is true." He speaks these words, but I see him not. He speaks sentences most easily, but will he reveal himself? I see a smile, only. No face, no mouth, only a smile. How can there be a smile without a mouth? But it is so. Now a mouth grows around it and the face appears as it did the other day, as just a large head. Now a large figure, with an Apollo body and rayed head appears. It is more Apollo than Mercury. Yet it is Mercurius, fleet of foot and quick of mind, helmeted and booted, but otherwise naked. Speak my Lord.

"I have spoken. I speak all the time, as you know. There is no trouble nor effort involved, just as you know. You wish to know of tricks? There are no tricks. Only quickness and adroitness. Only movement toward an end."

"But I am sad, Mercurius. In the old days, such conversations would lead somewhere. Now I am sad, because they seem deceptive in themselves. No concreteness...and I drift off.

"Sad it is. You once believed. You once knew the Gods. You once read of us, talked to us. Now we are mere mortals, like you. Unchosen. Like you. Once you were Chosen, no more. Now, not even your Gods are chosen."

"Yes, Chosenness is not so important any more. Now wholeness is. Wholeness in spirit, soul and body. Hence work in magic, in body, in those things."

"Yawn. Mine or yours? Your dreams are less attractive, are they not? Something critical of the new way. Not yet so positive or hopeful as the past? Has old intuitive Mercurius fled the scene and become a mere statue?"

"Yes. I feel sad and a bit dead. Nothing to get at, inside or out. Can see myself sinking down. Just like the young writer I work with. It is always, 'over there.' God is just beyond reach, as is whatever one wants. Yet, I have experienced fulfillment and concreteness and the 'now' as well...

"No more chosen. It is like a death, isn't it? A little death. What is dying? The God man? The Chosen Man? The Creative Man? The Healer Man? All dying?"

"Yes, all dying."

I see now, a picture of a coffin, with a figure lying on top. An Egyptian type of God, Ankh or Horus. Dying. Dead. Only the ordinary man is left...So many years ago there was the youth who flew, like Mercurius. There was the youth whose mind was quick, like Mercurius. Now dead. Now a statue and a pole. No answer within, no answer without. A…God is dead…Not possible. Only old images of God die. What is the new image?

Let us mourn… Meditate.

SESSION 53: JANUARY 24, 1973

The session was a very good one. I feel very definite progress is being made each time. The armor is clearly reducing around the thighs, the abdomen, the chest, and now, even in the neck, as well as forehead. At the end of the session today, I felt my head much heavier, the neck muscles had softened and my head was finally resting itself on the cot, rather than being helped up by the muscles!

There was, of course, lots of screaming and such when he worked on the adductors, but that is necessary, and led to lots of laughter. Yes, laughter. I wanted to kill him sometimes, but the release was in screaming and laughter, at the paradox of it, rather than tears. He also tickled me in certain areas and rubbed, in order to increase the laughter, to help reduction of tension and armor. And it worked. There was trembling and movement and relaxation. It is slow, solid work, and I feel it happening. He also remarked that I was disciplined and stick-to-it in character, from my Taurus, of course.

Then, last night, I had an encounter with an old colleague who had come over to apologize for his lack of support of me years ago and for his own power drive at the time. He said that he had been a child then and unable to do it. I needed and appreciated the acknowledgement, but did not need the apology. He has grown a lot since then, created his own huge "center." He talked about his involvement with women, a recent big relationship, but to live alone if he had to. I laughed with the realization that what he thought was so unique was really a pattern. When I said so, he did not like it, naturally.

SESSION 54: JANUARY 31, 1973

At the session, I was more tense than I had been for a bit. We did Flat-foot Charlie and flopping first, taking some of the tension out, and then worked, as usual, on the thigh muscles. I screamed and shouted, getting some tension out, but I was more fearful and tense myself this time. He also beat me up a lot—more than heretofore—on the chest region, and there was definite relaxation going on. The trembling, this time, really included the buttocks as well as the thighs, and there were even forays up into the belly. There is progress, of course, and I know it. Parallel with the Reichian work, I feel the struggle in me at the level of rage, of the belly and its demands, of not selling out my belly for the sake of the heart connection, as usual. But the living of it—with people, seems to go slowly and painfully. But how and why should I expect it otherwise? I only feel frightened that I should lose what I have gained, or be in some self-destructive activity which undermines what is gained.

SESSION 55: FEBRUARY 7, 1973

As I take up typewriter to write about yesterday's session, I am more involved with the reaction of a patient's mother. I saw the girl with her mother this morning and felt the session went very well. Just now, the girl called and said that her mother broke down when they left, thinking that she was worthless, and then went on to say that I was a phony, that my intensity could not be real, was just a technique. That was painful. I offered to see them again tomorrow, for free, but I think that the daughter just wants to have a good time with her parents on the week-end and will just drop it, including the joint session with her parents. That too, hurts. It is dropped in my lap, taken away, and I get zonked! What a crummy profession! Why do they not work it out with me? This A.M. I did positive work with the lady psychologist, now independent. I get people to a point of spiritual independence and then comes a cut-off from me, too. I am better at stating my need, now, but it seems that I am too much for people after all. What a foolish thing!

The Reichian session was good, as usual. There is more and more falling away of the armoring each time. Now he is working on my chest and shoulders more, though his intent is to work on the abdomen and legs first, to pave the way for the more difficult chest. But I found my chest and shoulders relaxing. It is good.

But what shall I do about this intensity matter?

SESSION 56: FEBRUARY 14, 1973

The intensity matter was not resolved. The daughter, far from just wanting a nice week-end, did not feel up to taking up the challenge with her parents. A later time, perhaps. All right. It is not my intensity alone, of course. Today, I saw another man and woman, husband and wife. He, a tyrant and a playful child, she a moralizer and a slave. Well, I could show these sides to them, as they interacted, but I also had to admit them in myself, of course, particularly the judge and the tyrant. So, there it is, always working, inside and out. My own process, too.

Yesterday's session with Regardie was all right. We spent the first minutes talking about the fact that I fell into depression again on Monday. Well, once again Saturn is sitting hard on Gemini! That old, hard, teacher is pushing me down all right. This continues, it seems, until next August. I also spoke to him about my growing need to work with my hands with patients, Reichianly. He had no time to teach just now, but he gave me the name of his teacher. I called and will try to get into a teaching class with him. Perhaps the answer to this heavy Saturn is to find a positive teacher. I hope so. The old teachers are surely oppressive when I come upon them, whether in the form of the papers in journals, or hearing about them (had another experience this week with that). The old teachers, indeed, are merely weights about one's neck!

But after the discussion, we got down to work, and my chest was tighter than it has been, thanks to the mark of depression. But there was also a curious experience, after a time, of laughter and then crying, brought very closely together. Release in screaming followed by laughing and crying. After the screaming, particularly, there is a moment of near unconsciousness, in which everything surrenders. Breathing and prana resume, the tension does, too. But the yawning grows greater and I make more sounds. As I write this, I yawn again. So, the session was all right.

I must speak of the group of healers which met last week for the first time, and is to meet again tonight. It was surprising a little. Not the mutual discussion and warm place that my old colleague wanted, but more like an encounter group. R. was attacked by D. for being "dead"; I was attacked by W. for being religious. He said it was a "spiel." Foolish of him. D., too, was frightened by my intensity, wants to run away from it. B. is not afraid, but feels me withdraw when I grow angry. It is true, I withdraw my care, connection, and often, my willingness to listen. Perhaps these can change in this group, if it continues. We shall see.

Now, is there anything else to say? Is anyone sitting in my psyche to speak or tell me anything? Is my teacher outside these days...? Yes.

SESSION 57: FEBRUARY 21, 1973

We talked a bit about my training to do Reichian work. I had called his teacher, as Regardie suggested, and the former said that he would start a new group of five people, two hours a week. I thought the fee rather steep and Regardie agreed. He said that the man had become a millionaire some years ago. He said that his only criticism, and that off-the-record, was that he had become both money hungry and compulsive. He was, however, a good therapist. Well, I suggested to Regardie that he start a group of us. His instinct was "no," because he would have to prepare. I said I did not think so, that he could just do technique with a patient and we would learn from that. He agreed to think about it. His own training, he said, was simply from undergoing Reichian therapy himself, from many years of having and doing psychotherapy, and from reading, as well as his training as a chiropractor. That was encouraging to me, especially since I have had all but the last of those qualifications, but I am, of course, not trained in any body work, so would like some, particularly so I won't do damage. Well, we shall see if he agrees to this.

Otherwise the session was good as usual, although I had a lot of rage from earlier things: the Judge was active, inside and out, giving and taking. Regardie showed me that the "exercise" part was of no use, since the opposite was intended (relaxation), but that I could work on the leg-spread exercise, slowly, with good effect. This was generally a therapy when the person doing it on himself was counter-productive!

I did my usual yelling and pounding. I notice that after a particularly hard yelling and pounding, where the pain is being taken out in release of tension, I go blessedly unconscious for a moment and feel totally relaxed. This lasts only a moment however, and we start work right away. It is an experience I would like to have without all the yelling and pain! That will come, he said, after the yawning and such produce the clonisms, the discharge of tension. Slow, but in such a person as I, rigid and with all the horoscopic oppositions, to be expected.

Now, a day later, I am down, as I so often am. Up and down. Tension too...not relaxation, for the masseur said my muscles were particularly tight today, even though I was yawning a lot on the way over to the gym. Tight. With Saturn standing upon my Gemini back. Is there someone inside now? Does the cloud bear witness to a voice? And why am I down?

I think of Dion Fortune's remark about herself in her Qabalah book: that she was on bad terms with Saturn until she did the meditation and work from

Malkuth to *Yesod*, number 32, I think. She changed, I think, when she saw, at last, the moon rising on the earth. Saturn became a friend and guide, rather than an enemy. I wish I could find that too. Could baleful Saturn and my Judge be similar or the same? I think so. Let me call upon him.

"Oh Saturn, strong dark figure who sits heavily upon me, Judge who holds tradition and who keeps the structure, the form, look upon me and be benevolent to me, if you will or can."

I close my eyes, yawn. Saturn in the body, perhaps. My eye twitches. Want to sleep, perhaps. Lie down on the floor and just be aware of body.

Did that. Did the leg flop and feel more relaxed. Yawned a lot. Feel better now. More relaxed, as I say. Did not do exercises. Depression has lifted. Funny. Ten or fifteen minutes of relaxation work and depression lifts.

Yes, Saturn is in the body, all right. I work with it, and the depression lifts! Am I fully convinced yet? Is Saturn truly in the body? Just as the Anima was? Is it all coming down to earth in the body? Dimly aware of the truth of this.

The Jung dream, of a few nights ago, supports this conjecture. In it, I visited Jung at his "home," not in Zürich particularly, but his "home." We walked and chatted amicably, but I felt a certain shallowness of our talk, not at the "heart" of things. I say this to Jung and he agrees. He takes my hand, warmly. Then I hug him and feel a physical closeness, a body connection which is very good and deep. Now Jung starts to grow taller, to a height of seven or eight feet. I look up and feel the numinosity of this experience. Jung is, indeed, a "big man." He needs, now, to go off. He is tired. All through this was the feeling that I was visiting Jung just before he was to die. Now he is going upstairs, holding his small cane. His servant appears, a nondescript man. The servant says that I, and others who have known Jung (and now there seem to be many of them, there in spirit or in subtle body) should not make a fuss about it, keep cool about it. At first I listen to this, thinking that perhaps Jung would want it that way, but then I object and speak for all of us who have known Jung and insist that we must be true to the depth of our connection and what we experienced, denying the validity of the servant's wish to keep things quiet. End of dream.

This dream says it. "Jung" is dying, I suppose, as I now go on to Reichian and body work, as well as magic. But Jung is also getting more into the body, it seems. The spirit is coming into the flesh, more and more. With that realization, experience and union, the Jung spirit rises, grows taller, even more numinous. There is humaneness and equality. I am glad that I spoke against the view of the "servant" of Jung, the mere follower and helper that one must keep "cool" and unobtrusive. No, we must speak of our experience of the union of spirit and flesh. There is a dying and rebirthing going on at the same time.

Which brings me to what I felt today at the gym: I work on my body, improve it, fix it as I grow older and closer to death! Paradox: to improve the body vessel all the time, to treat it, help it, make it healthy, and then to die and leave it. All right. Because the "it" is not an "it," it is an "I." It is I who inhabit this vessel. And the vessel is not to be denied and rejected because it is a vessel. Does not the wine need a bottle to contain it? And the body registers all those pains of soul and spirit that were not and could not be transformed, cured and enlightened.

I will trust that this work with the body, this relation to the flesh is truly a death and renewing of the spirit, a dying to an old, only spiritual, path and a beginning of a new, in-the-flesh way. Lord, let my new words be there for You.

SESSION 58: FEBRUARY 28, 1973

I write a day later, as usual; harassed, vulnerable. The treatment was intense, although we talked a long time before. He felt that my armor was so rigid that he had to slow down a bit, no use being brutal about it. For my part, I experienced a great relief when there is work on the thigh muscles. I scream a lot and then lose consciousness for a moment, lose control and am no longer as "vigilant." The vigilance is the armor, he says. Some people go quickly, he said, such as the homosexual patient he has in his early forties who, after only twenty sessions, is already quite loose. We talked, too, about his teaching. He is reluctant, having taught enough, but I reassured him that it would be on regular patient time, would be interesting for him, too. This is in line with what I said about men not being interested in relationship or working on it. I am rather sure that he, too, does not understand me, thinking it only in the context of eros as a general love attitude. Well, the pain is that there is love in men of course, impersonal and unconnected, but the other kind...? Well, it is like my being a woman, in attitude, yet not homosexual!

Right now, as I write this, I feel inarticulate, teary, unable to really express anything. Is this from conflict in the men's group, or from patients hurting me? Or my pain from the woman who not only did not pay her bill, but also hung up on me and spoke of injunctions to stop "harassment," merely because I suggested we work it out?

I am in pain. I want to cry. No, not want to cry, but...inarticulate.

I sink into the cloud. The Scorpio boy is there, looking at me in silence. He looks at me as if to say, "You see how people are? How life is? That is why I stay in this cave, retreat. It is too painful. I just nod and say yes, I agree. This makes me a bit quieter. I sit down beside him and sit close. Not to hold him, no. He doesn't want that. Just close. Silent acceptance.

SESSION 59:MARCH 14, 1973

After skipping a week, I had my 59th session yesterday. Regardie began by telling something very interesting. He had visited a friend in New York, or rather had planned to visit him, but found that the friend had died in an airplane crash three days before. Sad. The friend, 45, had studied Kundalini Yoga extensively in India, and had hit upon a new way of helping people raise the Kundalini, namely, by induction. One simply meditated in his "field" and then raised one's Kundalini! The consequence, said Regardie, was that the raising itself affected the armor of the individual, and caused clonisms, and broke blocks! He felt that a previous work with armoring, in the Reichian fashion, was necessary, but that this was an important finding. Luckily, the dead man had trained others, including Regardie, in the method, so it would continue. My healer said that he was not in the mood just now, but in six months time, perhaps, he would help some of us accomplish such a thing. Here is a real combination of magic and Reichian work! He felt that this would be his true contribution, what he would be remembered for. I agreed. I got very excited about this. I was only half-ready to start a Reichian training, so a six month wait, including magic, seems right. By then, I will have accomplished more in my Reichian work, will be a bit further along in magic, as well. So, very good.

The session was painful, indeed. He worked on my adductors in such a way that I had continuing pain. I even have a black and blue mark on the left side. But it was worth while. At one point, after laughing extensively, as I now do very often, I began a rhythmical lifting of the pelvis in a kind of jerking or intercourse motion. A beginning of the orgastic reflex, perhaps. I also noted a certain fear of the total movement of the pelvis earlier. But there was increasing relaxation of my pelvis and belly, and I became aware of the tension in my chest, face, and head. At one point, I had a headache, which he "cured" by rubbing neck, eye sockets, and top of head. It worked. Headache pain vanished, but tension remained! So, I am making progress, and am hopeful.

Work on the relationships continues effectively, as well as the "therapists" group. But I have less and less need to write about these things. I am only reporting now. So, I will continue to "report" or write when I really feel like it.

SESSION 60: MARCH 21, 1973

Page 300 and session 60, a high mark. But not really. The session was much as usual. The chiropractor had previously found that there had been much progress in a month: my back and neck were both softer and looser. The work was stressful, with perhaps somewhat less pain and "unconsciousness" than last week. At the end, I felt a lot of hunger and a need to cry, but I couldn't. The work is going all right. It will take long enough, I know. But Regardie had 200 hours, and I suppose that I, too, will require at least that number.

The therapists group had been rough. O. wanted to kill me, his wife, and himself over the weekend. He also has lots of distorted fantasies of me and his wife being the cause of his depression, or his not being connected with her. The kind of projective stuff which hurts and angers me. How ironic! Where I had taken utmost care, and where she has also for years and years, where there is no basis at all, that is where complaints come! I took it during the session, and even allowed the others to encourage his anger toward me, not defending myself, but a day or so later, my anger came up in spades. Especially after seeing his wife. She too has had enough of "taking care" of him! She loves him, but enough of that stuff, she would just as soon live alone. She seemed strong to me. I am very fortunate to have friends like her and L., as well as my wife. Perhaps O. and I can work it through.

SESSION 61: MARCH 29, 1973

Feeling very good today! Yesterday's session was as good as ever, but nothing special to report. Except that I was chatty with Regardie about a training group with his teacher, too. He reminded me that the later was a moralist, as well as compulsive and money-hungry! We had a laugh about that training group not being the "real" thing, especially since someone as nice and able as J. could already be doing Reichian therapy after 1 1/2 years, without even continuing his own! So, the session was chummy, with intimations of "certain people," guess who, becoming friends with Regardie after therapy is over. Also, about the necessity for training, perhaps six months from now.

I have felt good since Monday night, after the group session with the other therapists. Not that I was nourished so much, but I could express myself better, take in what some were giving, and I could also express my negative views better to O. for example. That, plus the good experience with L. on Tuesday morning, helped a lot! She had also been compulsively hungry all week-end, and she attributed this directly to the night at the psychologists. It shocked her that these men were so armored. Well, the mutual validation with her was very helpful.

But I am writing like an adolescent girl, I think. The reporting, plus enthusiasm, does not convey much except facts and emotion. But I do not mind now. Perhaps one needs to be such an adolescent girl, for the sake of the anima!

SESSION 62: APRIL 4, 1973

I came to the session yesterday, after meditating in the waiting room. That, plus the intense charge from the previous night's regular tri-weekly meditation group, made lots of energies available. I felt the tingling, etc., before I went in.

The session itself was as much as the others, except that he also worked on my back a long while, which he had not done in some time. I screamed and moaned. He made much of my trying to pound the couch and going through pain. I tried and succeeded, particularly when I was lying on my belly and could not jump up, move away. I found that I screamed and yelled and then had to breathe, and this helped.

But the main experience was the temporary loss of consciousness that occurred after working on my chest and thighs. This "blessedness" as I called it, was truly a loss of ego. I was still conscious, but in a vague and non-focused way. It was different from other egoless states. Regardie asked me if I experienced this in intercourse, as orgasm, and I replied that I do at times, but not very often. I have experienced something like it, however, in meditation and other introverted times. It is an experience of egolessness, I think, as he says, but of the Self also, in a vague and diffuse form. I have often experienced the Self, of course, as a relationship factor, in active imagination, in I Ching, in dreams, in life in general, but it is in relationship, not as egolessness. This egolessness is experienced as blessedness, I think. I could not be there all the time, but it is very nice. At that point, too, there is total loss of tension.

The rest of the work was steady, hard, useful. Again, as I have so often done, I laughed a great deal, after the pain and the falling away of some of the tension. This laughter is sometimes deep and profound, carrying within it a sense of paradox. Here I am, allowing myself to be beat up by someone, treasuring it and valuing it, and glad when he stops! How slow the armor is dissolving and how fine it is when it does!

Otherwise, I move slowly in my work, in group experience, too. The healer's group goes along and is good for me, since I am not in control, in charge. I didn't profit as much this week, but it was all right. This coming weekend, I begin a three week-end sensitivity training at Arrowhead. Again, I will not be the "doctor" (more blessedness), and I also hope to get out of my role as husband and father. It is not that I dislike the roles of husband, father, doctor, etc., but I would like to see how I am experienced with strangers just as myself. I hope not to have to spill the beans about it.

SESSION 63: APRIL 12, 1973

I write the day after...tired, wan. It was, as it so often is, an excellent session, in that there was much release of tension, much reduction in armor; but today, I am down and tired. The session itself saw a great deal of laughter on my part, as it had been of late: a kind of paradoxical laugh, a Buddha belly laugh. Regardie said that tears come from there, too. An infant, for example, cries with its whole body and releases tension. But today he particularly worked on my chest. He used a little machine and got my upper chest going with such pain that I almost fainted. But then came that blessed state when the pain ends and there is a moment of egolessness! He also worked on my neck, as if for the first time. Such pain! But it was so important, because during the observation period, I distinctly felt that my neck and head were all hunched over my shoulders and chest. That was the first awareness of what was always there: the reduction of armor made me aware of it! Much to do there, too. So, a good session.

Sadness today, where there was only a little this week. Yesterday, working on the chest almost brought sobs. As if the tears are beneath the laughter, layer upon layer. But today, sadness. Think of relative impotence, of worry over practice. Sink into the cloud. Is it still there? Or gone with my hopes.

I sink. The cloud is tears. I go through it and feel wet. I look for the Scorpio Lad. I see a teenager, dark. It is he, silent. I see the girl of my youth, too, or her image. All is silent these days. All is in the unspeaking body. I feel my body, too. Will meditate later.

APRIL 23, 1973: (AFTER SESSION 64 ON APRIL 18, 1973)

I write some days later, after an enjoyable family trip to Hearst Castle with my family. I had a somewhat heavy heart after the last session. Not only was I beaten up pretty badly by his work with chest and legs, but I had also spoken to Regardie about my current relative impotence. His response was that this is usual with the work.

Last night I asked for a dream for enlightenment about the whole thing. I dreamt that I was working, oh so hard, on my chest, as was an unknown woman, also in treatment. I awakened in deep chest pain. Such tears and agony. The dream answer is "the work," just as it has always been.

SESSION 65: APRIL 25, 1973

After last week's "downer," this week was very "up." I told Regardie about the "downer," with the finding by the chiropractor of a regression, but he was not dismayed. It happens, of course. He was interested in my dream of questioning, in which the answer was of Reichian "work" with me and the unknown woman. He thought that she was the therapist, himself, but I felt that she was in the work within me, the *anima*, not Regardie. My "girlish" moods, I think.

I lose interest in words.

The session was good, but the pain, yet of value! There is definite softening in my neck and gradual change elsewhere. We spoke again about the possible use of LSD at an ending or changing point, when the softness is there, later on. The possible experience of mystical states on the couch is intriguing.

I made lots of "faces" again, and Regardie showed me myself in the mirror. I said, "poor kid," thinking of the pain and fear being shown, but I do not know from what period that "poor kid" came.

Tired now. Sleep, then meditate.

CHAPTER EIGHT

SESSION 66: MAY 2, 1973

I have been in fairly good spirits during this week, having mastered the "encounter" weekend at Arrowhead.

The session was good, but difficult. There was the usual laughter, some tears, but the main change was a period of definite blackout. I lost consciousness altogether for some moments during which, apparently, I did some shaking. "Good," he said, "ultimately you will shake all over!" Fine.

But I was left with a dim feeling of failure, of sorrow, of incapacity. Childhood, childhood, childhood. He had also worked on my back a little and I screamed greatly. He also made a remark about bringing in childhood pictures. The armor is fully formed by puberty, it seems. I recalled a picture from adolescence where I was holding my hands in front of my penis all the time. I had a perpetual erection, I recall, despite daily masturbation. Regardie made some remark about this repressive culture with its horrible morality. Different from last week, I thought, when I experienced him as a moralizer himself. OK

SESSION 67: MAY 9, 1973

I "report" about the session. We worked hard and I felt the usual effects, but this time, more fear. I felt it around the face and in my eyes, and shouted it out. I also felt it close to my testicles, as well as in the upper chest. The session seemed shorter than usual, but it wasn't really. The work is slow, my armor is great. My pain frightens me, as well as the need to overcome it. Yet there is still laughter during the sessions. This time, more laughter, no tears at all. But fear is the new emotion coming in more strongly. Goodness knows where it will lead. "Castration anxiety," he says, matter of factly. That old Freudian cliché will, perhaps, take on great meaning for me in time. All truths are correct in this field, and all only partial.

SESSION 68: MAY 16, 1973

After last week's session, I was irritable and then depressed. Later, I was at home with my wife, pulled weeds, planted and gardened, read, and was with her, including making love in the middle of the day. Beautiful. I always feel better if I am in good connection with her, including love-making. But the next night, going out and seeing films about middle-age crises (Jack Lemmon in "Save the Tiger" and "Pete and Tilly") brought me down. As well as being rather wooden with my parents on Sunday. Depression returned.

The session, however, was very good. Some with less pain, but there was movement, clearly, in the chest—about which Regardie was very pleased. There was also greater flow of energy in the buttocks. At the end of the session, I was much more relaxed and felt a certain peace. Those "blessed" spots, coming usually after the greatest pain and moments of blackout, are best.

At the end, sitting outside in the car, I waited a bit, and enjoyed a certain calm and peace. I even meditated a little and felt the energies flow...

But my dreams of the last couple of days have been on instinct. First one about a sexy anima changing and turning negative, and then last night, about a little animal living on my back, in a nest and eating stuff. Awful, want to get it off!

SESSION 69: MAY 30, 1973

This session, after two weeks, started out badly. I was in a terrible mood. I gave Regardie his book back with some snide comment, which was something like "you think Reichian is the only form of therapy" and also something to the effect that I didn't think that I would ever be able to do it. He didn't bite.

The session though, was good as usual. He worked on my neck a lot, and that produced a scream that was different, a new agony. But all right.

I had my birthday a few days before, even with a party, but I only partly appreciated it. Damn me!

SESSION 70: JUNE 6, 1973

I was in a better mood for this one, and apologized for dumping on Regardie the last time. He tut-tutted, saying that a therapist is for this, a garbage collector. I said that I did not think so; it happens but it does not have to happen that way. But I felt that my real discussion with him about those things would have to be after Reichian therapy was completed. I was uncertain if the Judge-morality was in him or me. He said that my horoscope problems would continue now until the end of the year. Uranus will trine Pisces and bring me my "magical will" and will blow up the Saturn-Judge in Scorpio for me next year. There will be more perturbations, since it will square both Neptune and Jupiter, thus more inner turmoil, but much creativity. And blessedly, Saturn will be a lead box which is blown open by those energies.

He also mentioned that the patient I referred him would be better then, too, ending a forty-year depression. He, a Scorpio, like Regardie, would come into his own "genius."

The session was quite good. The healer worked more on my back with the electric tool, and I got relief from the low back pain. Clearly it is tension, he said. I mentioned about the possibility of seeing an acupuncturist and he said it was fine, if not too expensive.

Well, we'll see. Regardie thinks that the worst of the armor will be dealt with by the end of the year, so that Uranus energies won't blow me apart. That will be three years worth of work by then. It is slow, but happening.

SESSION 71: JUNE 13, 1973

I went to the session after spending several hours with a colleague, B., at the Booksellers' convention, where his new book was being spoken of and where he was interviewed. Came back from the meeting feeling good for my colleague, and somewhat hopeful for myself.

Session was more or less as usual, though I feel he did not push as hard this time. There was somewhat more trembling up from the thighs, and the latter are definitely softer now. Also the blessed blackouts, which Regardie says are anoxia as a result of hyperventilation followed by screaming and no breathing. Anyway, I experience a shaking in it, though he says that only my arms shake. I do tremble though, and consciousness goes. He says that more energy should be flowing up there now. Session was okay. Also okay with my wife, making love and feeling connected, despite my having to tell her about my other dream and the fact of my struggle with sexual energies in my work.

SESSION 72: JUNE 20, 1973

Session was, as usual, good. Nothing special to report. Relaxation greater; slow, slow work.

SESSION 73: JUNE 27, 1973

The session brought out tears in me, for the first time in a long while. There was only a brief "blackout" blessedness, and the tears came only after work on tensions which were not painful. Rather, they emerged only after a time in which I felt I wanted to cry but couldn't. Later they came profusely. The emotional content was a deep longing for my father, a memory of bleak days as a child when he was not around and I was subject to the nagging and what I felt as demands from my mother. But the tears also were connected with the memory of adult life when father was ill, seemingly near death. He then had great dreams of the forest (Astral?) and one of Europe destroyed in the Nazi time and only the lectern for a Torah was left. And my father wept and then there was new life, to rebuild from the youth. I remembered how moved I was by his dream, my need to embrace him, and how he recoiled from my embrace and spoke about my sister. He rejected my love for him. I understand that he was embarrassed, couldn't take it in, but it hurt. And I wept a lot, now, in memory of it. But there was pain, too, from my back being worse than usual, even though the chiropractor said there was improvement, even from one month ago.

Regardie was quite supportive through this, and I was glad that I had brought the pictures of my childhood to him to see my early armor along with the pictures of mother and father. I guess the pictures of me looking at my father lovingly, added to the situation, as well as their loving honeymoon photo.

Once more, I drop the words and try to sink into myself, the Cloud and cave. The big-eyed lad is there like my son, now 14. I think of how my son is suffering and how I am helping him now, where my father could not help me. All right.

SESSION 74: JULY 11, 1973

The session was good. He showed me again how my horoscope is so difficult; that Saturn is really a corker. But it is lifting next month, which should help, and Uranus is coming into things a year from December, which will really change my life! There is a threat to relationships, but a whole new and creative thrust toward magic, toward a real change in the oppressive Saturn. My horoscope, with its Grand Square is very tough, but there will be very good trines, also.

The session was hardly painful. He had me wobble my legs some, rather than the usual exercise, and I was soon feeling the thigh muscle go. He says that lots of work has been done, so that it is fairly easy to get vibration now. I then got a tetany in the arms, which brought about huge relaxation after thrusting. Much relaxation without pain. It is all going fine. One and a half years and I will soon be close to being armor-free!

SESSION 75, 76: JULY 18 AND 25, 1973

There was little to distinguish these two sessions. Quiet work, not much screaming, but much relaxing and getting the back down, the belly loosened. Long, slow work. Back hurts still, but I feel the loosening going on. Slow work, also in group, in my own practice, which now includes more Reichian stuff. But this reportage has become less and less interesting to me.

I have felt the need to do active imagination. Reading Jung's letters shows how central he believed it to be, so I try and coax my patients into it. Perhaps, think I, I should be doing more myself.

Example: the dream in which I should mediate between a black Ambassador from Eritea (body, feeling) and the Israeli Ambassador (thinking, consciousness, intellect, chosenness). The latter hurt the former without knowing it, and I should mend it. Well, I did a bit, in fantasy, and the two strong men embraced each other. Funny how it seems fine for the union among men to be a big hug. But where am I with my active imagination, my dreams and fantasies? What has happened to the cloud, which was so important and full of the boy, now a youth with eyes so transparent that the collective unconscious could be seen in them?

The cloud. In it, I see the smiling face of the African, the Eritrean. He is not Ethiopian, really, I wonder why.

"Because I am between Ethiopia and Israel, like your own African, part black, part Jew." Yes, I can feel that. And the Jew is contented to be your friend, too. "Yes, indeed." But is that all that is in the cloud? There is not much conflict in that, at this time, I think. There is a wholeness in it. Yes.

SESSION 77: AUGUST 1, 1973

This was a good session after a week of bad, bad back pain, so bad that I had to go to the chiropractor. The latter helped, but Regardie did his thing quite well. Not much active manipulation, but much breathing, exercises, etc.

This time, the streamings went up into my chest, a band of several inches. He noted that there was some relaxation in it, too. This was probably at a time when I was having fantasies. I don't have them much on the couch, hardly at all since we started, I think. But today I did, because he had mentioned assuming a "God-form" when he saw me meditating in the waiting room. He suggested Osiris, and I got excited. Is this a way to do the magic?

He also noticed some violent vibrations at one time. That was in connection with the desire that he break into the armor, not just let me breathe and exercise. Anyway, the session went well again.

Now I am thinking about trying to get into the God-form, Osiris, as he suggested. I am attracted, yet frightened. I don't want to be defeated by illusion again. I can read, however, and see what this God-form was like.

SESSION 78: AUGUST 8, 1973

This, the last session before the summer holiday, was similar to others, the exceptions being that my belly was loosened a lot, that Regardie said that he definitely would not teach Reich (I could do it with C. or by experimenting and reading), but would teach some magic to L. and me, individually. So, that was that.

But let me check the cave and cloud. Let me see if all is as it was.

I fall and climb at the same time, into cave and up to cloud. They merge in a cave way up in the sky, on a cloud platform, but it is open to the sun. The cave melts down to make a solid platform. The dark lad is there, eyes open, black, no longer closed in, no longer just cave-like. He smiles and I know that he has moved away from the darkness. He is not in the light, but even enjoying sunlight, although he is still way up and not directly in human life.

He is there. Is the bull? I do not see him. Rather, I see a smiling dog, tongue out, collar on. Happy, fairly tamed. I think maybe it is a bulldog, but no, it is some other kind. Wait, it is a kind of bulldog, but better looking. And the form of Mercury? I see only a statue there, of Hermes-Mercury. He is not there. Nor is the anima of my youth, A. Where are the woman and the God, I ask the boy? He shrugs. "Gone on holiday," the words form noiselessly.

At that moment, the phone rings and a friend calls, needing help with his dreams, marriage, etc., which I give, gladly and well. Trying to bring him down to earth and yet keep his vision! Like me? My vision, up in the sky? Or below earth? But anima and Self (Mercury) already gone on holiday! Okay. My young self, however, safe up there, and moving into air, light, life. This shows in fewer blow-ups, more seeing of what is happening in relationships, able to listen better now, without rages. Good. See you later journal!

SESSION 79 AND 80: SEPTEMBER 12 AND 19, 1973

I came back after the holiday rather a wreck. My back and neck had hurt terribly. My body got rigid. It was bad enough that I went to another "healer," a homeopath, for him to do acupuncture on my poor back. He did, chatted nicely, prescribed a homeopathic remedy. Not much help so far, but I will go back a little. No great deal and no rejection either.

But the 79th session helped a good deal. Regardie worked me over from below upwards and I relaxed a lot. The 80th session, I was quite rigid again, and we talked about it. Apparently, it was both the worry about finding a new office, starting fresh in Reichian work (as therapist) as well, and, importantly, being rejected for articles I wrote, as well as routine home things, such as tonsils of my son, etc.

I look at what I wrote before holiday. I was in better shape then. I have to breathe from my chest. Rigid, need to loosen it. I don't want to write anymore! Defeated. Nothing to say!

Lord, you who made me want to speak, now have shown me that I have nothing to say! Is God dead? Is my image gone?

I turn away, even from fantasy.

SESSION 81: SEPTEMBER 26, 1973

My quick glance at the previous session's notes shows that my mood is substantially the same today. I have more hope with Reichian work (last session made me feel good), there is a future for me doing Reichian training and therapy, the new office with L. is in the offing, but also despair.

Where am I? Can not speak much. Who was that Lord who made me do all these things and took away the fruits of victory or work? Who was it that made me do things which hurt my wife, and then punished me for it? I know. The same Saturn who kept me rigid. One Lord or two? The Lord giveth and taketh away.

My neck hurts. My back hurts. My soul hurts. Oh, my God, where are You? You, God of the Jews, who did not answer them for two thousand years and then answered in both terrible blood and terrible joy, where are you for me, an insignificant soul?

So much illusion, so much illusion.

SESSION 82: OCTOBER 3, 1973

I write before my 84th session. The last session was all right. Regardie felt that we should really work hard on the chest, which had regressed. He was concerned about the "blackouts" I undergo when he works on the chest. I yell and pound and then faint partially. For me, I experience a kind of twitching all over my body, like an epileptic fit, a relaxation and a blessed unconsciousness. He says that there is not much twitching really. Rather, it is a loss of blood to the brain, followed by a motoric discharge at the brain level, which feels like muscle action but isn't. He would rather I stay conscious in it. In future, we will do this in short spurts and return to it a lot.

Other things have happened in the interim. After much disturbance and irritation, we have committed ourselves, L. and I, to buy that little house next to Regardie, for our offices. Cheap, a good buy, but certain fears and difficulties. Leaving Beverly Hills, noise, money, and all that; good but chancey.

I want to get deep in myself again. Feel cut off from introversion. I also want to make love or something. Want to feel good. Wife in a bad place, too. I feel oppression in my chest. I sink into that oppression. Mandala, Chakra, Anahata. Flame. Deer or is it a gazelle? Yes, gazelle. Go in. I breathe heavily. Look at my wife's picture. Beautiful body with the deep eyes. So much love there, to and from. And my sensitive daughter. Get book for her, the darling, wonderful girl.

SESSION 83 AND 84: OCTOBER 17, 1973

Session 83 and 84 constituted much work on my chest, with real gains being made. Most notable was in session 84, when Regardie asked me to raise my arms in longing as he worked on the "pointed" area at the lower part of the chest. I did so, with the usual breathing, and asked for the recognition and earthing of my spirit in the world. The pain stayed around my neck and shoulders, however, and he asked me to focus in the lower part. When I did so, I began weeping and praying for the good of Israel, now threatened by the Arabs. I got much more in touch with the kind of prayer which asks for help for specific people or others as groups. I do not normally pray like this—I do not normally pray at all in the usual fashion. But now I did so, and for the first time, I felt Regardie also weeping, or fighting back the tears, I think, (though why fight? I ask myself; he must not have been doing that). In any case, I felt a connection with a "third" between us for the first time and told him so. He neither confirmed nor denied this, but we got into a talk afterwards about earthing the spirit, the *unus mundus*, and further talk about getting into the magic after the therapy is over. It was a good experience.

SESSION 85: OCTOBER 24, 1973

Worked on chest, reduced the apex triangle even more. Got in touch with a great rage also. The energies moved up into my face, and I felt the tension now more in my neck and jaw. Movement.

Good connection with Regardie, who encouraged my Reichian work with patients.

SESSION 86, 1973: OCTOBER 31, 1973

Good work. Much involvement with chest. At one point, Regardie asked me to pray, request. I did so, for others, and began to weep. Before that, asking for myself did not feel right.

SESSION 87: NOVEMBER 7, 1973

Raged, worked well in the session. Chest definitely better. Worked on thighs and pushed against pressure. Rage. Help!

SESSION 88: NOVEMBER 14, 1973

Worked well again, gains kept. I began talking about how to do this work. He shows me areas, talks about seeing the tensions, how to proceed. He also spoke about Reich's monogamy: erectile potency is merely repetitive sex. Orgastic potency is total orgasm which is usually enough once and usually enough with one person, but not necessarily so. I felt relief in the work; new areas of uncovered flow. Into belly and chest.

SESSION 89: NOVEMBER 28, 1973

After a two week period, because of Regardie's Thanksgiving holiday, we resumed. I had been ill in between, with intestinal spasm and some diarrhea, and it showed during the session in sore stomach muscles. The session was okay, my chest is still soft, and the work continues. End of bad retrograde Mars, but still blockages, frustration—in getting the house for practice, etc.

SESSION 90: DECEMBER 5, 1973

Session seems short, easy. Regardie talked about his concern for the crazy lady in the neighboring house we are buying; she had not had her light on for the week since Saturday. I, too, was concerned and called up the owner that evening. He said that she won't answer or do anything.

Dream at night had to do with starting Reichian training, which I do today: fear, incompetence, sex in it, confusion, leading even to a psychiatric interview on me by a social worker! Where am I? Worried about depression coming outside; economy is muddled, doing Reichian work, moving of my office. Want to sink in deep, as in a dream I had where there is a beautiful window at the end of a passage, blue and gorgeous, representing active imagination.

I do sink down. Or up. It is a large, sphere-shaped cave, or as in a ball, floating in the sky, some thousands of feet above the earth. The lad is in it, in his early teens. He is dark, long-limbed and tall now, slim. I visit him in the cave by walking through the wall of it, slipping in. I can do this. As I do, I think of my work with a young patient on phantasy, actively in it with him, even leading, showing him that one can float and fall and not get killed or go mad. It is in the same spirit—at home in this fantasy-magical world. I talk to the inner boy.

"I am lonely," I say, "and confused. The world out-down there is in trouble now, more than usual, and so am I. In a way, I envy your sitting here, safe and out of it."

"I am not safe, only separated. I can see what goes on, can be effected, but I chose not to be involved. It is better for me."

"Yes, better for you, but I have had a dream about my concerns: Reichian therapy, timing, confusion, study."

"I understand."

He is silent now. I sit down and am silent too. I start to do a Middle Pillar meditation, as if words are just more futility. Yet I do want help, I think. Money, worry, Reichian. No, I must just learn about the technique of Reichian therapy and see where the energies lead. This quieting, centering, is helpful... I look at the boy. He is silent.

I go up close and look into his eyes as I once did when he was smaller. Again, I see the deep blue sea and sky, with birds flying above it. It is serene, even though white-caps play on the water and the birds soar. That is where he is. Peaceful, quiet. I do need that. I did not get it yesterday with the reading. I did not get that... I was cold, from weather and fasting. I am cold now. Be quiet.

SESSION 93: JANUARY 9, 1974

I have missed writing about two sessions, have had holiday from Reichian therapy myself for two weeks, and here it is a month since the last entry. I have not done this before. At least a line, a note, something. What does it mean?

True, the time has been hectic, difficult. The house for our practice has still not been available. There has been wind, rain, depression outside; fear, insecurity inside. Anyway, I do not want to use this as a place for reporting stuff, psychic or otherwise.

The holiday resulted in great things in a way: staying at a Cistercian monastery and helping those lady Trappists and myself. Yet, the return shows me stiff in pain. Regardie said on this day that the chest armor was not significantly worsened, but I surely felt and feel the tensions in back and neck. Chiropractic, massage, and the Reichian treatment all help, but still...

Reading the *Journal of Orgonomy* does not add much joy or understanding. God, they are judgmental and rigid, too! I am back in a depressive phase. Yes, Saturn is in my Sun sign again, and will be until April, at which time, as Regardie says, I will feel like coming out of prison!

In between, though, I have done Reichian work on others, including in the class, and successfully. If I go slowly and learn carefully, perhaps I will feel right about it at last.

SESSION 94: JANUARY 16, 1974

I arrive at the session in a state of hurt and anger, but Regardie tells me that the old lady who refuses to move from our new office next to him had died! Not only has she died, but she has been dead for three weeks! She apparently died shortly after being delivered the ultimatum by the owner. Sad, horrible, yet strangely appropriate. No ghosts, I hope. Regardie has offered to do a consecration ritual for the place, which should banish the ghost possibility pretty thoroughly.

The body was discovered by one of the workmen we have hired to do some remodeling. So, we shall, in due time, be safely in the new place. A change time, a transition. Poor woman, could not complete transition either, but died peacefully, I hope. She seems not to have had any relatives or friends. God, the pathos in the world!

SESSION 96: JANUARY 30, 1974

Heavy work with thighs and rough with back. Much pain as finally he is working hard on adductors. Anxiety, he says, has diminished sufficiently for him to work there. In the past, a mere touch would bring reaction. But there is much pain, too, on my lower eye muscles. Leading to tears for the first time in months. OK. We now have our office and need to hurry and get in before Mercury goes retrograde. A huge mess was left including many bottles containing excrement! She seemed to have been even more disturbed than anyone knew.

SESSION 97: FEBRUARY 6, 1974

Session 96 had a big effect. Chiropractor noticed the change in my lower back, softer, as did masseur. Told Regardie and this session was more of same. Really on my way with it. Feels good. Feel his particular style—austere, allowing introversion. This is in contrast to my teacher, also good, but more involving, relating verbally, actively, also softer touch. Regardie is more of a magician, a lone worker. The teacher is more of a lover, involver, seducer. And I? Nothing yet. It is easy, yet most difficult. How will it be when I am really in that new office?

SESSIONS 98 AND 99: FEBRUARY 13, 20, 1974

Ditto. Much work on adductor muscles. More open to it. Receding space. Also seeing patients, now, in Reichian work. Feel alternately on the right track and good, and then a bit of a fraud.

New Office is full of problems, but we will surely be in there soon.

SESSIONS 100 AND 101: FEBRUARY 27 AND MARCH 6, 1974

Continuing with many things. Sessions have been excellent. Deeper work with chest, etc. Connection with Regardie is also deeper. I dreamt that I was his therapist! Compensation, I think, for holding him so high. But my Self says that I, too, can be there. And he supports my work with new people. One man I see had a year with Regardie's therapist! I may see him for both Jungian and Reichian work. I resumed work with S., an early Jungian patient; he is now and early Reichian patient!

SESSION 102: MARCH 13, 1974

In this session, there was clear fibrillation of my chest for the first time. Regardie greeted this with pleasure. Also much work on adductors, which are less apprehensive now. He apologized for his rigidity, last week, in being opposed to Rolfing. I understood, but would have done it anyway, had I really wanted to. A discussion ensued about transference, and about being with one therapist at a time. His was in the more traditional place, which I understand, but don't agree with. I know that he excepted me in it, as "psychologically and spiritually" independent , but it confuses beginners. Maybe. Later, I told him of my dream of working on him, which he felt a good sign, too. I thought it as compensation to my feeling so inadequate as a Reichian. But maybe...Well, I don't feel like "teaching" him just now. Need more teaching and feeding myself in connection with the lower chakras. He is doing it fine on the non-verbal level. And there are his works on magic...

SESSION 124: SEPTEMBER 4, 1974

I write six months after the last entry. Only twenty-two Reichian sessions, but so much has happened. Shortly after my last entry, we moved to the new office and we like it very much.

The Reichian work has gone very well. During the session for which I write, Regardie did very little. I merely breathed and my chest began to fibrillate. Little clonisms began to happen all the hour. He worked some on my belly, and I became aware of the feeling that the chest meant, "doing it by oneself," whereas the belly meant, "I need help." They were in opposition. I felt deeply grateful to Regardie. He's saying that now it is merely a question of time, the organism is cooperating and the healing, cleansing, breaking up of armor has cooperation! It is wonderful. Yet, there is repeated "falling back."

Regardie says that this back and forth, up and down, will happen until Mercurius is finally broken or finds his place in the body. The symbols of broken legs, or wings broken, is one: that is to say, until there is a true stabilization. That happened to him at about age 50, some 17 years ago. So, it is possible, nay, certain. But I do have these extremes of up and down, full and empty.

Now, when I must also prepare a paper for psychology and the occult, I am seemingly unable to really work at it. This morning, I was totally wiped out. Hadn't eaten breakfast, it is true, but felt finished, depleted. I seem deeply cut-off from myself. No introversion, says L., and she is right, of course. So where is my soul?

I return to the cloud. It is soothing even to think of it. But it is high up. The lad? Silent and large-eyed. I begin to breathe heavily. I see myself crawling along a road, dragging myself. I am in tatters, a beggar. My hair is dark, but there is a growth of beard. Then again, this dark-haired, curly-haired, hairy fellow, is not quite me. Yet he is. I see him crawling along dirt roads in India. He is dry and dusty. Is he crippled? No. I help him up. He can walk. He walks, hands out. But he gets nothing. He sits down at the side of the road, head in his hands and weeps. He feels defeated. I sit with him, too, feeling the same...

As I sat, I sank in and down deep, but I could not keep consciousness and so I fell asleep. This has happened before. I awakened with a quivering, a clonism of my legs. Could not sustain it. So, I fell asleep for more than an hour. Don't know where I went. But now, I feel hot and full, from the heavy lunch, which I needed, but it sits there now. I first was with the body, listening to it. Then asleep.

Now, let me try again. I climb to the cloud. But what of the beggar in India, sinking to the lowest place? He is there still, sitting on the side of the road, head in hands. So, I climb or, rather, fly up to the cloud, which is a flat disk, powered with a boat motor. A wooden platform, sailing along, I stand on it, hot. My feet are bare on it and they hurt. I put my shirt down and sit on it. Hot, alone. Apart. I put my head in my lap, bring my knees to my face. It is the same as the Indian beggar below. High, above the clouds, or on the land, apart from men: hot, uncomfortable, begging, or needing, alone. So, alone. I yawn. Sleep again? I long for a cool place. Not Calcutta or exposed to the sun. Cool. In the old cave.

I go down to the cave. It is cool, but a blast of hot air, from outside, keeps me from the coolest part. Again, alone, lonely. My introversion is lonely and alone, but not helping. Cut-off...legs cut-off? No. Cut-off from...? I think of sex. Something. Nothing. Then read, at least.

Did. Mead, Crowley. Nothing.

SESSION 128: OCTOBER 9, 1974

Four more sessions have come since the last entry. Much the same. Have bicycled twenty-two miles in two and half-hours, and think that I could do the distance to L.'s, seventy miles, easily. So...

Where then, are the "clouds," the boy and snake or dog, the old anima? The last cloud showed me battered, a tramp, or cut-off, high or low, begging. How is it now?

I sink down to the cloud, now. My Buddhist friend, Mokusen, calls. Long talk. Pleasant.

Back to the cloud. It seems like an open elevator, now some five feet below the ground. Below the ground, indeed! I get on. It is corrugated iron, has a trap-door type top. I go down on it. I think of our dog, Cleo, and her perennial desire for company. Is my inner dog, bull, there? I am not sure. Only cardboard, not real. So be it. So, I go down on the cloud-elevator, and come to the basement. Only two floors below. A door opens up, like that at my parent's apartment. I am at their place. All right. I go upstairs. I ring the door, at my parents. My mother answers. Surprised to see me. I go in, sit down. How are you, etc. But I want to talk about my childhood. I say that I still have negative feelings about the body smells of other people, particularly. I say that I think that it had to do with my toilet training and wonder where mother was with that, thinking of an incident of my soiled pants thrust in my face. I say that I can understand her irritation. I have felt that with my own children, and most recently, certainly, with our dog. But could she help me heal that place? She seems defensive and helpless. Then she grows arch and seductive, and that terrifies me. At this point, I know that it is not my mother, since she would not do that, but the incestuous character of it is apparent. Love me. Do not find me disgusting, even if I find you disgusting! What a difficult thing to ask!

The seductive mother is there. Perhaps it is she, or my own incestuous longing. Perhaps she was like that underneath. So, I respond. No, I don't think that will help. Neither would being held by you or comforted. I would like to have a human relation with you, mother, for you to understand me. That would help; and for you not to judge me or be so opinionated. But, would that heal my armor? My rejection of body places, smells, fluids? I don't reject my own, I think. Not anymore, anyway. So? But now I see that the sexual seduction is there in me as what comes up to heal the body rejection. I see that in my work with patients, my attraction to women. I sometimes use sexual imagery in trying to heal the rejection of the body. But that is only useful and will work when people are committed to a transformation process. Accept my own body? Self? I do. I certainly work with my own imagery. But not when I look in the mirror and see that chubby old man. Sometimes I see that athletic man, too. But, stuck. Ask the woman-mother: "Why do you think that will help heal the body rejection place?"

"I don't know any other way."

"I see. Neither do I. So be it."

PRIOR TO SESSION 131: OCTOBER 30, 1974

I sit alone. I sink down once again, to the cloud. Or rise to it? Last time, I sank on the elevator and came to my mother. No answer. No answer about love and longing, about the body, about any of it. And then I thought of different kinds of Healer: hungry, mediumistic, proud, failed, body, soul; all types of healer. But where is the cloud?

I see it. High up. On this beautiful day. High up, with sun on it. Good. I zoom up and sit on it. It is smoky, warm, heat—no, there is fog, or something rising. I see myself alone there. No child, no ox or dog, nothing. With a book. What book do I see? Jung? No. Astrology? No. Vision, Golden Dawn? Have a look and see. Read, what strikes the fancy.

For some time, I was reading in Regardie's Golden Dawn book. I read particularly on Skrying and Clairvoyance, and Astral Projection. It is rather like active imagination, plus some special rituals, prayers, and utterances of divine names. Could do it.

I am back on the cloud in fantasy. Reading again in the book. But it is a black one, the cover is black. It seems—by feel, not by vision of a title—that it is my own book, The Tree. It seems that I should be reading and writing my own book, not others. Is that so? I look up to the sun, far above the cloud and feel its warmth. But physically, on the material level, I feel cold. Just so. The visionary world does not seem to penetrate the physical. That is, just my difficulty and trouble in all spheres just now: food, sex, body, smell, etc. Therefore, there is still difficulty. But I cannot seem to bring myself to do the rituals of magic in it. Why? Must I first soften my armor? Must I make the vessel more adequate? Probably so. Yet, I can write if I wish.

But what do I truly wish? To write? To travel about in fantasy? To heat my bones now. All right. Ride my bike? Yes. Pleasure.

Later, I return to cloud and book. I try and see the title more clearly. Doesn't show. Now I climb down from the cloud edge and hang on it, as if it were—and is now—a disc made of metal. It moves. It goes along like a flying saucer. I climb back on and look to see what is happening. I am high up, and the disc is at once a flying carpet as well. But there is not enough "reality" of the astral in it, so I return to my typewriter. Change.

(TWO MONTHS LATER): JANUARY 7, 1975

A New Year. But old conflicts. I am much affected by reading the Seth Material, two books (so far) by Jane Roberts and her spiritual contact, Seth. It affects me since the occult now makes me conflicted about the psychological approach. Are they similar or different? Does one extend the other? Underneath, even as I type this, I feel a certain leadenness, a lack of inspiration, a lack of capacity to express.

Right now, a patient has failed to appear. But I have also given over my lunch period, when I would ride my bike home and swim, to writing and planning. Here I am in the same old rut.

Where is the great creativity which was "promised" me in terms of the horoscope, the appearance of Uranus in Scorpio from Christmas on? Don't see it much.

What does the Self want? This question, a psychological and older one, is different from the occult one, which is, what do I want? Well, I want to be creatively involved, in writing, in advancing my occult capacities, in healing myself. But I don't know how to bring these together. Self, please present something. Yes, I know the last image was one of Mercurius standing in the middle of a large field, facing each direction alternately, and throwing out and retrieving as set of cards with pictures on them, just as a card sharp would flush a deck of cards flamboyantly, spreading them apart with a flourish. That suggested, of course, that one could go in any and all directions, that each direction had its own set of images, but all started from a center. Yes, just take one perhaps. But something stops me from doing that. I am not sure what.

Let me sink into myself and see what the situation-landscape is. I see the face of a smiling man, with a large jaw. Is the jaw a symbol of determination? Will?

I try to look at him more carefully, clearly. The rest is vague, only jaw and mouth are clear.

"Well, who are you," I ask.

"I am what you think I am, of course. Namely, Will and Power."

"I suppose, then, that you would help me, if I asked, to assist in a direction that I would decide to take."

"Of course."

"Of course…I don't know why I am not excited or propelled. Perhaps I fear that further work would only be more illusion."

"Yes, I think that you feel that."

"And what do you feel?"

"Whatever you think I feel."

"That is annoying. Only projection, no dialogue. That is the trouble with the occult. It seems to be only one-way action. A teacher teaches, little dialogue or exchange."

"Yes, that is true…So far."

"And, perhaps, my contribution is to wed the two, the occult with the psychological. But I seem not to know the path."

"Yes, you seem not to."

"Who can help me?"

"You can."

"But how?"

"By deciding for yourself."

"But that is the thing I seem unable to do!"

"Yes."

"This seems like a comedy routine!"

Patient comes now; I have to stop.

Some hours later, after seeing patients, and a walk, I am back with where I was, not knowing which way to go. Each way is a little intriguing. I could, of course, go all at once.

Resistance. First, want to call up my answering service, then to read. To sleep. All right. What does the Self want? Once again. Hey, Will-power man! What would you want? "To serve you." Yes, I heard that. All right. Mercurius man, what do you want? "To serve you!" All right. Then serve me! Help me find the way to go that seems best. Yes, then. What do I want? To go in all directions at once.

Intrusion of a patient, a Japanese man, wrong hour! What confusion. But still, makes me want to continue on my own trip! Good, resent the intrusion!

Patients come and go, but I had a chance to look at the book of St. Ignatius, and it depressed me. I spend time looking over the entire manual. I am doubtful whether, indeed, I can use it. All the contemplations, etc., are all right, but there are so many and the main thing is that I can no longer put myself through a "Catholic" ordeal, I think. It appears to me that I can no longer go through the various systems, religious or spiritual, as I had in the past. Perhaps I have already done that enough. To do it again, even if in a new form (e.g., the

Spiritual Exercises), is no longer numinous or meant. That is a heavy burden. What then? Am I doomed for nothing? No, I could, of course, merely continue with images which do appear, as in Jung's Active Imagination. But, then, where is the new? I seem not to be able to fit into old forms any more. Sad, but not sad. Sad in that there is no movement; not sad in that my soul wants its own freedom, perhaps.

So, then, Self, or Entity, or Higher Self, or whatever that larger totality which knows best where I need to go, please appear and give me a hint as to direction.

I see, again, that jaw and smile. "What do you say, jaw?"

"I say, as before, it is up to you."

"But now, I see that the use of forms does not go. I want to write meaningfully, but it does not...I see my own sadness as a hell, as a trap, as...blockage."

"Well, then, shall one give up?"

"Shall I, oh Jaw, and smile? Shall I?"

"Give up what you want or not. 'Do what thou wilt. That is the whole of the Law.' "

"You say it is, but I do not seem to be able to. I want to use the forms, e.g., Catholic, but I cannot. Something comes up to interfere. No longer suitable or something. So, I cannot 'do what I wilt' I merely wilt! What say you now?"

"I say what I have said."

"No help there. Let me speak to the obstruction!"

I try to visualize the obstruction to doing what I want. What is it like? Feelings of failure, of seeing myself as uncreative, stuck. But what is the image? It is a desert landscape, but the earth is caked mud, with great cracks. Water has been there and is no longer. It is dried out. All right, a dried up place. But, follow the occult method: change it. I call upon the waters to flow. I see the rain coming down and some flowers spring up. I also plant seeds for more flowers and trees. It starts to grow and I am soon in the middle of a rain forest, which is partly like a place in Switzerland I recall, and partly African. But it seems equally ineffective. What, then, do I really want...? I don't know.

I experience frustration, rather than freedom and creativity. Changing it does not seem to change the mood. All right. I do experience my own limits, then. So, Jaw, I feel that. Do you see?

"I do. And I feel sorry for you. It will change, surely."

"Thank you for your concern. I hope so."

SESSION 140: JANUARY 22, 1975

I am writing on the day after the session, which was a quite valuable one for me. I had been despairing a bit again, about my armor, the pain in my neck and back, and thinking that I would never get free of it—this, along with the confusion in the usual places about creativity, the place of darkness in the psyche, the occult, sexuality, hunger, etc., all my usual struggles.

Regardie chatted for a minute, about the fact that I had more or less given up great ambitions during the holiday, enjoyed the momentary things of sun, flowers, friendliness, etc. Following this, at home, came a "downer," so I was again with extremes. Regardie said that ultimately, one comes to have the same attitude toward those extremes that one has toward the little things. "Detachment?" I said, and he agreed.

Then we started to work, after I said that my neck was killing me. He put me on the chiropractic table and worked some there, first massaging, kneading, and trying to adjust the many places in neck and spine which were out of line. He said that they were out, and that it takes a long time to retrain the spine to stay normal after it has been out for so long. Needn't go every month for adjustment, but not a six month gap either. Then he started working in full earnest on those painful places in my neck and shoulders and back, and I really yelled. Then, on the couch, the breathing and work continued, and I got great relief.

The central thing, however, was the experience I had on the couch, of really feeling the Jesus-on-the-Cross in me and my body. I lay there, moving my head from side to side, wanting to stretch, to get rid of the armor, to get rid of being the victim, scapegoat, just as I had, jokingly, earlier called out "Jesus Christ" to a pain, and a "God," to an unendurable pain. I am sick of being the victim of my own armor, of the world too, and of being identified with the crucified God-Man. I feel the God-Man idea as a truth, but I want to get out of the Jesus identification, particularly the crucified. Seth says that Jesus never really allowed himself to be crucified, but let some other nut do it, since he insisted. Well, I wanted to be out of it. And I was, to some degree, but I felt how frantic I was! All my efforts for exercise, getting freed, when what I should have been doing was to relax, breathe more deeply. The very armor of strain keeps me in pain. I have known that, but knowing and being able to change are two different things.

I think, now, that this writing is zero. I breathe deeply and try to get out of this struggle. I feel pain in my belly, now, as well as the pain radiating down my arm.

Let go, go smell the sun and the world.

My last two sessions have been very heavy with the feeling of neck and shoulder armor, along with the deep realization of the "Jesus Within" as a living, breathing, agonizing, hero-victim where even the struggle merely accentuates armor! Such a need to get out of that, yet not lose my religious attitude! Such a need to be fully human, with joy, and not lose creativity, depth, and intensity!

This session was, like the last, much on the chiropractor's bench, adjusting and manipulating, as much as working with armor. All the same, says Regardie. Armor begins from the date of birth, and layer after layer gets added on. Look about, he says, at 40 year-olds and more, are they not rigid, armored, sick, not alive? Yes, indeed. And this armoring process continues, layer upon layer, until death, usually. Whatever else Reich's theory is, his discovery of the technique is genuine. And, Regardie continues, all the other methods of relaxation of tension, such as mental ones, merely get it psychically, there is no reaching the body armor at all! There it is.

And there is all my struggle, too. Now, wanting to be free of armor, wanting to be creative, wanting to integrate the magical with the mystical. That is where it is at: I stretch, want my shoulders back, feel the neck go out so quickly. Yell!

JANUARY 28, 1975

I write now, in my Unhealed Healer's journal, because I feel unhealed, depressed. We had a nice weekend with friends in the country, but last night, on the way back and this morning, I have been depressed once more. Is it their depression hitting me? Perhaps. Here is my friend and former patient, who has worked hard in analysis many years, on her own process, has become herself a very good healer, and is down, depressed, can hardly free herself from a bad situation. And here is her husband, himself a brilliant, able man, knowing everything intellectually, unable to heal himself of depression and depersonalization, despite stints with so many therapists. He shops, goes to one for a time and then leaves, unfulfilled. He is fulfilled more by drugs than anything, it seems, but is equally trapped in his relationship with his wife.

But why am I depressed? Is it the vision of my former patient, still depressed? That of a colleague, depressed? My own depression returns. Of course, it was aggravated by the looking at a journal of psychology, with articles and awards for people I knew as a student. Here I am, out of it. Depressed, too, by the drop in my practice, and even in fear of economic depression. I am concerned that this same fear and depression is self-generated, that it will, as Seth says, bring on the very experience that is feared.

So, shall I call upon the God of Healing? Shall I ask for the cloud people, Mercurius, Lad, and Ox? Or shall I let the depression bring me down and look at what I see. Perhaps it is just the lack of introversion, or the lack of food (haven't eaten in 36 hours, after so much heavy gluttony before). Let us see.

I see a little boy, sitting on a curb. He seems to be a strange little lad and also hearkens to myself at about 8 or 9, serious. "What is it, little boy?" I ask.

"I am just sad," he says, "because life is very sad. There is sunshine, there are flowers, there are dogs, but life is sad. There is loneliness, hunger, failure."

"What has happened to you," I ask, "to make you so sad?"

"Nothing, or not much, to me, really, but I see what I see. I see unhappiness, failure, disappointment. I don't know if life is worth the living."

"I, too, am sad," I tell the boy, but I have nothing to say. I sit down with him on the curb, and am merely silent. Words do not help very much or mean very much right now. What good are words, I say, to myself, yet I also think of him. It is clear that what he says is true. I also believe, a' la' Seth, that the very belief in sadness, darkness, failure, etc., produces this. But my feeling is that even telling the boy this will have no effect. I am demoralized as is he. Better, then, to sit and be with him, at least. He said he was lonely. I don't feel especially lonely so, in that we are different. So, I just sit with him.

As we sit on the curb, in front of the house on Potomac that I lived in from the age of about six to ten, I think that here I am, some forty years later, healer, teacher, married happily and a father, with friends and meaning, and I too, am sad. No fame, like appearing in that prestigious journal, but not even knowing why I am repeatedly sad, since fame is less appealing now. OK Just sit there.

We sit, and my fantasy goes back to my childhood in the flat, when I used to dreamily sit at the piano and pick out sad Arabic, Jewish kinds of melodies, all in a minor key. I was sad then, of course, not sure why. Is this me, then? Why are you sad, son?

"Son?" he says. "Are you my father? I have no father and no mother. Not my real parents, they are up there (pointing to the flat), but I don't mean them. They are OK, as far as parents go, and I think you know, better than I, since you have known them for forty years more, that they are fine, human, but that is not my true, spiritual parent. I have none. I am a spiritual orphan. Nothing to believe in, no way to go."

"I guess, little boy, that is me, now, too. The Gods fall away. Since I was little, I have had different sets, but now... Seems to have..."

I watch the lad. He sits, as I do. Now we are silent. Nothing to say. Nowhere to go. Nothing to believe in, once more, not in healing, or being a healer, not a Jungian or Reichian, or anything. So we both sit, waiting for our Guardian Angel. He came before, but now?

As we sit there on the curb, there appears before us a large figure. He is strong and muscular, has huge wings. But these wings do not look as if they can carry his weight or be used to fly in the air.

"Are you our Guardian Angel?" I ask, just as the boy asked if I was his father.

"I am," he answers, but this does not carry great conviction for me. The little boy has big eyes. I think, well, the child in me, the naive, expectant one, is almost always looking for a new savior, perhaps, or at least some messenger from God who will show the way or give the answer. It is still there now, I can see. For me too, although I am less sanguine about such things these days.

I look again at the Angel and say, "Well, if you are, please save us, or guard us, or help us, anyway, to stop getting so depressed. I am a healer who no longer believes in healing, and here is a lad who has no Guardian Spirit or way."

The Angel seems saddened by what I say. He tells me that, in fact, my perception about his wings was true, he can no longer fly nor soar, and these wings are now just so much wax and heavy weight of the past. He is, in short, an Angel who is no longer an Angel! He, too, is depressed, a failed Angel! He sits down on the other side of me, and I am forced to laugh a little myself. Imagine, first the boy, then the man (me), and now even the Angel of God are all disappointed, frustrated, saddened, and depressed!

I sit there, between them, wondering what can save any of us. Perhaps God Himself. What does God look like these days, I wonder? What has happened to my image of God? What has happened to my image of the Self? Is it still there, or is it depotentiated, too?

I propose to the boy and to the Angel, that we say a prayer to God, to show Himself to us, we who are depressed, downhearted, and no longer able to play (boy), to heal (me), nor to fly in heaven (Angel). But they do not respond. There is more silence. The only difference now, is that there are three of us depressed and defeated. OK, just sit some more. I have the sense that I can not write nor ask any more, but just accept that boy and man, man and Angel, are all defeated, and that we just accept it. All right.

CHAPTER NINE

Last night, I had a dream about healing, which is hard for me to recall. It was something about working from opposite points of view.

Here I am with the Unhealed Healer, all right. I realized that the boy and the Angel are continuations of the Lad and Mercurius of the cloud. I am, indeed, continuing my healing saga, with the same figures. Only the dog was missing in this last work with fantasy, and the feminine. But no matter. That is how it is. I wonder if I can find my way back into my dream of last night, or get at its content? Let me try.

I sit again, with the boy and the Angel, on the curbstone. We have accepted our defeat. Now, I say, I have had a dream about healing, my friends, and I am trying to remember it. In it, I think I am healing someone, or trying very hard, and finding that I can not do so. But that is alright, it seems, because the main thing is to do all that I can, summon all my knowledge, skill and care; the rest is up to the the patient and God. Indeed, if my own inner healer can not do it, then the person's inner healer will have to come in, which is the point anyway, is it not? Are we not, as healers, trying to get the person in touch with his own healing forces? Are we not dedicated to that, knowing that the Healing God is bigger than all of us and resides in each of us, and that our task, as committed healers, is to excite, arouse, create, teach, and effect that condition to happen in our patients? Yes, I say, as I usually answer a rhetorical question with an answer, but at the same moment I am sensing that I am less certain that the work that we do is a healing one at all, but perhaps a teaching, or an unfolding of the path to enlightenment.

But, back to my dream. What was it? Yes, I am healing someone and working hard and not succeeding. But something else happens. There is a healing from somewhere else and this is working. Where is this healing coming from? From the patient? From God? I shrug my shoulders. I look at the Angel and the Boy. They do not know either.

I experience several interruptions, from my mind wandering, from other concerns, from doubts and criticisms, but I return to my place at the curbstone.

I sit, now, with the lad and Fallen Angel, but I sense the warmth of a spring day, the colors and intensity of life, just as I did long ago when I recovered from a sickness, mumps I think, and came out into the Spring sun after two weeks of darkness and weakness in my room. Darkness? Maybe it was measles and I could not read much—care of the eyes and all that. Anyway, I sense the richness and vitality of life. That is healing in itself, and I breathe deeply. I want to walk in the hills. But now, in my actual outdoors, it is winter. There is the winter sun, which is alright, but not that Spring sun.

I think, too, of those days at that other house, when I was five and was alone, lonely and afraid. I was afraid of the probation man or what-do-you-call him, the man who would come and take me to jail if I did not go to school. And why did I not want to go to school? I who was always such a good student and all, I who did well in Kindergarten at three (my mother lied and said I was five). I may have been humiliated, I think. No, that was later, when my drawing of a book (Pilgrim's Progress) was not put up on the blackboard. Only mine and one other was not. I was humiliated as an artist, but I hadn't read that book anyway...

SESSION 141: JANUARY 30, 1975

I write the day after the session. I had less pain than usual at the outset, but experienced more armor in my neck and back afterwards. Next day, L. says my back seems less armored, after years, but I feel as if I need massages and Reichian work every day. My neck still hurts; I move it, twist it, without result.

And yet, during the day, working with psychological aspects of sexuality and aggression with patients, I seem to be all right again. I do not want to write just now, though. Nor do I want to go back to the boy and the Angel, there on the curbstone. Seems all right the way it is...waiting, no savior, no seeking, just quiet and open to the sun, nature, smells, and sounds.

JANUARY 31, 1975

I am restless, hungry, impulsive, after seeing the patient who struggles with overweight. Fantasies of degrading her. Didn't tell her what they were, but did speak of the degradation part and anger, which turned out to be just right. So often, my Healer God sends me just the fantasy which is relevant to where the patient is. This should not be so surprising, since psyche is open to it, can either detect or polarize into the opposites, for example. Not surprising, yet hard to express and formulate. When I do write about it, though, it is usually not fully understood or appreciated by others. Maybe I will need to write another paper on this, sometime, though I think I can not reveal or express all that I feel about what goes on in therapy. Besides, I am moving over to an asymmetrical position, more and more, in the Reichian work, so perhaps my views will change again...

But my own neck hurts; I have hungers, too. How can I be true to what I say and do if I can not achieve healing myself in my own psyche and life? The body continues to demand this.

Where was I? Last time, I was seated with the boy and the Angel on the curbstone. We were depressed, waiting, no savior. Well, then, where are we now? I feel hungry, restless, though I ate too much last night. Now, my thoughts wander, although I am quieter, just by writing these notes. Still. Is everything alright with you guys in there? Boy and Angel? They nod. Seem to be O.K.

FEBRUARY 4, 1975

I had to get another chiropractic adjustment yesterday—the pain in my neck and then in my lower back had gotten just too bad and difficult. Awfully depressing. The treatment helped a lot, both the adjustment and the use of sine-wave and deep heat. Feel better today, though I was in a lot of despair. Will the armor ever melt and leave? Will I ever have the joyful, healing approach?

This is aggravated by an experience with a pupil today who sees me as in senex consciousness. I struggle with that disciplined, materialistic consciousness and need to transcend it. It felt right, but not from him; not loving enough. But we will deal with this some more, no doubt. It feels inflated from him, as if he thinks his consciousness is so wonderful. I can not be sure if this is an accurate assessment or merely his own negative senex, judgmental consciousness. We'll see what happens.

My teaching class at the University (new semester) is very good. But where am I with the Unhealed Healer? Last time, it felt good to write, that stilled the impulsive, hungry, restless state. I am feeling not so restless or impulsive now. Where are the lad and Mercurius?

I see them, still seated at the curbstone... My thoughts go to the letter from a colleague, wanting help for his Healing Center, but I am disappointed that I was not asked by them to give a talk there.

... Interrupted by a young girl patient coming early. Saw her, worked well. Talked about animal consciousness and ended up feeling connected with the issue of working on consciousness (changing thought patterns) as well as body (changing body by exercise). We were on a good frequency, which I told her, yet I also about my doubts of how to work with her: like a "father" guiding, directing (her step-father pays for her sessions, but is not around), or how? This way, I felt fine. I think about my daughter and our place of difficulty, now. But that is easy to remedy!

I am really in a quandary and puzzled. My changeover in consciousness is slow and weird and shaking. I don't know what is right. In the meantime, I worry about practice, money, etc.

I look at the lad and Angel. They seem fairly happy: sitting on the curb, enjoying the sunshine, warmth, even the air. They sniff the air contentedly and enjoy life as it flows. At this moment, I break wind, actually, and I think about my own problem with smells and sniffs—bad smells such as other people's body odors or bad breath. What to do? Well, give 'em a thing for the mouth, as I did with one Reichian patient. And take care of myself. No use punishing myself with it. O.K. Let it be.

...Another call was from a priest I once worked with. He stopped at a certain point, later worked with another colleague for a year, now calls for advice about a person in his parish. Just went on, following his own path, not against me, just seeing his own place. Fine. Can he call me from time to time, consulting? O.K., but I felt hurt the last time. I think, too about my own desire to work with a group of religious. I assented, but...why didn't he call the other therapist? What is my relation with religious people now? Seems to be changing, also.

Where is the Healer? Boy and Angel are sitting and sniffing with pleasure. I? A little tight around chest, connected with the religious and with practice.

SESSION 142: FEBRUARY 5, 1975

I had to go to the chiropractor this week—my neck and shoulders and, finally, lower back, were hurting badly. The adjustment, sine wave and ultrasound helped a lot, but there was a repeat when I got to the session. Regardie worked superbly, as usual, and I was aware of trying to watch his style. Mainly, however, for me, was the intensification of the belly reflex, the orgastic-like response which was accompanied by dry sobs and need to break and scream (break, that is, out of the armor). I yelled a fair amount, throwing out screams and little cries of agony. My legs trembled greatly. Some headway, but, as Regardie said, 40 years of armor building! My, what pain to reduce and get rid of it!

Now, my writing is "reportage" once again, lifeless. I have been feeling confused and in-between. Waiting, waiting, for change. I asked for a healing dream last night. What I got was animals. One was a horse, climbing the outside of a house. A cat was exiting the same house via a man-made, sheep-skin cave, hanging from a window. The message of the dream, I felt, was that animals need two exits always, in case one is blocked. Two ways to go. But the horse, I thought? The horse is just climbing up. That, maybe, is my loyal body energy, devoted, just keeps going one way, whereas the cat is trickier. Anyway, the message seems to validate my "two-sideness," the two of everything that I thought was of the spirit, Mercurius, and here is also assigned to the animal level. Perhaps they are coming together.

And the lad and Angel? They sit, still, on the curbstone, quiet. They look a little sad, rather than waiting or enjoying the breeze and smells. I wonder why they are sad, but they do not answer. I am moved to stroke the boy's head and the Angel's neck. They seem to like this, need it. O.K.

FEBRUARY 6, 1975

I am feeling sad just now. It seems to be my inner Healer who is sad, following the work I did with a patient who is very shy, withdrawn, has had much psychotherapy and also some Reichian therapy. His dreams and fantasies are rich, he makes good films, but he is afraid of people, longs for friendship and love but, in his middle thirties, has still to form a deep love relation or even have sex very much, or to form lasting friendships either (although he does have long term friends living elsewhere). I felt sad for him and for another young man who feels similarly alone and isolated, believing that he is boring to others.

I was reading Roberts, *The Nature of Personal Reality*, however, and noted that her inner guru, Seth, says that feelings follow beliefs—about oneself, the world, etc.—and not the other way around. We create our own reality, he thinks, and the feelings are a consequence of beliefs. I examined my own feeling of sadness, as he suggested, and not in an active imagination a' la' Jung. What I found was the belief that I can not heal others of their depression; I am impotent to do so. And the reason for this is that I can not heal my own depression. I need the Reichian work to do so and this is long, slow, only partly successful. Well, what about the belief? I certainly have not been able to heal my depression following the methods of active imagination or dialogue. Nor by interpretation.

Maybe Seth is right, the difficulty may lie in the belief itself. For example, I ought to be able to heal them, since they pay me. Sounds right to me. Also, how can I heal if I am unable to heal my own condition, which is also right? Well, then, how does one change this belief?

I read more from Seth, but do not have the answer. Maybe he gives it later. My impotence, however, may also mask a sense of deep inner power, like I am the "world's greatest healer." No, I don't believe that. I believe, however, that my worth is not recognized. Maybe it is not of "this time" sufficiently, etc. I can see how all this would lead to sadness. But how does one change the belief? I can help some, and do so, by giving what I have, by my knowledge and connection as well as humanness. I can't help everybody, obviously. Now that is also the truth and, as I write this, I feel immediately better! There! There it is! I come out with a balanced, real belief in my skill and what I do have that is helpful and feel better!

FEBRUARY 10, 1975

Went to a party at Regardie's yesterday evening and drank too much. I got sick in the evening and woke up with a headache and hangover. Horrible. Took aspirin, did Middle Pillar meditation, walked a bit and got rid of it. Felt better.

Continue reading Seth. Shaken still, about belief systems creating reality. When he talks about the impersonal level of beliefs, he sounds more like Jung, as he also does when he talks about animals. I wonder if Roberts has read Jung. But I feel personally so stuck and swamped in food-drink-depression-armor.

My feeling, again, as in the last entry, was of one of powerlessness. I can do nothing, it seems, about my food-drink-depression cycle. Feast-famine; deprivation-gluttony; exaltation-depression. All oral, no doubt, and seemingly unhealable by me. Let's try Seth.

Belief: I am unable to do anything about my excessive feast-famine swing and depression. From whence comes this belief? From repeated struggle with these throughout my life, from continual effort and success to many defeats in it. Beyond my capacity to settle, "once and for all," although I have not been fat, really, since I was about 10, and have been a bit chubby only at the time I was married. Still, it is a struggle to stay within any kind of "ideal" limits and, indeed, any limits at all. No sooner do I accept a limit, when something in me wants to go beyond it.

I can see that I also hold a contrary belief or, better, an ideal: the natural impulses are quite right and are the best thing to follow. Eat when hungry, drink when thirsty; the body has its own wisdom. I can see how this belief would add to the feeling of impotence. Not only can I not control my desires, I really ought not to, from an animal viewpoint!

Furthermore, I hold spiritual viewpoints: it is not right to be fat, it is a sign of gluttony, is unattractive; nor is it right to drink more than a little, as it is a sign of moral weakness, leads to alcoholism.

And, yet again, a dilemma: consciousness is a great blessing and high value (control, restrict, be aware); and unconsciousness is, too (go with flow, naturalness, spontaneity).

Yes, as I have been long aware, there is a conflict in me between these views. This is nothing new. This leads to a further belief: there is a continual struggle in me between the animal and the spiritual, body, and soul. I value both and disvalue both in different proportions at different times. But mine is a psychology of conflict of opposites, of no union in this struggle. I also embrace this as my nature and my horoscope (nothing easy, many gifts but many blockages, too). I have reflected on these beliefs quite a lot.

What then? Give up the belief in struggle? In opposites? Perhaps. Give up the belief in horoscopes also? Feel blocked now. Limited. Sad. Sick. What is this feeling? Helpless and hopeless. I can not do anything more. I have to go to the Self, to God within, for this. The Jungian way is to sink in and have a dialogue with this mood, or seek out the God within for help. This I have done, often. The Sethian way would be, I think, to further examine beliefs, but I am not sure how he would propose to change them. Until I do, let me sink, once again, to my inner place.

I see the lad and Angel, on the curb, and ask them their opinion. The boy seems to say that his needs do not get recognized enough: namely, play, sensual pleasure, joy, abandonment. The Angel says that it is partly his fault, because he has been an instrument of the Lord primarily, and that takes precedence over play, pleasure, and good times. He did, after all, summon me away from pleasure, too. He no longer feels that way, having been defeated himself, a fallen Angel, no less! His wings don't work. And he doesn't know what the Lord wants. Yes, he knows that he is a part of the Lord, and that...enough of thoughts and words. He is stuck, too. And waiting.

Once again, I sit down with them and am helpless like them. I feel this strongly. All I can do is write it and feel it and sit with it. I even wonder if maybe this is not what is meant. Perhaps I am learning to just accept and surrender, which would be a change in the Struggler myth. Here, though, I am surrendering to an impotence in changing negative and uncreative beliefs.

Well, then, let me long for an image or idea of a Self who can, indeed, not only reconcile these opposites of animal and spirit, flesh and soul, but also be kind and loving, creative and gentle with me. Even as I think it, I am aware of an intuition which says that even if I had this within, the outer world still does not cooperate, there is always such a battle with getting what one wants-needs-deserves from outside, also. Not entirely true, I have been able to make a rather good living as a therapist and have had a fair amount of recognition, but not the recognition that I desired.

So, then, where is the Healer-God who can heal me, soften me, enable me to enjoy life like the animals and still be true to the Spirit. Seth says that the body is a living expression of the spirit or soul and not in opposition. Yes, I wish I could feel that. Just now it seems to be true, but my body expresses only the conflict, not the union!

That is why I began this journal, this work with body-armor, and so on, just because the images of union, Self-hood, etc. that I achieved did not manage to reach the animal, body, instinctive level! Here I am, Lord! Here I am!

And here we are, Lord! Here we are! I sit here with my young boy, longing for life and joy, with the Angel, who has given up and been defeated, and myself. We look to you, all three defeated ones, who tried to do Your bidding, gave our health, vigor, humanhood, and Angelhood to your service, your calling, and are not healed. We are defeated and unhappy. We have fulfilled so much of your task, in so many ways. Yet here we are. Help us. Come to us.

I think of the Animal-Man-Healer, as described by Roberts in her book. She merely mentions this as an image from Seth out of the past, when men and animals were on better terms. Men were even healed by animals, by Animal-Men who could do this. I, indeed, would like to see such a one.

An image comes to me readily. I see a figure of a hairy animal-man, a healer, with great compassionate eyes. I see him taking off his animal skin, as if it were a coat. What is revealed is a bald-headed man of some vitality and vigor. But I don't want to be bald, if that is my healer image! He laughs. He says that he is not me, that he is a Healer image, as asked for. Furthermore, he says, I am in rather good shape, actually, referring to me.

Yes, I respond, but I when I drink and eat too much, I get sick and also beat myself unmercifully. He nods and I am reminded that in my dream prior to the "crowning," that I was beaten by two knights with two trees or branches of trees. Am I still being beaten by these trees? Of knowledge of good and evil, perhaps, and the Tree of Life, too? I suppose I still am. The one tree making discriminations and judgments, good and bad; the other Tree is one of the unity of life, in diversity and flow. How long must I still be beaten, I wonder?

Now, I feel even sadder, tired, and a little sicker. The bald-headed healer touches me gently, but he is not kind and soft. He is merely aware. He is tough. He looks armored, actually, and not that free. I wonder if this is not still another idol, another image of a Healer that I should give up and banish. Yes, I do so. Healer, I banish you from me as an image of perfection or ideal. Merely being energetic, physically strong, and in good shape, without kindness, without warmth, and still loaded with armor is not a satisfactory union of animal and spirit, body and soul for me!

The Healer looks at me, puzzled. I am sending him off. He is not used to being banished or rejected. Yet I do, it seems, have the power to send him off, to reject him as an image I would embrace. His power is dependent upon whether I accept him!

There is a possibility of union or reconciliation between what Seth says and my Jungian healing stance; I feel impotent all right, but I can and do have the power to reject images of value! I am not powerless in the acceptance-rejection of images, even though I seem to be unable to change my beliefs! Seth says, "change beliefs," but does not tell how, yet. Jung says, "relate to inner images," and change them that way, by dialogue and accepting their reality. My way, just now: relate to the inner image but I need not accept their authority.

The bald-headed healer seems to shrink up and become like a little ball. I think that this may be all his armor coming down into a piece, but the ball is that of mercury, and I know that my old friend, Mercurius-Hermes is there in the picture. But I thought my Angel was he, defeated.

I look to the Angel, who seems still quiet and defeated, although he seems more fleshy again and animal-like. But just a glimpse. What image then? Of Regardie laughing, armor free? Yes, but that is still a projection of the Healer to the outside, a transference glow. Where is that inside that will do it? Regardie is a good healer, but other things in him are not like me; I need my own Self.

Nothing. I am left with a little ball of mercury. The changeable, evanescent, transitory, Gemini-ruling, God of Mercury, with his pseudonyms of Mercurius, Hermes, is still there. Images are ruled and changed. But I am back to square one. Who is there to help me rule the flesh or unite with it? The old images are dissolved and there are none to take their place. Only changeable Mercurius Himself, the soul-maker, image-bringer. All right then.

We three: child, Angel, and myself, sit looking at the little mound of mercury. Out of it, a flower grows. The flower becomes a tree. The tree branches and moves and combines and becomes a veritably maze of branches, but the twigs are dry and of winter. Now the leaves grow on it and we see a a wall of a tree, as if it were a trained bush, or ivy having grown over a large wall. I am aware that the wall of limitation is of Mercurius Himself. God is the Wall. I remember when the wall once spoke to me, with a mouth. His words were like those of Scripture, firm and commanding.

All is of God and the Self and all is of Mercurius. Wall is, healer is, desire is, blockage is. But, Lord, I reject that, too! Lord, I reject it! Too long have you told me that all is of You, all variety and complexity, all of good and bad, hope and loss of hope, pleasure and pain! Too long! I reject this image now, as not having brought me enough joy, enough fulfillment. I reject it. It is no longer healing! That Nature is all of these is only a burden now. Speak to me, Lord, in a new form, a new voice, one that will reconcile the warring spirit in me, soften the blockages, open the wall!

Now I see a fire come and melt and burn the tree, with its maze of branches. First the leaves are seared, then the branches, and all is melted down until, once again, we three: Boy, Angel, and I, are faced only with Mercury.

Now the Boy pats a dog at his side, and I remember the old Bull, Taurus of my vitality, and how he got reduced at the start of this venture, how he became like a dog. I remember. But now there are Boy and dog, Angel and me, facing the mercury, the little ball. There is cold and there is defeat. And now there is rejection from us. Oh God, or All-That-Is, whether you are my Higher Self, or beyond and greater, there is more that is needed right now. More. Once you summoned me, chose me. Now I summon You. I call upon You, to bring me healing, bring me wholeness, show me the way to joy and union, pleasure and creativity, and deliver me from this dilemma. No longer can I feel Jesus in my muscles and bones and feel happy with it. No longer. The God-Man is ready for a new image of a God-Man: Creator, Enjoyer of Life, vital and alive, ready for healing! We wait, Oh Lord, we wait.

FEBRUARY 12, 1975

It is just before my 143th session and I am in pain. I thought I was going to write about my pain of the other night, when I was in darkness and despair, waking up about 4 o'clock, but I recovered later on by swimming, being in nature. Furthermore, I had a dream last night, in which I was with someone, an English-speaking person, in Germany. He was being complimented on his understanding of German and ability to speak the language. He was now going into a hospital for both treatment and to teach. End of dream.

I understand that I was with my shadow in the land of oppression (depression, despair, trapped, no escape for the Jews, the "chosen ones"), and that now there was understanding of that language and the capacity to be both healed and to teach. I felt positive about that.

But, this afternoon, I was once again deeply hurt by a friend, after spending a couple of hours hearing her pain, her "feelings." But they are attributions, pointing to me! Later, when I spent just two minutes telling about my own pain, she popped right in with her calling my honesty "brutality." Naturally, I blew up at that. It was no help for her to say it was her "feeling," my not having to accept it. That whole psychology, a' la' Fritz Perls—that everyone take care of himself—is what disgusts me. It conflicts with my "mutuality" idea. I ought to know that by now. I should stick to relationships where there is capacity for it. Not H., right now, since she is in continual pain and need, nor L., who is rarely available to me these days. Nor even to my wife with whom I can rarely speak about these matters, nor my male friends.

SESSION 143: FEBRUARY 13, 1975

The session with Regardie was powerful. We talked first about my masochism. He was strong and adamant about stopping this. Good medicine.

The session itself was potent also. I really yelled a lot as he worked on my back and neck. He spoke of my bull, my Taurine ascendant, being imprisoned in the stockade. I merely had to let it exit. I felt the stretches and the angers, rages, need to break out. Growls were heavy, but they also turned to yelps of a sort or meowings of a pussycat.

What about this bull? What about it having gotten smaller and smaller, tamed into a little one, and then even a doggie? Is it there now?

The boy and the Angel are still on the curbstone. No bull there. They shake their heads in response to my non-verbal request as to whether there is a bull there. No. So, I go off to find it.

Soon I find myself in a big, empty field, something like the empty field on Jefferson, during that other period of loneliness and dread in my childhood, before Potomac and "curbstone." There is a stockade, like the one that had horses, that my friend Martin painted. I see the bull inside, but it seems to change back and forth to a horse. Now, it is fully a bull. It is big, powerful, full-shouldered, and fierce. He is foaming a bit, wanting to get out of the stockade, but he is rather menacing and, I think, dangerous.

It would be foolish to let such a creature loose in the streets and am even frightened about going into the stockade myself. I go up close to the fence however. The bull looks at me fiercely, but its eyes go very soft and sad. I reach in and stroke the front of its face. It is soft, like the snout of a dog, and there is also saliva there. His big tongue comes out and licks my hand. He is, indeed, very much like a dog when I am close. When I move back he is fierce, combative, aggressive, snorting, and frightening.

An interesting fact: closeness makes him tame. When I am close with him, he is sad, warm and cuddly. When I am distant, he is fierce and frightening. Dare I go into the stockade? I do. I climb under and through the bars of the stockade and go inside. At first, the bull stands back, paws the ground and is fierce. He looks around and snorts, but he does not attack me. I make special note of his big and powerful shoulders, very muscular. I feel my own shoulders and his are very close in feeling, as if were I to stroke his shoulders, my own would feel it. I do so. I even jump upon the bull's back and squeeze his shoulders, as when I do Reichian therapy. The bull sighs and breathes with pleasure. He raises his head and enjoys this. His shoulders and mine are similar, although I do not feel his pleasure in my own shoulders. I do, however, sense his body, his short hair, his warmth and power.

Now, I start to turn on and feel sexual desire in me and imagine women to fulfill this with. Feeling the bull, of course, is to feel my own sexuality. I get off the bull's back and am now walking around with him, inside the stockade, with a rope through his nostrils. He seems more like a horse now, or a steer. I don't like it. I untie the rope and throw it down. Again, I see the fierce bull. But he comes up and licks me again. Does he want to go out? Seems not. Seems that what he wants is to be close to me! All right.

Now I see the boy and the Angel just outside the corral. They look at me and the bull, interestedly. I invite them in. The bull will not harm them if I am close. They come in. They, too, come and stroke the bull's flanks, back, and snout. He seems to enjoy it. All is peaceful and serene. We three get on the bull's back. He can carry us easily. He walks proudly and gracefully. Now the gate of the stockade opens of itself and the bull walks slowly and majestically out, with the three of us astride his back. We are close, three upon a bull. The boy is in front, then I, and the Angel behind me. The wings of the Angel are quite apparent now. But we sit astride our Bull, as he walks down to the sidewalk. He walks right on to the school grounds, inside the fences there, and we come to the place where I was briefly in kindergarten. As we arrive there, I see a little boy, who was myself at that time. He is intently and seriously working upon a drawing. He is drawing a cowboy. The lad who is with the Angel and me is astonished to see him; as if the latter is different from Boy, as if from a previous time. He, too, is interested: here is himself before he came to Potomac "curbstone." As if he, like me, is also looking at an earlier time in all our one life! The Angel is merely quiet and thoughtful. We watch.

As we watch, we see the boy bring his drawing to the teacher, who makes a face at it. Not very good. The little boy is crestfallen and sad. The teacher sees that he is hurt and is sorry, pats the boy. The latter smiles, but he is clearly covering up the true extent of his feeling demolished. He goes back to his seat, sits down and folds his hands. He is now a "good little boy." He smiles, does not show his pain and hurt. He is just good. The teacher, not at all mean or insensitive, smiles at him warmly. She has no idea that he has put on a mask for her. The class goes on.

Now we see the children doing a little dance: called clap, clap, bow. It goes: "clap, clap, bow" and repeats; then "stamp, stamp, turn around." After this, the children join hands in couples and dance about. The little boy does this very well and feels proud that he is fast and effective. He seems to feel very good again.

But why are we seeing this just now? The boy does not seem so destroyed. Hurt, yes. A temporary, "good boy" mode, but his stamping of his feet so sturdily and with such joy show him that he is not badly injured. What are we seeing?

We are seeing that he is all right. Yes, there was a period when he was frightened, not liking school, but not so injured. The bull was there then, as a calf; warm, appreciative, proud and wanting approval, but not injured. Not a sick child. And we are to know this, so as not to mourn an event which did not, indeed, take place. But then, what about the stuttering child, the frightened child, the child angry at his mother? Well, Boy says, that was later on. He remembers that. So, we leave the school, atop the Bull's back and come to the curbstone and sit. But the bull runs back to the stockade. He prefers it there to city streets. There is grass, nature, a dusty smell, the feel and look of hills. Bulls don't like it too well in cities. Come and see me, he seems to say, when you like; ride on me when you wish, but I do not feel the need to stay in the city, on concrete. O.K., but I know now that he is there, uninjured and all right. Furthermore, I see that Boy is all right, too. His eyes are dark and dreamy, and sometimes fierce, like the bull, but he is all right. If there was a wound there—and there was no doubt, in those years—it seems to have been healed. All right. Peace.

FEBRUARY 20, 1975

I write a few days later, after the 144th session, after a bad Wednesday, after... Feeling down. First, I thought it connected with separation. Now, not so sure. Wondering about healing, others and myself. Sense extremes: good work, and— not bad work, but a sense of not wanting to be a healer at all. Hate taking care of the little kid and animal in everybody. Hate having to attend all the time, hate having to put up with...And why put up? In my own head. Because fear of economic insecurity or disaster. Will—at least feel I will, but won't probably— put up with more shit in order not to lose patients.

Long for healing. Long for end of armor. Long for end of struggle about money, fame, security, senex consciousness. Wish I was "really writing."

In this *144th session*, Regardie even put alcohol and ice on my shoulders, in order to start a trembling going. Didn't work yet, but it will, it will, he assures me. Pain and such in my shoulders now, and neck. Need to throw armor off there.

Yes, I do good work with people—women, men—though have not helped the depressed, isolated ones enough. Though I am there in the pinch. And it is better than the past, when I was wiped out inwardly.

Today I had an extraordinary experience with a Persian woman with whom I had worked, off and on, for some time. She had overcome her situational difficulties and we found ourselves chatting about "unity" and about Jewish/Muslim conflict. I had said something about Muslims not being likely to be friendly to a Jewish person's presence in their holy site (I had been reading about Ka'aba, the holy stone in Mecca), when we both had the idea of going there together. We "flew" there in fantasy, but I was not allowed in. She then sang a famous Sufi song/poem which goes something like this, in translation:

Every door that I knocked on,
      You were the owner
Every place that I went,
      You were the light that lit the abode
In the wine house and in the shrine,
      You are the beloved
My goal, whether I go to Mecca or to where
      there are stone idols, is You
You are everywhere!
The Sufis saw the essence of Your being in
      everyone and everything
I am the madman who goes from house to house,
      searching for You

As she sang this song, we both wept deeply. Needless to say, we were allowed "in." We felt the "unity" You are, Lord, and to which You summon us.

FEBRUARY 21, 1975

Today I have an even greater sense of failure, frustration, and sadness. The Healer that I am goes unrecognized, except in a small way, and I worry about money, security. Perhaps I am, like the article I just read of Jung's, an hysteric, someone subject to extremes of opposites, needy of recognition and status, because of some real inferiority. In my case, it would not be so much an inferiority of feeling, but one of sensation, of outer reality. That seems to be continually the place where I run up against difficulty. All my wild fantasies do not result in fruition.

Here I am, the Unhealed Healer. This morning I was sick from overdrinking and eating last night. But exercises and swim found my back less hurting, my shoulders less sore. The swim and the walk at noon have helped my feeling. Again, nature, sensation in a non-human, non-"worldly" form seem to help. They calm me, make me appreciate what I do have. They reduce my inflation, soften my pain a little.

When walking, I thought again about my "crew" in the inner world: the Boy and the Angel, plus the Bull. No woman is there. Has she vanished into the depths? I think of Jung again, with his diagnosis of the lack of the feminine in the German psyche. And I think of my work with the feminine, oh so much. But now she is gone. Is she, like the girl of my youth, vanished from my world? Is she only outside in relationship with actual women? Is she gone?

But, as I was with the Boy and Angel, who were still sniffing the air and enjoying nature, I found peace. I saw myself holding the boy, now only a small youngster of 8 or so, and I felt his warmth, his need, and our closeness. I was reminded of my own beloved son's childhood, and I started to weep. The tears came easily. I thought of Father and Son redemption. I called out to God and asked for redemption, renewal: some way to leave this long-delayed and long-exiled place of non-acceptance. This need for recognition seems so great. Lord, are you there? Healer God, are you there? Summoned or not, it was once said, God is there. I suppose. There is emptiness, non-achievement, abandonment and lack.

Now I sit between the boy and the Angel, an arm around each of them. I feel their warmth and closeness, and I start to weep again. I sob, wordlessly. The boy on one side, the Angel on the other. I am between a lonely and tender, but eager and creative, child, and an Angel, on the other side, who has lost his wings. No longer an emissary of God, no longer chosen. We sit, the three of us. Just quiet. And I sob now and then.

Does the Angel sigh? Yes. He shrugs his shoulders, which seem heavy and somewhat pained, like my own. It was easier when he could fly and soar. Now he can not, so he just sighs and sits on the curbstone, sniffing the air, feeling the wind and enjoying the smell of dust, flowers, earth. And the boy does, too. Do we need a Healer? It would be almost too easy to summon up a Lady, a Goddess, a replacement of the lost anima, the feminine which seems not to be here. Too easy and contrived. But so would any other Healer be so contrived at this time. There seems to be no inner Healer available, only the outer one of Regardie, warm and true, still hopeful, still banging away at the armor of my body. But, that inner Healer? The one who seems to work on my own patients at least, whether in a Jungian or Reichian fashion. He/she must be there in that. Or is it only my own integrated work of years and not at all a special figure? Feels like that. But it, too, gets nervous when not recognized.

But enough. Still, all that is there are boy and Angel, with the Bull safely in the corral, ready to come out whenever I wish. The boy and Angel are content. Perhaps, this poor old Healer, this poor old sobber, this poor old unrecognized one, is learning just to Be, just to sniff the wind, taste the dust, smell the flowers, just as the creative boy and fallen Angel do.

Alright, my friends, all right. I, too, am a boy, sad but still hopeful, and a fallen angel, no longer an emissary of God. I, too, am just here, learning the way of Being. All right. And tears come once more: tears of failure, defeat.

But now the boy and Angel put their arms on me and pat me. They stroke me and comfort me. It is not so bad, they seem to say, not so bad. One can be ever a child, naive and open, energetic, but easily hurt, and ever a fallen angel, chosen by God and rejected by God, and it is all right. It is alright to just sit and sniff God's earth until He, in His wisdom, decides otherwise.

But now I wonder why the Angel fell. Was he like a devil and full of arrogance and pride? I look at him with my question. He shakes his head sadly. No, that is not the reason he fell. What then? Why did he fall?

Fell to become man, are the words that come. Humanized, I suppose. Perhaps my "chosenness," God-likeness, was, indeed, not human enough. Well, then, all the suffering would make it so. But I have rejected that old image of the God-Man crucified. I am trying to get that masochistic God-image out of my bones and armor. I am trying to be with a creative God and the joyful God!

Yes, the answer comes. I, the ego, need to come to that, but the Angel, himself, has another need, another task. To simply live and be human. Here, with unused wings. All right. Acceptance.

MARCH 3, 1975

Last week, after my body pain and despair returned, I thought about the old conflict with local Jungians. That came up after I had decided to write a letter to von Franz, whom I admire so much, when I heard that she was coming to Los Angeles in the Spring. After that, I had a dream in which there was profound discussion, and I had the idea to work out the whole thing, once again, as a court-room fantasy.

Now, last night, I had a dream of my first analyst, who became my friend, the analyst of my wife, and one who betrayed me, among the others, at the time of the Judgment of the Jungians! I feel particularly weak here. I can not write very well, I feel ill, and without power. As if this whole complex does indeed render me impotent, despairing, and uncreative! These are the "three faces of Marvin" all right! The Despairing Healer, the Uncreative Writer, and the Powerless Magician!

The phone rings and H. cancels the afternoon hour; she, too, is beat up, needs rest. All right, then I have an extra hour and a half to write and work on this. More than enough time. But still, feeling all these wiped out places.

How shall I begin? With Z? With a trial? No, I can't take that, yet. Though, in a way, the impotence needs a higher power, a greater Judge than the one who hurts me. But, perhaps, I should start merely with where I am: sad; powerless, defeated, despairing. Tears are felt but do not flow. Pain still in my neck and back, even though I saw the chiropractor today and he helped a lot. I am close to tears. I think of my father's words yesterday: Life is more suffering than joy. Even my father said that! Even that father of mine who has been a symbol for me of the person who enjoys life, who lets evil and pain roll off his back, who really appreciates what is pleasurable! Even he! And he said, when good things happen, look out, because something dark will be next! My father said that! Hard to believe that he thinks that. So, even his joyful, appreciative attitude to life doesn't hold up altogether. Just like me and my students. When I told them that I don't have it altogether, they had mixed feelings: appreciative of my honesty, but wondering, after somebody like me, after half-a-lifetime, twenty-four years of analysis and work on myself, is still despairing, doesn't have it together, then what? And it is true. I don't blame them.

But, perhaps no one has it together. At least not on a deeper level. No one I know, of course, but whom do I see? Patients, colleagues, friends: all in the field of specialists in suffering! No doubt others, more hedonistic, don't have that. But maybe not. Perhaps no one, as Jung says, escapes pain and suffering. Jung said, I think, that pain and happiness are about equal in mix for most people. Maybe so. I don't know.

But right now, I want to deal with the present pain: the judge, the Jungians... I just thought that Jung might be a good judge for that trial! But I can already hear his Judgment since the Jung in me seems to know all about the whole thing. He says, "Let that whole mob go! Most of them don't know what it means to be an individual. Therefore, they persecute somebody who is! Let them go, Marvin!" That is what he says to me. But I can't seem to let go. Or rather, something of them doesn't let go of me...! Such as Z. and the Judge, internally.

All right. I see Z. there, of my dream, looking as he did: saying that life is mostly suffering.

"Z," I say. "You talk to me and seem to want to reconcile with me, but you seem to forget, or never realized, how much you betrayed me by judging me when you had no right to do it, and even betrayed my wife and your work with her by entering into that judging place and depriving me of my rights, actually."

"I did not judge you wrongly and I had every right. I was on the Board at the time, and we all had the duty to judge you. If you only had the sense to wait, to submit and do what we said. You would have had everything!"

"You still don't understand. You still don't realize that if I had submitted to that unjust group meeting and decision, that the whole spirit would be zero, negative, meaningless. It would have been no longer Jungian psychology or anything. I was ready to dialogue with you, try to help you to see, to hear you also, and to work out some kind of union among us. But all that you and K. and R. could do was point a finger. Pretty horrible. Resulting only in further splitting and further suffering... And still you don't see. Still you hold on to..."

"Jung tells me to let go. Perhaps that is right. But I do not seem to be able to... But you, Z., you do not even listen to me. You want to reconcile, but you do not even hear what I say. I don't see how you can want reconciliation. For what purpose, and how?"

"Just admit you were wrong. That's all."

"How can I admit that? I was wrong, I think, not to fight you more in the Society as a whole. But that band of weak sisters, incompetents, and rigid ones could hardly be expected to hear or act, either. So, even that seems not wrong at this moment."

"But, you still suffer, don't you? If you were promised an end of suffering, would you submit then?"

"Now you sound like a Devil, all right. Sell my soul for a little respite of suffering from the harassment? My God, is that it? Am I like the poor women of the middle ages, being required to admit that they were witches? Must I admit that I was a witch, 'aggressive,' and 'wrong,' so that you will be freed of your own struggle with your own wrongness and witchery? You find it easier to project that on me. But I am no witch. What do I project on you? Judgment? I seem to judge myself enough, for my own betrayal and lying. I do not have a way of forgiving myself, either. I am not guilty of lying much anymore, but I am still caught with Judgment.

"But, what do you want, Z.? What?"

"I still want to reconcile, to be friends."

"Then be my friend, really! Be a friend enough to realize that a friend doesn't judge a friend, doesn't deprive him of his legitimate rights."

"You judge me."

"Yes, after the fact. Must I sit and take everything and be a saint or masochist—the same, perhaps—and still be your friend? What do you think I am made of?"

"Same as me, of shit and flesh and soul and pain."

"All meaningless words... I remember, many years ago, when I had been working with you for only a short time. I thought you were very wonderful. And then I dreamed of you as Devil, as sneering at me, rather than with the warmth and feeling you had. And I thought it was my projection! But it was true! You did carry it well, later on, alright! And my inner devil of self-judgment, brutality towards myself is not much better... I confess, I still can not deal with it, inwardly or outwardly. I do feel impotent."

"Because you can not hurt loved ones, is one reason, yet were unfaithful then."

"Who says that? Is that you, Z.? Or something of myself...? Perhaps all. I can not be as unjust to another as you can. And yet, I have, in a way. I sink down and down. Seem still to be trapped. Best to just lie down and rest for a bit. Pray for something helpful to appear to move this wall-like barrier!"

I nap a bit, but still awake in darkness. Words are something like "surrender," but not to the outer Judge. Surrender rather, the armor, "surrender," as Regardie says.

I get up, not having the stomach to write more. Read, perhaps. I pick up two Regardie books: *My Rosicrucian Adventure*, [now titled *What you should know about the Golden Dawn*, Falcon Press 1989] and *The Art and Meaning of Magic*. In the beginning of the former there is a quote:

> The Voice of my Higher Self said unto me: Let me enter the path of Darkness; peradventure there shall I find the Light.
>
> I am the only being in an abyss of darkness; from an abyss of darkness came I forth ere my birth, from the silence of a primal sleep.
>
> And the Voice of Ages said unto my soul, I am He who formulates in darkness, the light that shineth in darkness, yet the darkness comprehendeth it not.

These words, as a dedication or forward, which he quoted when he was only 31, seem to relate to me, this man of 48 who is also in the darkness. Where is my Higher Self? Let it enter the path of darkness and find the Light! Perhaps this same Higher Self is all there in that darkness. Was it there in my little nap, as the symbol of that 'primal sleep'? And was it that same Voice as 'He who formulates in darkness'? Yes, the dark comprehends not.

All right, Higher Self, you who are above Judges and Devils and Gods and Angels and Witches: Please enter that Darkness. Please speak in that abyss and primal sleep. And let the darkness comprehend You!

"I am that Light," a voice speaks. "I am that Light, but I do not speak just yet. I am there, have faith. But not yet. Not yet. Read, as you will."

"All right, I will read, as you say."

SESSION 146: MARCH 5, 1975

I was down for this session, feeling great body pain. My neck and shoulders were aching, and I was despairing about ever getting rid of the armor. This, even though I had seen the chiropractor on Monday and got some relief.

But Regardie worked well on me, in the session, on both the chiropractor's couch and the regular one. He deftly manipulated the muscles, pushing here and there until the right side, at least, let go. I felt such a contrast between the great tension I felt moments before and the sense of letting go. My shoulders, particularly on the right side, felt great. Regardie was of the opinion that this recurrence, this clamping down of the armor again, although not a regression, and now worse than before, was the system's reaction against the threat of previous sessions, when new breakthroughs were possible. My chest was no worse, but the clamp down was heavy. He showed me how to push back my shoulders during the day and then relax them. This would tend to relax the trapezius. This exercise, along with the hanging from the bar, would help my shoulders. Slow work, but it will come. I agreed, but still despaired of the pace at which I was working.

In my own mind, I thought of my former patient, Hyatt, whom L. and I had referred to Regardie. He had about as many hours as I, but he was getting leg clonisms and belly spasms. Actually, his character had changed; he was now softer and warmer than he had been. He had called the other day and said that he cried for the first time in nine years. Well, he is a good deal younger than I, though his armor, too, was heavy. It will come for us both, I pray.

But, that night I had a dream which took up the same issues at a psychic level. I dreamed of the Jungians. The day residue for that was that I had received a questionnaire put out by some Jungian in Texas. The questionnaire asked whether receptivity to Jungian psychology had increased in the last ten years. It was a rather thin and shallow instrument, and lacked any attention to problems of reliability or validity. I noted this on the questionnaire and also added that I thought that the greatest barrier to increasing acceptance of Jungian psychology was Jungians! A bit snide, of course, but I couldn't help saying it. Then, why did I need to answer it at all? Clearly, I am not free of them. All right, the dream:

I am at a gathering of Jungian analysts, a kind of convention. I do not know any of them, nor do they know me. They all seem rather pale and not too lively. They walk around, each with a button on with a fractionated number, such as 1/2, 1/4, 3/4, etc. I have no such number. Then a man asks me where I am from. I respond that I am from Southern California, the only person, apparently, from that region. He makes some snide remark about the area, much as people in the east do about the west, and Europeans do about Americans: primitive, ugly, without tradition, etc. I respond that much of what is new comes from California, only later to be taken up elsewhere, that whatever else is wrong with the place, it has vitality, and I, myself, have a considerable amount of it. I say this quite firmly, but not aggressively, noting, in my own mind, the lack of vitality in the people around.

Then I am with Regardie. He looks well and alive, but is saying to me that, at the conclusion of Reichian therapy, one has an enormous amount of sexual intensity. When a girl walks in, he demonstrates, one truly feels the huge power of sexual excitement. I look at him and see his energy, but I am rather ambivalent about the value he is presenting. It seems just phallic to me, a place I have been, and not as great a thing in itself as a more related, or romantic or individualized sexuality. End of dream.

The dream seems clear enough, and was even clearer after I talked it over with L. this morning. The Jungians, the representative of the senex, a limiting and hurting position for me, are showing their partial personalities (fractionated numbers, dead appearance). This time, in response to a snide comment, I am able to speak up for myself, instead of being paralyzed and hurt. I speak for both a region and myself. O.K. I stand for vitality and life, as opposed to false standards of tradition and death. But then Regardie, who seems to carry the pleasure principle in my dream (in reality, yesterday, he was very kind, not just phallic), as well as an impersonal eros (which, I think, is fairly true of him), and is even more alive, makes me ambivalent. Once again I am between the extremes: can not seem to leave or separate myself from the one opposite, or embrace the other. They both seem to lack individuality or individual relationship, at this point. My "judge" is certainly not too individual or related, either; witness how my students experienced me "stereotyping" women the other day when I was not consciously intending to. And what it does to me is similar to what the Jungians do, put down my sexuality, my desires, etc. And yet, my powerful "pleasure place," (Regardie), seems also to be one-sided, though more alive and vital than the senex Judge.

What can I do now, with my psyche, to further the process of change? Must I just wait for the change in armor, a product of the long, slow labor of the Reichian therapy? Perhaps that is the truth, that I can do little, really, and that I must allow the fourth function, sensation, to take its own course. Perhaps, even, the 'letting go' of armor. The dream is a 'just so.' But let me see if an active imagination will help at all... No, comes the answer. Imagination, now, belongs to another part of me. Let the healer, "unhealed," go on with this reportage, this waiting for pleasure, this telling of dreams and facts.

But no, another voice says, you should at least get an internal image of what Regardie is carrying so that you can deal with it, and get the projection off of him.

I think of the image, and it changes to a short man, vital, a little ape-like in his arms, curly haired, hairy. I embrace this man and feel his warmth, hairiness. We laugh together. We then toast together, having a glass of wine, to life. But then I think about my excesses with alcohol, too, and wonder if he is to be trusted in this, or do I, in point of fact, need that senex, Saturn, as a factor of limitation, a positive way to avoid the discomfort of fat, unwanted drunkenness, bloat, etc. The Vital Man seems to think not; he is enough. He listens, he seems to say without words, to his needs, his body energies, and knows his limits. Just be aware enough, he seems to believe, of moment to moment sensations, and one will limit naturally. Instinct has its own limits. Yes, I think, I have always wanted to believe this, but I have not been able to achieve it.

I now think of my little band of friends, boy, unflying Angel, and Bull. How can this Vital man join them or infuse them with his energy. Better, how can he infuse them with his sense of instinct, of natural limitation. Then I see him, on the back of the Bull and merging with it. As if he and the Bull are one. Here is another Ape-Man, but one who has natural limits. Perhaps now it is more important for the man to merge more with the animal than the reverse. And yet, this man is more human, differentiated than the bull... Now I see it, this man is bull-like himself, much as my own physique is. Perhaps he can take the place of Bull, or at least, ride him peacefully. We shall see.

And what of the judges, the senex? Is there any place for them? The answer comes that the only place now is for me to be able to speak up, just as I did in the dream.

CHAPTER TEN

MARCH 11, 1975

The answer which has come has been more pain and more despair. I have had to see the chiropractor again, and still pain. Tomorrow I see Regardie, and I have set up several sessions this week with the chiropractor, but still pain, and the despairing that goes with it. Yesterday, with my group of students, I felt better, felt I was working on the Judge issue better, too, but this morning, pain, and a dream which showed me not able to deal with the Judge in the personal connection.

The dream: I am a patient of my first analyst, Z. whom I loved and who betrayed both my wife and me. He seems fairly well and fit, despite the fact that he has been ill, in actuality. He talks on a bit, about himself or his ideas and the session is at an end. He is about to leave and I am aware that I owe him for a session. End of dream.

I awaken with sad feeling, and body pain. Can't seem to free myself of Saturn-Judge, nor truly find the right place. After the last dream, where I relate to the Jungian collective with some sense of my identity and ability to respond, here with Z., I do not respond and am only aware that I owe him. What do I owe him? That he was kind at the outset, that me taught me a lot, that I loved him. But I acknowledged that to him then and since. What then? That I did not pay to work out my relation with those guys? That I did not, for example, agree to wait six months or something, provided they try and work something out with me? I wish I could have said that then, but I did not. Perhaps it would have been senseless or hopeless. And now I think about a forthcoming meeting with von Franz, but before that, I hear my wife saying those guys are not worth it...etc.

I fell asleep for a few minutes and it felt good. Ten minutes of no demand, no pressure, allowing rest, acceptance... Now I see Z. looking at me and saying it is all right, it is fine to rest. He encourages me. The judge lets me be. He can at least recognize my states of physical fatigue and let me rest. That's enough just now. Maybe I'll be ready for a dialogue later.

(Later). A most remarkable synchronistic event has occurred since I wrote!

I have seen Z! Yes, the Judge, my first analyst! I saw him with his wife, at a meeting I attended, and he came up to me during the intermission. When I first saw him, I almost panicked, in the urge to leave. But, once seeing him, I was calm and easily offered my hand to him, as I did to his wife. We chatted briefly, and he said, almost guiltily, that he was getting "his portion"—a kind of Biblical phrase which referred, according to his wife, to what he deserved. That saddened me, since his strokes have left him, they say, much damaged. He did not seem damaged, however, when I spoke to him. And his wife was eager that we somehow resume good feelings once more. I understand it and sympathize. That night, however, and since then, I felt very sad about it. I felt so sorry for him, that he has to see this assault to his consciousness as his "portion" and I am pained that it seems to be attached to guilt. I imagine that he feels this toward me, but I would be glad to free him of this. I did love him very much, after all, and I recall with particular pleasure the years of my youth when I was his analysand. I recall that, plus the visits to his house, more than the friendship of subsequent years. The hurtful judgment of the analysts among whom he belonged seemed dimmer now.

So, that dramatic encounter, so long expected, anticipated and, in the ending of a pain of rejection and judgment, so easily healed or, better, washed away. There it is. We are going to have dinner together, the four of us, soon, perhaps to heal further.

SESSION 152: APRIL 16, 1975

I wept during the session. After considerable work on back and neck, I began the now-familiar belly clonism when I resumed the routine position on my back. After a time, there was great pain in my jaw and neck which, when I bit and grunted and growled, changed into sobs, heaves of the belly and screams of agony. Later on, I found myself moving my head back and forth, my neck twisting and wanting to stretch. The head movements felt like saying "no, no," and I felt myself sinking into a deeper state. It was a repeated attempt at saying no to something, but I did not know what. It was also a sense that my "nos" were of no avail. And then, after some heart-rending screams, I involuntarily put my arms in front of my face, as if I were trying to ward off some blow. There was fear in it, but I did not know of what.

Regardie was clearly of the opinion that this "no" and this warding off of blows was a direct body memory of mother's rage toward me. That, and the experience of her "nervousness," at the time, must have been of great terror and hopelessness for a little chap. The chest tension, he is convinced, my chief area of armoring, is directly related to that. He advised me to re-read Reich on "Expressive Language of the Living," regarding chest armor in this connection. He may be right, and it makes sense, of course, but that was not the content of my fear and "no" at the time. Actually, I felt the "no" more related to saying no to the pain, or to the crucifixion experience of opposites, and in truth, to the experience of the Crowning dream, long ago, where I also said no. I feel that it has a significance deeper than that of mother alone, that of my relation to God and the divine. There is, surely, still emotional residue from that very early period of my life, before age three, before the "hero" emerged, which finds itself non-verbally stuck in my body. I experienced some relief, at any rate, and a diminution of body pain. I think and hope that the worst of the recent flair-up of neck and low back pain are over and that I will gradually emerge out of it.

But now, as I write, a day later, I have fallen once again, into a depressed place. I have glanced at the *Journal of Analytical Psychology* and, as usual, get depressed. How strange it is, to be listed among the twenty or so consulting editors, leaders of Jungian psychology in the world, and to feel so out of it. It is no longer a depression because the psycho-analytic bent of the journal diminishes my appreciation of it, but rather my sense of being out of things and not knowing.

I am reminded of what else I said to Regardie yesterday: that if I ever healed that mother-pain that I might give up being a therapist. It seemed to me to be a profession of limited pleasure, and I mentioned Moody's theory that therapists take up this profession in order to heal the mother. If "mother" is healed within, perhaps one no longer has a need to be a therapist! Regardie said that this was not the first time that a therapist gave up that career as a result of Reichian therapy. But what else could I do to make a living? Write? Hardly! Teach? Perhaps, but not enough income there, or place to do it. I could, perhaps, do therapy with different ground-rules: assert that I was not going to carry the "responsibility"; that since I was going to be my full self, that the patient had to carry his own responsibility for himself, too. But this all seems weak, as I try and recover from the sad experience of reading the *Journal*.

I do feel out of it, depressed, with no "community," no certainty. An old swamp, triggered by the *Journal*. Feel like "cleansing" myself. All right, I do so...think, now, of going for a little walk. Get rid of the depression energy (possible anger) by walking and a little air. Go into it afterwards.

I took a twenty-minute walk, refreshed myself with the clouds, the trees, the spring flowers now blooming, stretched my back and breathed that smog-free air and, indeed, I do feel much better. It is true: the continual searching, struggling, combatting, looking for answers in the spiritual or intellectual world merely brings me down, as it should. It should bring me down into my body, into the truth of my muscles and armored tightness, into the truth of need. So, all that proscription against acting out may be correct or not, I do not know, but I do know that the pressure toward that self-same concreteness, that body-world-matter reality seems right for my soul!

Perhaps I will never know the "truth." Perhaps this "healer"—so benighted as he approaches his fiftieth year, after half his lifetime as a healer—has healed no one, has not even himself been healed, and does not know if others are healed either. Is it a will-o'-the-wisp? Is it merely an American Dream that there is a state of being problem-free in the joyful sense? Can one go forward to the state of Paradise? L. feels, rightly, that the magical world is everyday, that it is a question of viewpoint. One can go in and out of that sacred, symbolic state during the course of the day, experience the pleasure and joy in the path of integration through Well-Being. Well, tonight I shall have dinner with my two Gurus: my wife and L., both of whom are committed to the path of integration through Well-Being. My wife follows that path without a psychological commitment, whereas L. has it. I look forward to hearing them talk, to listening in on the gossip, attuning myself to their way, so that I can learn.

I shall try and be more aware of my own body, to subdue that head-consciousness which drowns out the body-consciousness... A call from an Israeli woman, who tells me that my former Israeli psychologist-patient from that country has given birth to a boy and wants me to know that he is well and fine. That is good news. Life goes on. She was, I remember, a most deep person, and we did a year of profound work. It is as if the answer to the question about healing patients comes to me: it is not just healing but a process of life, of development, of living one's myth and drama. I know that, of course, but when the Judging Healer descends negatively from the space of the spirit world, then I must recall it. Would that I could remember that teleological perspective of Jung, that depression means to drive one down into the unconscious which, for me, at this time, also means the body; out of my "head" (which is also part of the body, after all), out of my thoughts and worries, into movement and sensation. Yes... Shall I look at the state of the Boy and the Angel? Have I time before the next patient arrives? Yes, a start at least.

I see them as before. Seated on the curb. The boy smiles, he cuddles up to the Angel, who is large, muscular, dark, but of warm and passionate mien, like the actor Victor Mature, in a way (what a name! Victor and Mature!), or like myself when I feel good and healthy. The boy cuddles up, the Angel keeps his arm about his shoulders and they both smile. Does the Angel have wings? I can not see. Yes, but he does not use them. The two are silent. I squat there, before them. Do they know about what is happening in my own Reichian therapy? They look puzzled. Do they know about my patients? Again puzzled. They are content in my childhood and in my future, enjoying well-being, warmth, the prospect of nature and civilization on the border. The moment, as in my childhood, when I was healed of an illness of several weeks, and emerged from that darkened room into the glories of the day, sunlight, and smells. There was a beauty in childhood and I must not forget that, as I dwell upon the pains, the armor, the fears, the depression, the illness of soul. These two, now, are not anymore privy to my adult concerns of healing, but they are there, awaiting me. I have only to be with them, in pleasure and warmth, to leave the depression of the mind-expanding, the soul-diminishing, and body-neglecting world.

Next day. I have just had a session with a patient, a male psychologist, which emphasizes the problems of therapy, body, mutual process. I have not often written much, in these pages, about such things, but I feel I want to now. The man had a fine week after our last session. We had talked about his shame in connection with his parents and this week he stood up for himself in all sorts of ways, with his parents, his lover, his patients. He felt high, but also wanted more in his life. As I listened and we worked, I became aware of mixed feelings about him: I liked his soft eyes and his sensitivity, I felt disgusted with the physical aspects of his homosexuality and I had a phantasy of him standing up for me at a party where I had been hurt by a homosexual, bitchy man. I wondered whether I should share these fantasies. I was not sure if they were "mutual process" or merely "dumping" and getting attention for myself. I prepared my patient, himself a capable professional, by telling him these doubts and then I told him my fantasy. He responded by saying, defensively, that my limitations (the feeling about homosexuality and his in particular) would limit the distance I could go with him or take him. That hurt and infuriated me and I slammed my fist down on the table, saying so. I said that when I bring in a part of my own limitation, my own prissiness or child wound, he reacted quite self-centeredly by defending himself and rejecting me. My aim was the totality of our mutual process and here he was rejecting it and me. At that, he burst into tears. This weeping got him in touch with his own rejection of his body, his homosexuality, his own disgust, and he had to defend himself or his whole life would be wiped out. I embraced him and we both deeply connected with each other and the world of self-rejection. As we worked it through, there were many aspects: his mother demanding of him and giving nothing, his father's lack of understanding of him, both of them wanting him to take care of his brother and also themselves. It was a fruitful session and pointed up the value of mutual process. I see that if I ultimately remain a therapist, I will have to establish ground rules (for myself, anyway), that I can/must bring in my reactions, even if from a wound and showing my limitations, and that I am not there only to take care of the patient. Finally, I shall have to have a ground rule against my "responsibility" to be more than human.

SESSION 153

My own coming close to the feared Mother and the back pain and anger was not continued in this session, though Regardie did work for some twenty minutes on my back. I yelled and raved a lot, with all that pain from those strong back muscles which carry so much affect (unlike the weaker muscles in front, except for the chest), and I felt much better and softer there than ever. He remarked that he could now grab hold of those muscles. So, time and patience will do it. I hope,

In my practice, I worked with a man in a Reichian mode who is enormously filled with rage and contempt, for women generally and his mother particularly. I was afraid of him at the beginning of the work (and told him so, which made the work go better, since this was the first time a therapist had been honest with him), and the work has gone marvelously for almost a year. But now, I am put off by his sloppiness and by his smell, sometimes. I sense now, that I am like my mother, hating his dirt as my mother hated my own dirt. And I am afraid of his murderousness, just as I was afraid of what I thought was my mother's. He says that he is alright with me, since I am a man, mostly indifferent, combative, and defending, but sometimes a bit close. Anyway, it looks like the Mother-Son, Body-murder complex hits both of us and we are embroiled in it. But I do not yet choose to tell him my disgust. I think I see his disgust, contempt, and lack of care also (although in other ways he is very caring and considerate). We will, no doubt, have to talk about this. Today, however, I really worked on his back a lot and brought out enormous rage. I was also less afraid of it, after my earlier reflections about the case. So, there I am.

I think, too, of L.'s remarks this morning, about most people, herself included, really being kids, not having grown up much. She said it not judgmentally, but as a fact, and perhaps even positively—she would like, in some ways, to be even younger! In her case, it is her feeling which is at a four year level—cosy, playful, warm, and tea-time. My own child, I see, belongs with my ongoing Healer Fantasy, the eight or nine year old boy sitting on the curb with the Angel.

In between, I have seen a relatively new patient, a young Persian woman who astonishes me, thrills me. She is forthright, clear, and aware, stemming from the Gladiator in her, a spirit who is truly independent, courageous, and alert. She is also a therapist, but still does not have her doctorate—is some months away from it—but is ready to give up being a therapist altogether. She is bored with her patients (young dope addicts who are depressed, spaced, and whiny), does not get anything out of it, does not have her needs met in therapy, will not sell out for the money; indeed, she now doesn't care about anything. She wants to withdraw, except for me (most of the time), but realizes with her head that she should stay on the job for a bit and get her license. Her's has been the Way of the Heart, but now she is leaving it, after a great pain from a rejected love. She does not seem pathological nor rationalizing. I like where she is. I have said so and been more and more myself with her, as I have been with all my patients. But I do worry at times, that I will, as a consequence, have no patients, will leave therapy altogether, myself! But then what? How to live?

But I must return to the boy on the curb. I realized, in my talk with L., that the boy is my own happy boy of eight, with all the needs for a group (gang). I had it to some degree then. He is probably in the therapy too, or anyway, looks for union there. The Angel is that high spirit who functions also. But these words do not convey...so, stop them.

SESSION 163: JULY 16, 1975

It has been some time since I have written in these pages, and today is going to be my 163th session. I have been making slow and steady progress, primarily in the breathing, which is now full and deep. Regardie has been using a device for a few weeks, which massages the back as one lies upon it. A roller effects the lower back and works its way up for several rounds. Then he focuses it upon my two difficult areas—the lower back and the shoulder blades. It seems to work rather well, in that the "grosser tensions" are relieved, as he says, and I build up quite a high in the fifteen or so minutes of deep breathing, Reichian style. I am much less hindered, now, by my neck stiffness or pain, so I am hopeful once more. Asked when he thinks things will improve, since it is now almost four years since I began, Regardie says that from September onward, for six years, I will see big changes in myself. The passing of Uranus into Scorpio, which happened briefly from last December until February, will again take place in September and remain for six years. This will see great changes in me, particularly in the influx of creative energy. Presumably, this too will help break down the armor. That is exciting.

Also exciting was my experiment yesterday. I lay down, in the middle of the day, fatigued, ill-humored. I did Reichian breathing for some ten or fifteen minutes, and thought to do a Middle Pillar Meditation along with it. This resulted in an enormous increase in energy, a kind of high on my own oxygen intake—the kind of trembling and circulation of energy, concretely, that happens when I am midway through a Reichian session! An exciting feeling. I plan to meditate regularly in this fashion, combining breathing and Middle Pillar, and see what happens.

I have neglected to mention two important events which have taken place during this time. The first one was rather sad, in some ways, but brought to an end my grievances toward my first analyst, the Judge who had betrayed me. As promised, my wife and I went to their house for dinner and I was reminded of my magical experience there, so many years ago, when I was just a new graduate student of twenty-two and went to his house to hear about Jungian psychology. He told me a dream, which was a cross between a fairy tale and a personal drama, and I was totally entranced, resolving to having analysis with him when I could afford it. I did so, two years later, when I became a teaching assistant at the University. What a wonderful time that was! And how sad it was now, to see him wiped out by age! He seemed to hardly remember the past and we all gently related to him. His wife was gracious and I appreciated her tenderness toward him, but wished that she, at least, could make some gesture of understanding the destructiveness of what he did to me and my wife also. She did not, but perhaps I expect too much. I came away freed of the "Judge" and my own rage, I think, and filled with the sadness of seeing a good man brought down, one who had surely pursued the Self and the unconscious as best he could. My warmth toward him was rekindled; I only wish that we could truly talk and share those events, in order to heal the "Judge" between us more deeply. Alas, it is a desired event that can not take place.

The other event was also enormously positive. When von Franz came to town, we met and had a marvellous encounter. She invited me to dinner at her hotel at the beach, and was totally supportive of me and my work. She seemed to understand what I had gone through with the Jungians, and responded just the way that the inner "Jung" did: totally in accord with my individuation and dismissing of the institutional mind. It was like what my friend Hyatt had said, the Judge is not so much concerned with justice but with his own position, and this easily produces lies and deceit: both to himself and others. A good point. But the evening brought back memories of when I first met her, as a youth of twenty-five, and of all those seminars in my Zürich years.

The wonderful evening with wine and great conversation was followed by two potent dreams. In one, I was crossing a Renaissance bridge, in a European city, leading to a futuristic, utopian city on the other side. Midway on the bridge, I encountered a crippled beggar, with only the upper half of his body, rolling along on a kind of skate-board. The beggar told me he was God! I nodded and invited him for a drink at a kiosk on the side of the bridge. As I acknowledged him, his crippledness vanished. He took on a full body and we toasted each other with wine. Following this, he poured gold and silver coins, from every time and place, from his fingers into my hands.

The second dream, a few days later, was more one of being informed about the nature of God. I was told that the entire universe was like a huge worm, an uroborous, circling upon itself. Its organs were the galaxies and the cells were all the forms life everywhere existing. There was a pattern of inhalation and exhalation to the entire process and all those beings, including me, who were fortunate enough to be at the special vortices of this process, could have mystical experiences.

What a pair of dreams to have at this time! When I told von Franz the dreams, she said that I "must have suffered greatly" and referred me to Jung's *Mysterium Coniunctionis* on the worm symbolism, which validated her remark.

JULY 23, 1975

I have had a chance to reflect further on the two "big" dreams and am deeply impressed with the imagery of God taking on body as I acknowledge Him. It seems as if all my "crippledness" in body, these last years, has been a true image of that process, that the incarnation of the Self in my life has required even this. Finally, the reward of gold and silver coins, masculine and feminine values, is both a truth and a promise. I am, in turns, astonished, awed and grateful to be part of this.

Last night, I had an unusual dream. In this dream, I was doing Reichian therapy with an older man, perhaps in his fifties. He was difficult and demanding. I was working hard with him, rather effectively, but he seemed to need more. His armor was great, he had a large chest, and was involved in gagging. Depression was his symptom, from the large chest, and something also needed to be thrown up. End of dream.

I do not recall dreams in which I had been doing Reichian therapy until now. I have indeed had dreams in which the theme appeared, such as the man who criticized me severely, but this is the first, I think, wherein I, myself, am doing such a work. This comes more than a year after I began doing this therapy, and at a time when I am wondering how effective I am in this work. I seem to be doing better in my verbal therapy, better than ever, but several of my Reichian patients are afraid of the pain, are reluctant to come, and I have lost others in the past months. So, this dream comes at an appropriate time. It seems right for me to continue with this work, partly to help others and partly to become more attuned to energies, to non-verbal ways of connection and effect. This seems to come ever so slowly.

In the dream however, I am dealing with this depressed, chest-elevated, throwing-up man. I can see him as the bitter, defeated man that I have felt myself to be, but feel less of these days. Now, *I* am working on this image of the "senex," the old man of rigidity, pain, judgment, and depression. He is, indeed, very demanding, as all my own work upon myself has told me. His armor, too, is extremely resistant to softening, as I painfully realize through all my own undergoing of body therapy. But now, at last, my ego is active in the work. I am not only "being worked on" by my healer in a body way, but I am also active, in my soul, in trying to heal, change, soften, help this rigid old man. That he is in his middle or late fifties seems to be the way that I might have become without the body therapy. Thus, the image is both accurate for what I have been, in part, and an image of a future self that I might have become without intervention. I am glad of the change, and look forward to more development here.

JULY 28, 1975

Just a note "for the record." This morning I went to the chiropractor for an adjustment, some three weeks since the last one, and I seem much better. There is my chronic condition, plus the chronic chattiness of the Doctor, but I do feel much better. In addition, I have changed the handlebars of my racing bicycle, so that now they turn up rather than down. Not so stylish and svelte perhaps, but better for the back and neck. As I rode from the chiropractor to my office, a long stretch, without using hands, I realized that the handlebars now looked like horns. I thought of my bicycle now as the Bull, and here I am astride his back! Even as I whistle a tune, riding with no hands on the handlebars, I am like the Zen fellow in the Ox-Herding series, riding upon the back of his bull with no reins! So, I laugh: not exactly an enlightened one, nor even one whose body is without blemish; but at least I am in far less pain, feel healthy, and can ride my "bull" with pleasure and "without reins!"

My bike has given me enormous pleasure, as a matter of fact. I am particularly pleased that I was able to ride the entire seventy-plus mile distance to L.'s place in Laguna, in less than seven hours and almost a year before my fiftieth birthday, as I had promised myself.

SESSION 165: JULY 30, 1975

It is immediately after the session. I have not taken notes or written immediately after a session since several years ago, when I was eager, hopeful, and full of the mystery of the Reichian therapy. Now, more than a hundred-and-fifty sessions and almost four years later, I do it again. I do so because I am excited. I am a bit groggy—more than a bit—from the hyperventilation, but I can gather my thoughts a little and want to record this excitement at once.

During this session, Regardie worked hardly at all on me aside from the breathing. I spent the early warm-up on his machine—ten minutes of the bar-massage on my back, after which I was already a little bit hyperventilated. Then we returned to the work-couch and he soon had me flopping my legs, which he had not done for a long time. I was quite anxious when he squeezed the adductors but, after a time, the trembling began in my legs, and I went to the "croak-pause-flick" maneuver, as he calls it, without any hindrance. We went on this way for the entire session.

At the end of the session, which saw only one small flick of my belly, the energies were flowing freely all over—or almost, that is. They flowed from feet and legs into belly and chest, all the way up my neck. I felt only a band around my neck, while my face had energies, too. It was exciting—no pain in lower back or "wings." Trembling had taken place all the way up to my back!

When we spoke, Regardie was pleased. My chest was perfectly fine, soft to touch, he did not have to work on it, hardly at all! The croak-pause-flick was now going to be the main exercise, and the work was going well.

In a few minutes though, the low back pain returned, along with a sense of a line or armor around my chest and upper back and neck, but there was a break-through, and I felt a great resurgence of hope. Maybe, even the calcification of my back will melt!

Next week is a holiday for Regardie and, after that, one for me, but I feel hopeful that when I begin the fifth year, some true changes will occur.

SESSION 168: SEPTEMBER 10, 1975: (SIX WEEKS LATER)

I think it is a long time since I have written about my sessions. Perhaps once, briefly, but not often. Oh yes, there was the recent session when enthusiasm re-emerged. Yesterday's session was also one of those enthusiastic times, not because so much new happened in the hour itself. No, that was fine, with the energies moving a fair amount, the discovery of a block in the solar plexus region, and the experience of movement and progress. It is nice to feel that, when I have so often felt despairing, hopeless, and blocked. But it was something else that moved me to write here.

Regardie spoke earlier about Uranus finally moving into Scorpio, after a brief sojourn there early in the year. This, he repeated the other day, would be the beginning of the most important six years of my life to date. A total change and transformation would take place, which would surely effect the armoring, too, and bring on new life. The changes might be experienced as both negative and positive, but the ultimate result would be positive. I would (also considering my Jupiter in Mid-Heaven, which is very benefic), get what I want. These changes would be not only for me and him, too, a Scorpio person, but also in the nation and the world. This Uranus cycle was partly unpredictable, but it was certain that changes would occur. Also, Saturn would be moving, Saturday coming, out of Cancer into Leo. This would help me, too, in feeling a load removed from my shoulders and neck. I have no planets in Cancer, but it is aspected and the change would help. Saturn will be in Leo for three years—a new challenge for L., but nice for me. So, these great Uranus changes would bring great new energy (as if I have not enough already!) and direction. That is very exciting.

Additionally, at the end of the hour, Regardie mentioned a new meditative method to me. I observed that I was not very aware, proprioceptively, what was going on with my body. For example, at the end of the session, during the observation period, I was not aware that my chest was flat and fairly relaxed. Pretty armored still, but relaxed, and I did not notice the difference. I also had the sense of wanting to lift my shoulders a lot, which was not the way to release tension. Thus, he said, my impulses along that line were not to be trusted. As if I had been fed the wrong food early in life and had to learn to eat the right kind. It was at that point that he mentioned a Buddhist method of meditation which trained proprioception. "Mindfulness" is what it is called, plus another name which I forget. It consists, essentially, of sitting quietly in place (or lying down) and observing carefully what is going on with the body. One should also verbalize these sensations, else one "goes off" into something else, fantasy or such. This "mindfulness" leads to relaxation and, I presume, to some kind of enlightenment or, at least, greater awareness of sensation and proprioception. He mentioned an author who wrote a whole book on this as a meditative procedure. Well, this excited me greatly. I do not know, now, if this was partly a consequence of my "high" on air itself, namely hyperventilation. It is, however, a method I plan to experiment with. I feel a little resistance to it, now, as well as a slight embarrassment, speaking words when alone, but I shall try.

SEPTEMBER 16, 1975: A WEEK LATER

I write now with a sense of joy, of energy, of purpose and direction. It is midday. I have seen several patients, doing Reichian work with two and Jungian work with two. It was excellent. I worked hard, was relaxed, honest, felt the effort, but good flow of energies. This is particularly remarkable since I did not work for the previous three days and got into a depression. The depression may have several causes—it did, indeed, pick on old problems, dilemmas, failures. But this hardly matters, since as soon as I began working in earnest, once more, focusing upon the psyche and bodies of my patients and bringing to bear all my interest, energy, and concern, my depression lifted and I have felt fine. It is now clear to me that I need to do this healing work not only to "make a living" in a sense of earnings, but to "make a life," that is to use these energies in the service of life, which is a union of spirit and body and soul. When I do this, I feel well, useful, alive. When I do not work, I feel depressed, down, half-dead.

So, then, I am a healer in the sense of the old healers, a shaman, indeed! They, when they did not work and heal and serve the soul, under God, would get sick, would often "go under." I see, now, that I, too, must do so. I must serve nature, must be a "physician," a healer, in the sense of letting nature work through me: nature heals nature, as the old alchemists said, and as Jung taught us. But Nature also wounds nature, said those same alchemists, and this is also true. I shall try to be on the healing end of nature and help nature heal itself of its wounds. For are we not of nature also? We people? Yes, indeed. And, in so proclaiming, I follow my old master and teacher, Jung, (although I had only a few hours with him, his spirit filtering through others has been my guru).

But I also must not forget my current "gurus," Regardie and Reich, the body men. I must also pursue this new found consciousness and work with the body. (As I type, I make errors: I type "gody" instead of "body." I must serve "Gody" in both spirit and flesh.)

A moment ago, as I wrote about nature, I noticed a squirrel running about on the lawn. An hour earlier, when a patient was speaking about dreams in which animals appeared, including squirrels, with whom he wished to play, and when he also ran away from a shark to a roof, there appeared, on the neighboring roof (Regardie's!) a squirrel! It never happened before. A synchronicity, and a right one. A meaningful coincidence of allowing the unconscious, as playful and conserving, to enter into the mind (roof), and bring together opposites. Nature spoke. It has often in the past, but my drapes have been closed too much, not allowing it in. I must allow more of this; during verbal Jungian work, anyway. Nature can appear in the body itself as we work in the Reichian way, which needs the protection of drapes against nudity. But, I feel fine. The Healer, not yet healed, has found his vocation anew in his healing. He must *heal in order to live*, and *live in order to heal*. In this he is the servant of nature and God, and in this, he meets the meaning of his own existence. So am I, and so will I be.

EPILOGUE

(FIFTEEN YEARS LATER)

The note taking and reflections of *The Unhealed Healer* end at this point, although the actual therapy continued for several more years, until Regardie's retirement, as a matter of fact. My colleague, L., and I, were faithful to the continuing process, even though we both found the therapy to have more of a "maintenance" character, in contrast to the production of significant bodily changes. My voluminous note-taking and writing continued unabated, however. Rather than being "confessional" or "reporting" about my "true life" experiences as one undergoing healing or trying to become a published writer (my companion book at this time was *The Unpublished Writer*) I resumed the fictional writing that I had done previously on psycho-mythology. I now engaged in a fictional work with two other "failures," namely an "Empty Teacher" and an "Unfrocked Priest." I had already completed the companion work to the present one of *Unhealed Healer*, namely *The Unpublished Writer*, around the same time the *Healer* book drew to a close.

Lest the reader become too downhearted in sympathetic sorrow for my two real-life "failures" of Healer and Writer, I can reassure him and her that the process continued productively and even has had a "happy ending." Ultimately, the two "true" figures of the Healer and Writer join with the "fantastic" figures of Teacher and Priest and come to the cave of "The Powerless Magician." Here the failures share their experiences and finally become "The Successes," but that is a work which is for future publication; indeed, it is not even finished yet!

In between are several years of notes and experiments in the magical arena, which was the original interest in propelling L. and myself to visit Regardie. These, too, may see the light of publication in the future. I leave the faithful reader with the knowledge, however, that enough healing took place to make the effort worthwhile, and if the "Healer" rediscovered his vocation, he was also able to give greater definition to his limitations and to continue on his healing path.

After a few years, I gave up doing Reichian therapy, since I did not feel suited to it and believed that I should undertake much more education in the "physical" area in order to do a proper job. My Jungian work, however, was enormously impacted by the experience, as it continues to be.

I must also add that during the editing of this book for publication, more than fifteen years since its completion, another powerful synchronistic event occurred which has propelled me further. A doctor of oriental medicine has come to work with me, referred by a former pupil. He came "armed" with a "letter" he received, on a psychic plane, from Francis Israel Regardie. This letter was addressed to me. In characteristic Regardie language, he informs me that he has already infused me with the magical information during my years on the couch. Considering that Regardie had been dead for a number of years, that my new patient knew practically nothing about him beyond what was given in his final Interview book, and that this letter contains both style and content which could not be known to the young doctor, I offer this information to the reader, knowing that he or she will be as incredulous and astounded as was I. The letter, supplied with the literarily necessary deletions of some of Regardie's colorful but culturally unacceptable language (also quite unknown to the young doctor) follows:

Dear Spiegelman,

Don't you get it? We did the work! I was always there: beast, shadow, and all. At my worst, I was my best. You are supposed to be angry. Placidity breeds fat sows. While you breathed outside, I lectured inside. Nothing was left undone.

The work still continues, whether you like it or not. I've impregnated you with my seed. You have the choice to abort or deliver, not if you're going to get pregnant or not. You're knocked up.

The apprentice sweeps floors and carries water while he simultaneously dreams the work. Every time the energy passed between us the magic was taught. Now get your d... hard and retrieve the magic out of your unconscious and stick it where it belongs...in your conscious mind.

By the way, being upfront never got a man into the virgin's bed. Nor is it the way to turn the novice into the master. I lied, I withheld and f... you over when you needed it. I also f... you when I needed it. I'll do it again, when you need it...or when I need it.

Just remember, the mind is a dung heap. It is a good place to hide the jewels. Nobody in their right mind goes digging around in that crap. Just be thankful I'm not in my right mind and neither are you. End of "letter."

I have taken this unexpected "letter" seriously, on a psychological level, as a message from the unconscious and assure the reader that I have no opinions, pro or con, whether this is "really" Regardie or not, treating it as a meaningful expression of the psyche, just as Jung taught us to do. Since the theme of my Unhealed Healer book, as well as several others, hinges on the relationship of body and soul, physical reality and psychic reality, I merely continue on the path of finding the transcending symbol or path which unites them. The many changes which have occurred since editing the book, now in the reader's hands, gives me the necessary impetus to continue along these lines and I will be giving the results, in some fashion, in the "success" book of healer, writer, et al.

To give the patient reader some idea about how these various experiences have come together in the work of this Jungian analyst, I have included, as an appendix, a lecture I gave, in the spring of 1991, at the C.G. Jung Institute in Zürich, about the development of this "unhealed healer." It was given as the first part of a two-part "report to alma mater," some thirty-two years after graduating.

I conclude with the fervent hope that my fellow "wounded" or unhealed healers, particularly psychotherapists, will take some solace from my experiences and I hope that my contribution to our shared myth will add to the collegial feeling so often lacking among shamans of all kinds.

APPENDIX

THE UNHEALED HEALER AND THE UNPUBLISHED WRITER: THIRTY-PLUS YEAR REPORT TO ALMA MATER: SPRING 1991

In the spring of 1959, after three-plus years of intensive work at the C.G. Jung Institute in Zürich, Switzerland, and nine years after I had begun analysis in Los Angeles, I completed my studies, was awarded the Analyst's Diploma, and returned to California. Now, in the spring of 1991, more than thirty years later, a month before my 65th birthday, I am returning to my *alma mater* and have decided to give a report, so-to-speak, about these many years of life and work since then, so that current students and fellow graduates might have a glimpse of the experiences of one such *alumnus*.

The titles for these two lectures—"The Unhealed Healer" and the "Unpublished Writer"—sound rather unpromising, I admit, but I hurry to inform you that the results are not so grim as it may appear. I employ this heading since two books of mine with these titles are being published soon, written twenty years ago but appearing only now, synchronistic with my return to Zürich and certainly bearing on the theme of what can transpire for a dedicated psychologist and psychotherapist, deeply immersed in Jungian analysis, when he returns to the land of his birth, tries to practice his craft and live the symbolic life.

I will begin, as most Jungians would, with a dream. This dream summarized my experience and rather uncannily predicted some important aspects of my future work. I had it at the end of my analysis in Zürich. Here it is:

I am in the consulting room of my analyst, C.A. Meier. We are deeply engaged in conversation and then begin to roll about the room together, in a kind of ball. We wrestle and generate both light and heat. At last, we stop and my analyst kneels at my feet, recognizing me with a bow, but also with a touch of scorn. I shake his hand and leave the office. As I do so, I also see the Institute secretary, my friend, Alice Maurer, standing there and I bid her farewell also.

Outside the office, I encounter my maternal grandmother, who points, with great significance, to a bricked-in room which has no windows or doors, but is open to the sky. It is a sunny day, but above the room appears a night sky, filled with myriad stars. Inside the room is a dark and intense man, writing passionately and occasionally looking up to have a conversation with a non-visible divinity. I see this man through the walls. I then nod to my grandmother and proceed onward. Now I find myself on a ship where I serve as first officer (chief mate), to a captain who is as much a luminous presence as an actual person. The ship has a circular deck where we stand, which rotates slowly in relation to the sun. The ship somehow manages to go across Switzerland and Italy to the Mediterranean and from thence sails around South America to California. At the port of Los Angeles, it changes into a truck, drops off a young sailor in Pasadena, and then proceeds to the beach at Santa Monica. The captain and I now stand on the beach. A Greek temple is nearby, in which a red-haired woman has experienced a near-fatal fire. We now look toward Asia and are astounded to see the sun rising in the west. End of dream.

This dream, as I have said, was strangely predictive of certain qualities or events in my work as a therapist and writer. In these two lectures, I will be speaking about these events, concerning my therapeutic work in the first meeting and writing in the second. Before I do so, however, I wish to comment briefly about some of the symbols in the dream.

First off, there is the presentation of my analysis with Professor Meier as a sort of wrestle, rolling in a circle and generating heat and light. This, I think, was an accurate portrayal of what my psyche underwent during this formidable three-year period of intense analysis and I am deeply grateful both to him and to Zürich, to the Institute and to colleagues, for such a profound and fulfilling experience. At another level, this struggle with my Analytic Self was to continue as a wrestle long afterward, rather like Jacob with his Angel, but also like that of a Japanese sumo wrestler. My therapeutic Self has indeed embraced me and challenged me, as we shall see.

Secondly, I did not know it at the time, but that wild-eyed and intense writer in that bricked-in room was to break out in earnest some seven years later and has embroiled me with his passion and intensity ever since.

Thirdly, the small detail of the young sailor getting off in Pasadena upon my arrival back in Southern California was humorously accurate. When my wife and I returned from Zürich, penniless and pregnant, I needed to get a job of some sort while building up a practice. Well, I did so—in Pasadena! I took a position as a psychologist with a management-consulting firm, thanks to a former student of mine. I had taught him Rorschach in my earlier days at the University and I had been known as a capable diagnostician, a skill which I was ready to abandon now that I was an analyst. They hired me, though, to assess executives in connection with jobs which were offered, something for which I was very poorly equipped, being knowledgeable about psychodynamics and diagnosis, but not at all about business. I did the best I could for some months but ultimately resigned this position. Suffice to say, however, that this was indeed a youngish aspect of myself—a kind of side issue—that was engaged in Pasadena!

Finally, the astounding aspect of watching the sun rising in the west, coming from the Land of the Rising Sun, was concretely realized within two years of my return. While I was teaching once more at UCLA (Rorschach, largely), a visiting Fullbright scholar from Japan, Hayao Kawai, took, my class and soon embarked upon an analysis with me. After about eighteen months of work, he returned to Japan, ultimately came to study in Zürich as well, and has become a famous person, bringing Jungian psychology to his nation and serving as a model for many psychiatrists and psychologists. When he completed his work with me, he referred his friend, the Buddhist priest, Mokusen Miyuki, to me and this analysis lasted four years. Dr. Miyuki then also went to the Institute in Zürich to study, became an analyst, and returned to California. We have been friends and colleagues ever since. After Dr. Miyuki, a steady stream of psychologists and psychiatrists have come from Japan to work with me. I realized, after a wonderful visit there with Professor Miyuki, some years ago, how one can become a sort of admired grandfather under such conditions, an unmerited Wise Old Man. So the dream predicted that event also.

Sadly, the fearful fate of the red-haired woman in the Greek temple was also predictive. As it is with many analysts, one woman patient, in a life-and-death struggle and producing very rich dreams, was particularly challenging, and the emotional and passionate uproar it produced in me almost cost me my emotional balance. Before I tell about that, however, I want to suggest to students who are near graduation to pay particular attention to your final dreams, since you are indeed living in a kind of special place and condition, conducive to predictive dreams, I think.

Resuming life in California was rather mixed, at best. I missed the introversion and ordered life of Zürich and felt the stress of driving long distances on the freeways with our Volkswagen, pretending to be a psychologist to business. I did as best I could, however, and, earning a rather good income, established a practice in Beverly Hills, slowly building it up. I continued the consulting job for some ten months until I had the following dream:

I am in my office in Beverly Hills, talking to the wife of a colleague from Switzerland. She is very attractive and well-dressed, showing every inch of her wealthy background and personal security. The telephone rings and I answer it. Apparently, my job is to provide membership cards in resorts and country clubs. I speak for a time and hang up, returning to speak with my friend. She now looks haggard and ill. I ask her what is the matter? Speechless, she points to the telephone, obviously agonized as to how I was on it. "But I was only being natural," I say. She then nods significantly. End of dream.

And end of job! The next day, I resigned from the consulting job and spent full time in my practice, although I was soon to resume teaching at the University, as well. As all of you will readily recognize, it was all right for me to do this industrial psychological work, even coming home sick and crying pathetically in the bathroom, as long as I was aware of the conflict and doing as best I could. As soon as it became "natural," I was lost. I am grateful to this "wealthy" anima, not seduced by money, who let me know when the time was up.

How, then, did this practice go? Was I inundated with interesting, Jungian-type clients eager to do active imagination and actively pursue individuation? Unfortunately, no. Although I had a few such patients, most of them were much like those suffering individuals I had worked with in the Veterans Administration and the army, years before, more interested in symptom-reduction or improving their lives rather than in the psyche itself. Besides, an economic recession was on and my desire to be on a par with my financially more successful Freudian colleagues had to be abandoned. I continued to work deeply on my own dreams and fantasies, however, and enjoyed being a husband, father and friend. The *I Ching* gave the message of "Difficulty at the Beginning," so I was comforted.

Alas, after a time, my family happiness was impaired by my often coming home after work in a state of exhaustion, hardly able to enjoy these very relationships I treasured. I worked mightily on trying to figure out why I was so tired, since I had always been a rather energetic person. At last, I realized that this fatigue was not so much that I was drained by patients or the work—although this, too, did take place—but that I was exhausted by the endless efforts to maintain "analytic objectivity." I labored to be reflective, to contain my emotions and reactions, to provide a safe and non-threatening vessel for my patients. In short, I modelled myself on many Freudian and some Jungian colleagues. This was killing me. I then remembered that Jung had been quite spontaneous during my one interview with him; indeed after an initial period of openness to me, he talked most of the time. If Jung could be spontaneous, why not I? Indeed, why not? So, I changed and was much more reactive, natural and myself. Result? Exhaustion vanished. I gave full attention and energy to each analytic hour, but was able, then, to come home and have lots of stuff left to be with my family.

This increase in spontaneity had an immediate effect on my practice: I started to get many more "Jungian-type" patients. Giving up being "the analyst" and being myself, paradoxically resulted in more analytical-type work. It also compelled me to deal with the transference much more. Embroilment in the process required much more sorting out with the patient as partner. So, after about four years home and a reasonably successful practice, I was ready to go back to Zürich for some weeks and undergo what an American might describe as a 100,000 mile check-up.

I am amazed that I was able to save enough money to go to Europe and provide for my wife and two children for a month or more! But I did. Luckily, neither family nor patients felt abandoned. Looking forward to a period of intense introversion in Zürich, I found, instead, that my dreams and fantasies lead me to a true termination of my analyses with Drs. C.A. Meier and Liliane Frey. My earlier ending had more to do with finishing training than with finishing analysis, actually. I had continued analysis with some senior analysts after I was back in Los Angeles for about two years. Now, however, I could conclude my work with a very satisfying series of paintings and dreams which found me at one with my Self. So, off I went, back to America, ready now to "be my own man."

This sense of wholeness and well-being was challenged before long—as it is for many analysts approaching middle age—by an intense transference-counter-transference situation with a woman who was in a life and death struggle. I can recall, even now, the moment when the transference had changed its character. We had worked with great intensity on her difficult personal situation for a couple of years, in which much archetypal material had been revealed. In this, I had been essentially in a rather caring, interested and objective position, compassionate—even life-saving on more than one occasion—but still not "embroiled." Then, one day, this person transformed before my eyes into someone with a full body and power, perhaps both goddess and witch. Undaunted by this experience, I welcomed the archetypal transference, but the vicissitudes of that relationship did echo my dream of the woman threatened by fire in the Greek temple. I will mention two images which were crucial in this challenge.

The first image involved her need—nay, demand—that I be more fully in the relationship with all of my feelings and reactions, rather than remaining "analytical." Knowing nothing of alchemy, she had the image of a divine bird present in our relationship, with a fine thread which it wrapped around us. When the relationship was going well, this thread was harmonious and healing. When, however, I retreated or became objective, she experienced the bird continuing to wrap the thread about herself, now choking her. A dream of hers also pushed me deeper into what I later began to call, a "mutual process," with this analysand. In the dream, the woman saw both of us at the seashore, watching two fish come up from the deep. One, a "harem fish," entered into her genital, while the other, a "cat fish," latched on to my genital. The two fish then went back into the sea and united with each other. As I have said, she knew nothing of alchemy and I assumed, following Jung, that the harem fish was male (her animus) and the cat fish was female (my anima). I was surprised to find out that the reverse was true. Perhaps needless to say, a long period of intense mutual shadow work took place, the analysis finally ending successfully, but I felt in danger rather often.

This case, however, was crucial in my embrace of the idea of mutual process and I have written a number of papers on this theme (1,3,4,7). Almost all of these have been published, but it is also synchronistic that these papers will be appearing shortly in a book being published in Japanese, more than a year before it will be printed in English!

I did not realize it at the time, but my espousal of the idea of mutual process, plus my own emotional upheaval at this period, was propelling me toward a course different from that of many colleagues, particularly some senior ones. In retrospect—but not at the time—it is not surprising that when a close friend and fellow Zürich graduate and I came up for appointment as training analysts, we were both advised to wait for six months, since we were not considered to have a sufficiently tutorial persona. This came on the heels of a visit to our area by Laurens van der Post. My colleague and I were rather forthright in our comments at a public meeting, thus producing opprobrium from senior colleagues. We were both deeply chagrined by their rejection, which followed. He was furious because this appointment was supposed to be automatic after five years, unless there were serious doubts, and his view was that the current Board had an unrecognized image of how a Jungian analyst and training analyst ought to be, but were unwilling to discuss it.

My own chagrin was more connected with justice and reason. I had been Director of Studies for several years, had just got off this very Certifying Board itself, and was actively engaged in both teaching and treating professional therapists. It seemed bizarre to me that they should reject me because I was not only already functioning as a training analyst, but also had just been among those who decided who and when people were to become training analysts!

Our desire for dialogue on the issues was rejected, so my friend and I felt it necessary to retreat. At first, I merely withdrew, hoping that someone from the

Society would interpose themselves as mediator, but no one did so. We both then withdrew from our local Society and maintained membership in the International via our status as Graduates of the C.G. Jung Institute Zürich.

This separation from colleagues proved to be both painful and fruitful. First of all, it led to my fictional writing, or "psycho-mythology," as I call it, and I will talk about that in my second lecture. It also led to a deeper confrontation with my individuality, as both a healer and as a man. In a moment, I shall try and describe the results of this many-year confrontation, but first I must mention another deep encounter which occurred five years later, when I was forty-five.

During the preceding years, a colleague and I had been interested in the western occult tradition, often known by the name of "magic"—an unfortunate appellation linking this honorable study with both a parlor amusement and with primitive kinds of thinking, but in actuality including a long history of concepts and methods of a spiritual path which included alchemy, astrology, meditation and kindred topics known to Jungians as fields but less known by them as developed disciplines. My colleague discovered that a world-famous practitioner in this area, Francis Israel Regardie, although of British origin and a leading figure in the Golden Dawn Order, lived not only in the Los Angeles area, but even in our local part of it, Studio City! We telephoned him for an interview, which he granted. When we expressed the desire to study with him in his area, he said that the energies released in magical study and work were quite profound and that it would be wise to undertake, along with that study, a course of Reichian therapy.

I knew of an interesting book Regardie had written on the Middle Pillar meditation and its relation to Jungian psychology (he had undergone both an extensive Freudian analysis in England, as well as a two-year Jungian one), but we did not know that he was also a qualified practitioner of the methods of Wilhelm Reich. We were both a little skeptical about such an undertaking, since each of us had undergone many years of Jungian work, but I was intrigued since, when I had been informed of my Jungian colleagues rejection of me, I had experienced a deep pain in my back, which had responded to treatment only minimally. I had accepted this pain as both a symbolic statement of my feeling "stabbed in the back," and a dubious reward for years of poor posture, as well as a consequence of an athletic injury. Dr. Regardie, however, felt that more could be accomplished with this condition, let alone the deeper relaxation and opening up to be achieved with such a body therapy. My colleague and I both agreed to undertake this work and did so, for the next eight years! My eight years of Jungian analysis were now matched by eight years of Reichian work.

This was an enormously impactful experience, as one might imagine. I took notes and did active imagination in connection with this work during the first four years of it and produced a book, at the time, called *The Unhealed Healer*. I did it for my own edification, largely, but my publisher saw it last year and offered to bring it out. This year, once more in synchronistic connection with these lectures, the book is being published, some twenty years after I began to write it.

It seems incumbent upon me, in this *Report to Alma Mater*, to describe some of the effects of such experiences and how it has impacted my therapeutic work. I should say at the outset that I never had the remotest intention of abandoning my Jungian orientation and work—indeed, the body work seemed a reasonable extension of my Jungian process. This was true even though I also took some training in Reichian therapy during the latter four years of my own work. My therapist was reasonably friendly to Jung's orientation but he held "Jungians"— those he knew—in rather low esteem as being "too much in the head." I knew what he meant, from having attended some Jungian congresses of various kinds, but I also had my own experience, later on, of attending Reichian congresses. These, I often found, were like experiencing a convention of physical education teachers—perhaps not reflective enough about what they were doing. In any case, my actual therapeutic work was relatively free from polemics, even of interpretations, luckily, because the therapist both wanted me to have my own experiences and because he trusted my knowledge and grasp of the symbolic domain.

So, the bulk of my time was spent on the couch, undergoing the special kinds of breathing and body work characteristic of this field. Such work would routinely bring about increased relaxation, often clonisms of various kinds and an upsurge of energy which one can characterize as orgone or subtle body, depending upon one's orientation. Early in the work, there was quite a bit of emotion released and also some vivid memories from childhood. I did not, however, experience these emotions and memories as qualitatively different from my earlier Jungian work. They did have a more intense or "whole body" aspect, however, in line with the inclusion of muscle, blood and bone, so to speak. The psyche not only took on more body, it also seemed to arise from the body. I began to feel, in time, the validity of the *chakras* in Kundalini Yoga and the *sephiroth* in Kabbalah in Jewish mysticism. That experience and belief has increased over the years.

I sometimes even had mystical experiences on that Reichian couch—profound feelings of oneness with the universe, the benevolence of God, the unity of life. When I asked Regardie why this was not generally experienced by people undergoing Reichian therapy—they are not a particularly religiously aware group—he said that they did indeed have similar experiences but put them in a different rubric, rather like that of the oneness of Nature. Just as one can readily experience the archetypes in Jungian work, although not everybody does, Reichian work enhances this experience of cosmic energy, with or without specific content or imagery.

You might ask whether I experienced the kind of "end-state" that one expects from successful Reichian work, namely the orgasmic reflex. This is the kind of full relaxation, similar to that following a total orgasm or what one undergoes when shaking in a total shedding of muscular tension. This is equivalent in value, in Reichian work—in goal rather than content—to the importance of the working through of the Oedipus complex and achievement of genitality in Freudian work. The goal of comparable importance in Jungian work is the experience of the Self, wherein the ego fundamentally shifts its orientation to an internalization of the symbol of totality and is in ongoing relation to it. Well, I both did and did not experience this orgasmic reflex. That is to say, I sometimes did, but the effects were always temporary and I soon returned to a condition of some kind of muscular armor or tension. My therapist informed me—as I also discovered in my reading—that the orgasmic reflex was not the *sin qua non* of the work—since it could even be experienced by schizophrenics—but, like the relativization of the ego to the Self in Jungian work, was an important end-state for formal therapy. But, I am deficient along those lines.

I see myself as as still "in process" in this area, although I believe that there are structural limits to my capacity to achieve this desirable state. These limits come from postural defects since childhood, athletic injury in youth, and the effect of age itself.

During those eight years of Reichian work, I was also actively engaged in what had brought my colleague and me to our Reichian therapist in the first place, namely the work with "magick" or, more precisely expressed, the attention and devotion to those methods of spiritual transformation which belong to the occult field. These include various kinds of meditation, including Buddhist and Kabbalistic, as well as a course in working with images in an evocatory or directed way, such as guided imagery. Working with Tarot card images is an example, as well the daily practice of the Kabbalistic meditative method of the Middle Pillar. The latter involves the the circulation of a form of light through various "centers" or sephiroth in the body, while invoking and chanting names of the divine. Another is the "mindfulness" method of Buddhism, wherein one focuses upon and describes the sequential sensations of the body, leading to relaxation and, perhaps, to a mystical state.

Along with all of these "magical" practices, I continued, with religious devotion, my many-year practice of Jungian active imagination, even though the latter is opposite in character. In active imagination, as we know, we let the unconscious speak for itself and let it provide direction for our work, whereas the former attempts to specify forms and goals.

Unlike what I was led to believe about such combining of practices in my earlier education on the spiritual path of individuation, I did not find these diverse ways of approaching the psyche to cause undue disharmony or damage, just as I was able to do Reichian therapy with some patients along with Jungian work. Ultimately, I gave up doing Reichian therapy because it did not suit me temperamentally and also because it required an asymmetrical approach to the therapeutic relationship which was at odds with my continuing belief in the analytic process as fundamentally a mutual one, the processes of which could or should be discussed.

In addition to these activities, I also continued my writing of both fiction and articles. So, it was obviously a busy time, even though primarily introverted. The energy for all that, I believe, came partly from that withdrawn from my deep involvement with Jungian collectives, and partly from what was released in the Reichian and magical work itself.

It remains, now, for me to describe to you—as I promised earlier—just how all this study and work effected my efforts as a Jungian Analyst, for that is what I remained, throughout this "hegira." Not only did I remain true to the Jungian viewpoint, I have continued to see myself as a "classical" Jungian, as I have described both in my paper commenting on the multiplicity of positions in the international community at this time (6), and in my book, *Jungian Analysts: Their Visions and Vulnerabilities* (5). I am "classical" in the sense that I am archetypally oriented, as is Hillman's archetypal psychology, but am convinced of the fundamental importance of the Self, as both center and circumference of the psyche, as he is not. Nor am I so impressed with the centrality of childhood, as are the Developmental Jungians. I am of the opinion that much of that involvement constitutes an excessive preoccupation with the child archetype, often at the expense of the religious attitude. I also believe that the active relationship with the psyche, with such methods as active imagination, are of central importance for those who would like to prove empirically, for themselves, just what it was that Jung discovered. The Developmentalists and Archetypalists seem less so inclined.

Where, then, you might ask, does my individuality, as an analyst, reside? I would answer that it resides in my own preoccupation with the transference all these years, as my papers attest (1,3,4,5,6,7). From the outset of my analytical practice, I have been impressed with what might be called the "field" character of the psychotherapeutic encounter. As Jung remarked long ago, the psyches of therapist and patient are ultimately enmeshed, if they are not so at the outset, and the impact upon each other is proportional. Indeed, he felt that the therapist could only have an effect on the patient to the degree that the analyst was open to the latter's psyche.

Over the years, I have written a number of papers on this "mutual process" theme, detailing how I see it working, the conditions under which it appears and its limits. I would like to briefly summarize what this approach to analysis is like by means of examples.

I can think of my analytic practice as divisible into four categories, when it comes to the question of the degree of personal involvement in the transference. These four categories, therefore, are really division points on a continuum of mutual process, and each constitutes about one-fourth of the people I see in long-term analytic work. In addition to these, I, like others in our field, see a fair number of people for relatively brief periods—usually less than a year—for traditional psychotherapy. In those cases, the transference may or may not be present to any appreciable degree, but it is largely in the background, and interpreted only when there is some sort of interference or blockage; the focus is on problem-solution, goal orientation, etc. At any time, in such work, even in the very earliest sessions, the psychotherapy can turn into analysis proper, which I understand as following a process whereby the analysand develops a relationship with his/her psyche and gradually becomes united with the soul, following its peregrinations, deepening and developing the particular *religio* we come to expect in analytic work. Many patients, coming for counselling, never do this. These, however, constitute a small portion of my work, even though such work can also be interesting, exciting, even deep.

To illustrate how psychotherapy can change into analysis, I think of the example of a neuroscientist who came to me because of his interest in dreams, wanting to understand them better and develop his capacity for lucid dreaming. We worked happily for about a year, systematically interpreting dreams, but also dealing with his sense that people did not enter deeply into relationship with him, not seeing his soul and hurting him thereby. After these many months of good but not particularly deep connection between us, he dreamt of being stung by a scorpion, his sun sign and my moon sign. My psyche was then mobilized more profoundly than it had been with him and I said so. The next session, he spoke about his desire to terminate, to my amazement and hurt, and I called his attention to what had transpired between us in the previous session. He saw the validity of my interpretation, but also said that he had been thinking of stopping for a couple of months—therapy was expensive, he had other things to do, was not sure it was worth it. "Yes," I said. "Let's wait for some more dreams and decide whether we stop or not."

In the next session, he told a dream in which he had been wanting to buy a special tool so that he could sharpen his axe with it, one that he used to chop wood for his fireplace. It was expensive and he didn't know if it was worth it. In the next part of his dream, he was experiencing a terrible loneliness. I interpreted this as his coming to therapy in order to learn techniques of dream interpretation, ones that he could use in the privacy of his own hearth (fireplace), but that this was, indeed, now too expensive. If we went on, we would have to deal more deeply with his loneliness, also in the context of our relationship. We could no longer approach this as a learning technique. He agreed. So, now the issue was: do we terminate the therapy altogether or do we begin a true analytic work? Here, as in the analytic cases, the transference-countertransference situation is the dramatic, unexpected quality which decides the course of further direction. He decided to stop for the time being.

I now move to my four categories of analytic process, in terms of increasing consciousness of mutuality in the transference field. The first category is rather traditional analysis, of the type that M-L von Franz called, when she supervised me here in Zürich, a "womb analysis." In this situation, the analysis is a cave or womb, a vessel in which the analysand can safely explore and relate to the unconscious and the analyst provides a protective and supportive environment for it. The example that comes to mind is that of a highly creative writer I worked with, one who had had much analysis, was professionally well-placed, had many rich dreams, and worked quite well by himself. I provided dream comments or interpretations, only occasionally having to remark about what was transpiring in the relationship between us. Nor is this merely intellectual; the one image that sustained itself as as transference one for a long time was that of a giant lingam of light between us! Otherwise, however, the process proceeded without much discussion of our interaction.

The second category might be called "womb-interaction," perhaps, indicating that there is, indeed, more conscious attention to the relationship. The example that comes to mind is a former priest, who had suffered from serious depression and anxiety for years. After many months of work and our mutual experience of inability to change his condition, despite interesting dreams which referred back to his initial vocation and loss of connection with the divine, I finally revealed to him a fantasy I had. This involved us praying together before a Dürer print I had in the room, of Christ crowned with thorns. He immediately expressed a desire to do this concretely and we both knelt and prayed. As we knelt there, shoulder to shoulder, I felt a Christ-like presence, with an arm on each of our shoulders. I reported this and he responded that he, too, felt this. He was amazed. I then had the strong impression that my analysand was much larger than I was, even though we were physically about the same size. When I mentioned this, he was startled, since he had the same impression. Right away, he knelt lower, feeling that he was too inflated, and touched his forehead to the ground. I strongly said, "No, not at all!" He, after all, was indeed far larger than I in relation to a Christian manifestation of the divine, and it was exactly right that he acknowledge this. He wept with relief and joy and we embraced. This was a turning point in his analysis and subsequent sessions presented a great influx of energy, content and direction, which was experienced as rather miraculous.

The third category, which one can call "mutual process" proper, has a wide variety of conditions and examples, characterized by frequent and sometimes intense reference to what is happening in the analytic relationship. This can be the typical parent-child situation, many archetypal relations, the kind we are familiar with from Jung's diagram, but in which I differ by being much more explicit about it. It can range all the way, in my experience, to the use of mutual active imagination. I am thinking, now, of a very intense sexual transference with an older woman, in which the sharing and working through of these images led to a tremendous sense of wholeness.

The fourth category includes all of the regular mutual process I have written about, but added to this is the experience of actual subtle-body energies and effects on the various chakras or sephiroth—head, chest, diaphragm, etc. One woman I am thinking of, who had done much analytical and body work, experienced, with me, an intense period of work with sexual and other energies, leading to a revelation of a goddess figure in the background which was highly numinous and conveyed a priestess-type of vocation to this professional woman. Synchronicity seems to be characteristic in such encounters and exchanges.

All of these varieties of mutual process are of interest, of course, and often change back and forth from one category to another. My own desire to include subtle-body energies makes the last category particularly salient at this time. Whenever the numinous manifests, however, whatever the "category" or type of analysand, one realizes that this work is truly alchemical, as Jung discovered. I also realized, partly as a consequence of my Reichian body work and magical practice, that alchemy does indeed have an apparent material dimension, best characterized as subtle body, I think, and this is of continuing promise in our field.

Also of promise, I think, is what I have called "joint active imagination"—a natural outgrowth of mutual process. This arises when the transference situation presents a mutually constellated content. As an example, what comes to mind is the incident reported by Jo Wheelwright, when he was supervising someone in training. The latter's patient dreamt of him as a lascivious, sex-seeking person and the person in training was overwhelmed and apologized. He was no doubt correct in this and he was surely more honest and therapeutic than the usual analyst's interpretation that this was a projection on the part of the patient onto the analyst. But one might also suggest that the content in question, the dark sexual figure, belonged to both parties and could be jointly addressed. I have done such joint fantasy work frequently and find it valuable, particularly when the content is archetypal in nature. I shall discuss another development in active imagination in my second lecture (this lecture can be found in the companion book of this series, *The Unpublished Writer*).

In conclusion, I want to reiterate my thanks to all my analysts and teachers, as well as to the continuingly present spirit of Jung. This has truly supported me in the work when little else did so.

SOME PAPERS ON THERAPY AND MUTUAL PROCESS

1. "Some Implications of the Transference," in *Festschrift für C.A. Meier*, edited by C.T Frey, Rascher Verlag, Zürich, 1965, pp. 163-175.
2. "Notes from the Underground: A View of Religion and Love From a Psychotherapist's Cave." *Spring*, 1970, pp. 196-211.
3. "Transference, Individuation, Mutual Process." A lecture presented to the Jung Group of San Diego and privately printed, April 1972.
4. "The Image of the Jungian Analyst and the Problem of Authority," *Spring, An Annual of Archetypal Psychology*, 1980, pp. 101-117.
5. Editor/contributor, *Jungian Analysts: Their Visions and Vulnerabilities*. Falcon Press, Arizona, 1988. 181 pp.
6. "The One and the Many: Jung and the Post-Jungians," *Journal of Analytical Psychology*, 1989, Vol;. 134, #1, pp. 53-73.
7. "The Interactive Field in Analysis: Agreements and Disagreements, "Chiron Publications, Illinois, 1991, pp. 133-150.

Made in the USA
Middletown, DE
10 March 2023